ECONOMICS

WORK AND PROSPERITY

Russell Kirk

A Beka Book.
A MINISTRY OF
PENSACOLA CHRISTIAN COLLEGE
PENSACOLA, FLORIDA 32523-9160

Acknowledgements

The preparation of this textbook was initiated by the Educational Research Council of America (Dr. George Baird, President). The original plan of some of the chapters, and some of the substance, were prepared by Dr. Raymond English, when director of the social-science program of ERCA. Assistance was given by Mrs. Elaine Wrisley Reed, Miss Marie Richards, and Miss Agnes Michnay.

The author is especially grateful for the sagacious advice of Professor William Campbell on several points, and for graphs prepared by Dr. Campbell.

"The Goose That Laid the Golden Eggs" is reprinted with permission from *New Tales from Aesop* (1982) by Paul Roche, published by University of Notre Dame Press.

Photographs are used by agreement with The Bettmann Archive (BA), Ewing Galloway (EG), H. Armstrong Roberts (HAR), and Photo Researchers, Inc. (PR). The credits following are listed from top to bottom, left to right on a page, with any background photo listed first. 1-HAR; 2-HAR; 23-HAR: 24-BA (Adam Smith, title page of book); 41-HAR; 42-Mark Chester (PR), Joe Munroe (PR), M. E. Warren (PR), Renee Lynn (PR); 65-Lynn Lennon (PR); 66-Spencer Grant (PR); 93-Catherine Ursillo (PR); 94-Robert A. Isaacs (PR), Peter G. Aitken (PR); 119-HAR; 120-EG; 141-HAR; 142-Earl Roberge (PR); 167-Robert J. Erwin (PR); 168-HAR, Paolo Koch (Rapho-PR), George Whiteley (PR); 195-EG; 196-EG; 225-John Spragens, Jr. (PR); 226-Art Stein (PR); 247-Barbara Rios (PR); 248-HAR; 275-Mary Ann Brockman (PR); 276-Jill Hartley (PR), Carl Frank (PR); 301-HAR; 302-HAR; 343-HAR; 344-Steve Maslowski (PR).

CONTENTS

CHAPTER 1

Everybody's Economics

Chapter 1
Everybody's Economics

Why Bother about Economics?

Economics is the study of how goods are produced, distributed, and consumed.

If it were not for America's economic system, you might not be here reading this book today. In fact, you might not be alive at all, for human life can be maintained only by some system of economics. And a prosperous life can be maintained only by a good economic system.

This book is an introduction to economics. We are going to discuss the economic ideas and methods that make it possible for us to be well fed, well clothed, and well housed. We shall see how intelligent work can make us prosperous.

Everybody needs to know a good deal about economics. Why? Here are several reasons:

- to manage our own incomes and to achieve a decent standard of living for ourselves and our families;
- to run a business or carry on a profession;
- to save money intelligently;
- to understand governments' taxing and spending;

•to choose political leaders who are economically sensible;
•to see how nationwide or worldwide economic policies affect
us all.

When the ancient Greeks and Romans wrote about economics,
they meant the art of managing a household or a private estate. But in
the twentieth century, this word *economics* usually means something
bigger than running a household. As we use the word in this book, an
economy is a whole system of production, distribution, and consumption, extending to great numbers of people. Every nation has its
economy. Nowadays, indeed, there exists an international, or worldwide, economic structure.

We human beings are born into an environment that is hostile to
us in many ways. Think of all the care that is needed to keep a newborn
baby alive: well, the human race is rather like a baby in the hard world.
Human beings survive better than do other creatures because God has
given us intelligence, foresight, and ability to make plans.

Any people must create an economy in order to survive. Even
savages, who live by hunting and by gathering wild fruits and berries,
must have some economic system for distributing food within their
group, obtaining simple clothing, and sheltering from the weather or the
dangers of the night.[1] Also, they must have means for saving food for
a time when no game and no fruit may be found.

There can be no culture, not even the simplest sort, without an
economy.[2] Likewise, there can be no civilization unless a people
develop a fairly complex economy.[3]

In America today, we benefit from the most complex and productive economy that ever has existed. We tend to take our economy for

---

1. **Savages:** people who live by hunting and gathering or by some other economy that is very simple,
have no towns or cities, possess only simple crafts and arts, and usually have no writing.
2. **Culture:** a people's way of life, including their language, ideas, religion, work, government,
education, arts and crafts, and laws.
3. **Civilization:** a condition of human society marked by the existence of towns and cities, learned
persons, knowledge of mathematics and writing, efficient food production, elaborate arts and crafts, saving,
and much real and personal property.

granted, as if it had grown up by itself, like grass or trees. But really our economy, like all other economies, was created by the hard and intelligent work of many people.

Discuss

1. What is meant by the statement that the environment is hostile to mankind? Can you suggest ways in which the natural environment threatens human life? (Imagine yourself in a desert, a jungle, or the Arctic without the protections of civilization.)

2. Why must a person know something about economics to run a business or carry on a profession? Suggest what sort of economic decisions the owner of a large store must make.

Building an Economy: *the Pilgrims at Plymouth*

To understand how an economy is created or built up, let us look at one famous historical example of a group of people who built their economy, within a few years, out of almost nothing.

The Pilgrims, who landed in America in the year 1620, began their economy almost "from scratch," as the old phrase goes. These first civilized settlers in the region now called New England sailed to America for the sake of religious freedom. Also, they had economic reasons for settling in North America.

When the Pilgrim leaders sought from the king of England, James I, his permission to settle in America, James asked his chief secretary, "What profit might arise in the part they intend?"

"Fishing," the secretary replied.

"So God have my soul," declared King James, " 'tis an honest trade. 'Twas the Apostles' own calling."

The Pilgrims—most of whom were remarkably intelligent and hardworking people—knew that they must support themselves in the New World by profitable work: that is, by building up an economy in the wilderness. They intended to catch fish, dry them, and ship them to Britain for sale. They also intended to trade with the American

5

Indians, exchanging beads, hatchets, knives, and other things made in Britain for beaver skins, which were much wanted in Britain and Europe.

In order to reach America and establish themselves there in religious freedom, the Pilgrims had to obtain the use of ships, and they needed supplies that would last them until they could grow crops. So they borrowed what was then a large sum of money, seven thousand English pounds, from a group of merchants called the Virginia Company of London.[4] These "merchant adventurers" of the company were willing to invest money in New World settlements because they expected to make a handsome profit on their investment at the end of seven years. (Actually, as matters turned out, there was no profit.)

The Pilgrims hired a ship, the *Mayflower*, which they laded with tools and weapons, a stock of dried and salted foods, a few goats, pigs, and chickens, and goods for trading with the Indians. Among the more important articles put aboard were nets for fishing, that occupation being the colonists' chief economic hope. (These English nets turned out to be unsuitable for fishing in Massachusetts, so that the Pilgrims had to learn from Indians how to make efficient nets.) Some one hundred Pilgrim men, women, and children sailed for the New World.

Late in the year, the *Mayflower* reached Cape Cod—no very encouraging sight:

> *The breaking waves dashed high*
> *On a stern and rock-bound coast,*
> *And the woods against a stormy sky*
> *Their giant branches tossed.*[5]

On December 16, 1620, the Pilgrims landed at Plymouth Rock. They found themselves in a land of huge trees and dark swamps, and soon hostile Indians were shooting arrows at them.

---

4. **Pound:** the British unit of money, originally worth a pound's weight of silver. Until the Second World War, the British pound was worth nearly five dollars in American money.

5. This poem, "The Landing of the Pilgrim Fathers in New England," was written by Felicia Hemans (1793–1835).

Having driven off the Indians, the Pilgrims had to cut down trees, build cabins, and prepare to survive in isolation after the *Mayflower* should sail back to England. Having made friends of some of the Indians, they learned from those natives how to plant corn and to fish from the beaches. Soon came a "Starving Time"; half the Pilgrims died of tuberculosis, pneumonia, and malnutrition.

Yet some of the colonists survived, fished, and grew crops of corn. Through their own labor or by trading with the Indians, they were actually able to produce enough goods, only a year after their landing, to pay off nearly half their debt to the London Company. They had cut a large quantity of good oak lumber and were able to fill two hogsheads with beaver and otter pelts acquired from the Indians. Or rather, this shipment *would* have paid off much of their debt: for the small vessel carrying these goods, the *Fortune*, was taken in the English Channel by French pirates, who stole everything, "passengers and crew robbed down to their shoes."

Despite this sad loss, the colonists labored to make a success of their settlement. They knew nothing of deep-sea fishing or fur-trading, but they were taught by that hard master called Experience. At one time, the London creditors of the Pilgrims sent out a ship to foreclose their claim upon the Pilgrims' property because of their unpaid debts; but the ship was turned back without reaching New England. Common religious belief and a courageous spirit held the colony together.

For their first two years at Plymouth, the colonists lived by an economic plan called "The Common Course and Condition." This was a form of communism: all households shared equally in whatever the colonists could produce. But by the spring of 1623, the young governor the colonists had elected, William Bradford, decided that communism was an inferior economic system.

The Common Course, Bradford wrote, "was found to breed much confusion and discontent and retard much employment. . . . For the young men, that were most able and fit for labour and service, did repine that they should spend their time and strength to work for other men's wives and children without any recompense. The strong, or man of parts, had no more division in victuals and clothes than he that was weak and not able to do a quarter the other could; this was thought injustice."

Besides, Bradford went on, the older and more respectable men resented being treated no better than "the meaner and younger sort." The wives among the colonists "deemed it a kind of slavery" to have to cook the food, wash the clothes, and do other tasks for men who were not their husbands or sons.

Such communal economy runs against God's wisdom, Bradford concluded. Therefore, the colonists abandoned the Common Course and Condition. Instead, every family was assigned a tract of land (the amount of land varying according to the size of the household) and allowed to grow corn for themselves, not for the common stock.

This plan of private enterprise was successful very promptly. Sixty more settlers arrived at Plymouth in July, 1623, but, thanks to the new economic system, there was sufficient food for them, too.

"This had very good success," Bradford wrote of the new system of agriculture, "for it made all hands very industrious, so as much more corn was planted than otherwise would have been by any means the Governor or any other could use." The governor did not have to force people to work, and the settlers were far better content than before.

"The women now went willingly into the field, and took their little ones with them to set corn." Under the communal system, Bradford commented, the women would have complained that they were oppressed, had they been told that they must work in the fields.

Never again were the Pilgrims short of food. Thereafter, despite a harsh climate, poor communication with Britain, troubles with the Indians, pirates who took their cargoes, and other handicaps, the Pilgrims' economy began to prosper. Presently they commenced to pay off their debt to the London merchants.

In 1630, they were joined in Massachusetts by a large body of Puritans, similar in religion to the Pilgrims, who settled at Salem and

Boston. Massachusetts would become a thriving center of commerce and shipping among Britain's thirteen colonies.

Discuss

3. Sometimes the Pilgrims had to pay interest as high as forty-five percent on money they borrowed for their colony.[6] Why did lenders charge them so much for their borrowing?

4. Can you explain in your own words why the original Pilgrim plan for sharing alike, "The Common Course," did not work well?

Everything Has to Be Worked For

The Pilgrim settlement at Plymouth succeeded—though earlier colonies in Virginia and Newfoundland had failed—because the Pilgrim settlers knew that they must work hard and intelligently. *They worked harder and more intelligently when they were working for their own households rather than for the general community.*

The first thing to understand about economics is that all goods have to be worked for. The Pilgrims learned that lesson thoroughly.

Remember that economics is the study of producing, distributing, and consuming goods. What is meant by this word **goods?** We mean *material things or services that people will pay for—or will work to obtain.* Food and clothing are examples of material things. Medical attention and advice from lawyers are examples of **services** that people expect to pay for. So when we speak of economic goods, ordinarily we mean both services and material things.

To obtain goods, people must work. Most people are **producers:** persons who work to *provide* goods. All people are **consumers:** folks who *use* goods.

It is a fact of life that nearly all of us spend most of our time

---

6. **Interest:** money paid by borrowers to lenders as a reward for the use of the lenders' money.

producing and consuming—getting and spending. This absorption with material needs may be regrettable, but mankind never has found a way to survive without working to provide goods. Everything valuable has to be paid for.

The poet James Russell Lowell expressed this hard truth about our material existence in his well-known poem, written in 1848, "The Vision of Sir Launfal":

> *Earth gets its price for what Earth gives us;*
> *The beggar is taxed for a corner to die in,*
> *The priest hath his fee who comes and shrives us,*
> *We bargain for the graves we lie in;*
> *At the devil's booth all things are sold,*
> *Each ounce of dross costs its ounce of gold;*
> *For a cap and bells our lives we pay,*
> *Bubbles we buy with a whole soul's tasking;*
> *'Tis heaven alone that is given away,*
> *'Tis only God may be had for the asking.*[7]

Yes, economics is the study of that hard, material side of life, in which everything has to be worked for and paid for: the world of getting and spending. No goods are really free, because someone has had to work to produce them. Even our graves have to be paid for, because someone has to dig the graves—and that means hard work. Heaven is free, but heaven is not made up of material goods.

Discuss

5. Give five examples of material goods that you must have in order to stay alive.

6. Give five examples of important services that may be purchased in your neighborhood.

7. Can you think of anything besides God that "may be had for the asking"? Are there some things in life that people may enjoy without having to pay a price?

---

7. **Dross:** scum, refuse, rubbish. **Cap and bells:** parts of the costume of a jester, or fool, in the Middle Ages.

Economists and the Language of Economics

Economists are scholars of the production, distribution, and consumption of goods. They are experts, or authorities, on economic matters. Like experts in other fields, economists sometimes disagree among themselves.

As you study economics, you will find that some words with which you are familiar happen to be used by economists in ways that may be new to you. Already we have seen that when economists refer to a *good*, they do not mean something that is right or pleasant, like a "good job."

Instead, by a *good*, economists mean a material thing or a service that is valuable to people.

Economists say that a good is a thing that is created to satisfy a *want*. So what do economists mean by this familiar word *want?*

In economics, **want** means *a human desire to have a certain good or kind of goods.* When economists say *want*, they do not mean a desire for friendship or wisdom or heaven. Rather, they mean a desire for material things or services that people are willing to pay for.

Another familiar word that economists use in a special sense is *market*. We may think of a supermarket or a shopping plaza or a farmers' outdoor market when we see that word. But economists mean something bigger and more general (and vaguer) than a store or a series of stores. *This economic market is not merely one place:* instead, in economics, **market** is a *process* by which people exchange goods (including money) so that buyers and sellers can get what they are seeking for themselves. A very large number of people to whom very large quantities of products are sold is called a **mass market.**

Then there is the word *supply*. In ordinary speech, we may say, "She has quite a supply of meat in the freezer." *Supply* in this case means, of course, the amount of food a household has on hand. But when the economist says **supply,** he means this: the quantity of a good for sale at a certain price. (The economists' special use of the word *supply* will be explained more fully in later chapters, as will the other terms of economists used in this chapter.)

Or take the word *demand*. You might happen to say, "I demand my money back." In such a case, *demand* means to claim a right. But the economist means something different when he says *demand:* in economics, **demand** is the amount of a good that people will buy at a certain price.

Later we will come upon other words that are used in a special way in the study of economics. At first these economic terms may seem confusing, but you will grow accustomed to the language of economics as we move along.

Most of the study of economics is concerned with goods, wants, markets, supply, and demand.

The economist is a learned person with a special knowledge of production, distribution, and consumption. Studying goods, he emphasizes the human desire for more things. The economist does not say that all people are entirely greedy. Certainly he does not say that they ought to be greedy. Yet *in order to explain how human societies function, the economist assumes that a great many people in every society desire more goods than they possess already.*

Because they want goods, including services, people will work and save and invent and trade. Because they want many different goods, people have to choose what things they especially desire, as opposed to the things they can live without.

In economics, the idea of men and women as creatures with limitless wants is useful for explaining how people act in production, distribution, and consumption. But the economist's view of human nature is rather one-sided. This **economic motive** for human actions explains many of the ways in which people act, but it does not explain all human actions.

Discuss   8. Explain the following statement: "Human wants never can be satisfied."

> 9. Make a list of ten things you personally want but do not now have. Do you expect to obtain them? Will you be unhappy if you don't get them? Why or why not?
>
> 10. If an automobile dealer says, "There's a big demand for compact cars in my town this spring," is he using the word *demand* in the way economists use that term?
>
> 11. Do all the following fit within the economist's definition of the word *market?* The New York stock market, a stand where lemonade is sold by small children, a huge department store, little stalls in an Arab town where handicrafts are sold in the street, the buying and selling of gold in a London bank.
>
> 12. If you were to ask an economist, "Is there an unlimited supply of candy available?" what questions might he ask you in return? (Recall what an economist means when he uses the word *supply.*)
>
> 13. Can you name some human motives that are not economic? (Think of religion, defending one's country, helping old people or children, and other motives that do not involve money primarily.)

Economic motives are strong in the twentieth century. Socialists and Communists influenced by the teachings of Karl Marx argue that everything which ever occurred in the history of mankind resulted from materialistic desires.[8] And some defenders of a market economy seem much more interested in goods than in anything else. But society and human nature are not so simple as all that.

Goods, Wants, and Needs

Most people want more goods than they can pay for. That rather unpleasant fact presumably has been true ever since the Fall of Adam. Such desires are easily understood if a society has only a crude economy in which most people are hungry and ill-clothed much of the time.

Certainly this longing for more goods is true of industrial societies

---

8. **Karl Marx:** (1818–1883), radical social thinker, advocating communism. His followers are called Marxists.

in the twentieth century—even though not *all* men and women in today's society are eager for more goods. Some societies of this century are rich, producing and consuming more goods than people of earlier times ever dreamed about. Yet rich nations seek to grow richer.

Even in the more prosperous countries of our century, there never are enough goods produced to satisfy everybody's wants. People who own one automobile often want another; people who own two automobiles may think of getting a third. People who eat mostly beans may hope to consume steak; people already eating steak may think it would be pleasant to have a plate of caviar every day. In short, most people can contrive to think of more goods they would like to have— or think they would enjoy. In that sense, human wants never can be fully satisfied.

Although the accumulation of goods cannot produce happiness, nowadays most people seem to want a great deal—more, in some cases, than might be good for them. Many are more eager to spend money than to earn money. There is an old word for the bad habit of spending more than one can afford: *prodigality.* That word brings to mind the story of the Prodigal Son found in the New Testament. Here was a young man who demanded his inheritance and immediately commenced to spend it frivolously. His spending spree came to an abrupt end, however, and he soon realized the folly of his youthful actions. That age-old principle is still relevant today: one who spends beyond his means will eventually reap the consequences.

From the moment when, as children, we learn that things can be bought in little shops or great supermarkets, most of us tend to be frustrated from time to time. We remember the thrill of discovering that toys and candy were for sale—and the disappointment of finding out that certain persons in authority insisted on buying milk or bread or clothes until there was little or no money left for nice things for children.

All economic life is like that. *Economic choices have to be made and economic priorities set because all goods have to be paid for in one way or another.* And the amount that most people are able to pay always has been strictly limited. (The amount that most Americans are able to spend today would have astonished our great-grandfathers and great-grandmothers.) *Certainly all of us need to distinguish between our many wants, on the one hand, and our real needs on the other.*

What do we need most? What can we afford? How can we earn enough to get more of the goods we want? Such are some of the basic questions in the management of an economy—whether it is one's own household economy or the economy of a great nation.

Both a housewife and a member of the President's cabinet have to choose what material goods and services are truly needed, as distinguished from the many other goods that seem desirable. For wants, the economists tell us, are unlimited. But means of paying for the goods we want are very limited. Therefore, we must make choices among our wants.

Needs are not unlimited. Our needs usually are fewer than our wants. A woman may want to go shopping in Paris; but her need may be satisfied by sending an order to a mail-order firm; or she may get along by postponing her shopping until next month. A man may want a new set of golf clubs; but his need may be satisfied by using the clubs he owns already, or by borrowing a neighbor's clubs. *A **need,** in short, is a necessity: something it would be difficult to do without. A want is a desire, a longing, an appetite for something.*

For those goods we need most, we are willing to pay more than we would pay for goods of less importance to us. Suppose that one day you wanted both a square meal and a small photograph album, and that you had money enough for only one of those two goods. Probably you would choose to satisfy the want that is also a basic need: something to eat. The other want could wait, since rarely does a consumer *have* to obtain a photo album at the price of going hungry. *All needs are wants, in other words; yet not all wants are immediate needs.*

Even in the most prosperous of countries, economists tell us, goods are *scarce.* They mean that practically all goods are produced by human work, and so have to be paid for. *There is not an unlimited supply of any good.* Even in the richest country, the number of automobiles is limited, and so is the amount of steak available, or of caviar; even beans, which are relatively cheap, have to be produced by human cultivation and, therefore, are not available free to consumers. Everything has to be paid for.

So all of us, even the richest among us, necessarily have to choose first the things that we need most. And then, if we have money left over, we choose among our other wants.

Some wants may be harmful or evil. Often it is these baneful wants that certain people will pay most to satisfy. That is what James Russell Lowell meant by the "devil's booth" where "each ounce of dross costs its ounce of gold." Certain human wants have to be restricted or denied, if good character and public morality are to be maintained. So it is that almost all governments forbid or control the sale of certain goods that could do serious damage to society.

Discuss

14. What do Matthew 6:19–21 and 1 Timothy 6:8, 9 teach us about our wants and needs? According to Proverbs 28:27, what responsibility do we have toward those with legitimate needs?

15. Do you believe, with the typical economist, that people have unlimited wants?

16. Do you want twenty sweaters? Do you *need* twenty sweaters? Distinguish, in your own words, between personal needs and personal wants.

17. Suppose a candidate for office were to declare, "Americans need a minimum wage of fifty dollars an hour so they all can enjoy the standard of living they deserve." Would the candidate be talking, actually, about a *want* or about a *need?* Can you suggest any difficulty in satisfying claims for a fifty-dollar-an-hour wage, or do you think that the candidate's proposal ought to be adopted? Present your argument logically.

18. For a century and a quarter, the United States government has forbidden markets where slaves are sold. What other markets are unlawful in this country? Why is it any concern of government what people sell and buy?

Goods for Production, Goods to Use Up

Economists classify all goods under one or the other of two headings. One category is *producer goods* (or production goods). The other category is *consumer goods* (or consumption goods).

Producer goods are created because they are necessary for the making of other goods. A different name for producer goods is **capital goods.** Producer goods, or capital, may be used to make consumer goods or to manufacture more producer goods. Farm tools, factories, freight trains, and oil-well drilling equipment, for example, are producer goods.

Consumer goods are those produced for direct use by consumers: they are used up by the people who obtain them. Food, clothing, shelter, and most forms of fuel are among the more common consumer goods.

If no producer goods existed, there could be no consumer goods—or almost nothing for consumers. Even a piece of sharpened flint used by a savage to skin rabbits is a producer good, or capital.

Never, in any era, in any society, have there been enough capital goods or consumer goods to satisfy everybody. But the more capital goods exist, the more consumer goods can be produced. *Essential human needs can be satisfied when a society has been made prosperous by acquiring sufficient capital goods.*

How is it that the more productive countries of the twentieth century—lands that often are called the *developed countries* [9]—have managed to meet most of the needs and many of the wants of a large population?

The chief reason for this economic success has been that developed countries have created more producer goods. These

---

9. **Developed countries:** those having many large industries and scientific agriculture. In such countries, most workers are employed in manufacturing; relatively few work in agriculture.

producer goods, or capital, have turned out far more consumer goods than could be produced in the same countries two hundred years ago.

And how did they contrive to produce more producer goods? Through intelligent work and saving. Twentieth-century **technology**— the industrial skills and scientific methods that make possible efficient production—results from applying intelligence to work. *Most nations that are prosperous today are nations in which individuals or governments save part of what they produce and earn.* With such savings, they are able to make or buy more efficient capital goods.

Lack of goods is what we call **poverty.** When capital goods, producer goods, are very scarce, a society usually is very poor.

Discuss

19. Is there any good that you consume which was not produced by capital goods? Explain.

20. Can you think of any country that has few factories, little agricultural equipment, and only one kind of twentieth-century technology—and yet has a very large national income but a scanty population?

What Makes Goods Valuable?

All capital goods and all consumer goods are worth something. In economics, the **value** of a good is what people are willing to pay for it. *What determines the value of things?* That is, why are buyers willing to pay a price—sometimes a very high price—for things that may, or may not, be useful?

The value of goods varies according to their *scarcity* at a particular time and at a particular place. A typical citizen living in an American city today would not be willing to pay twenty dollars, say, for a glass of milk and a sandwich: for food and drink are plentiful in our society. But such a person would be willing to pay *something,* especially if it should be lunchtime, because everybody needs food and drink. Our

American city dweller might be willing to pay as much as three or four dollars, say, for a good sandwich and a glass of milk.

Yet a starving prisoner in a communist concentration camp, if he had money, might be willing to pay a high price for a glass of milk and a sandwich: for food and drink are painfully scarce in such camps. If the prisoner possessed twenty dollars, he might be eager to exchange his money for that food and drink. Under such circumstances, the value of a particular good is far greater than the value of the same good in an American city today.

Because new automobiles cost much money to manufacture and are in great demand, new cars ordinarily have a high value. Yet an old gentleman living all year round on Mackinac Island, in Michigan, probably never would buy an automobile, new or old, no matter how scarce or plentiful cars might be. Why not? Because Mackinac Island is the one public place in the United States where driving an automobile is not permitted.

The old gentleman living there would have no use for a car: so it would be worthless (have no value) for him. But the same car might be worth seven thousand dollars to a young woman living only a few miles distant, on the mainland. *Value, that is, varies not only in proportion to the scarcity of a good, but also in proportion to what use a consumer can make of a particular good.*

Economists are forever writing about scarcity. Sometimes all this emphasis on the alleged scarcity of goods seems ridiculous in a country like the United States, where a great many people eat more than is good for them, take long, costly vacations, spend large sums of money on formal schooling, own at least one good automobile, live in very comfortable houses or apartments (well heated in winter and perhaps air-conditioned in summer), and in many other ways have far more goods than any of their ancestors did. *In America, even the people officially classified as poor ordinarily possess television sets and other goods that would be looked upon as riches in many countries.*

Nevertheless, *it is the relative scarcity of a good, even in an affluent society, that determines the good's value.* Indeed, the more prosperous a society is, the more many people in that society are willing to pay high prices for something that is scarce.

Consider emeralds, the gems that today bring prices even higher than diamonds do. Emeralds, mined chiefly in the country of Colombia, have no practical use. People buy emeralds, usually of a deep green color, simply to wear in rings, necklaces, and other pieces of jewelry. Yet a small sack of emeralds, easily carried in a pocket, is worth a "king's ransom."

Why? Emeralds are pretty, set in gold or silver; but so are pieces of common green glass, set in gold or silver. Emeralds are extremely valuable because they are extremely scarce. Most people are proud to own scarce objects.

In the nineteenth century, the gems called amethysts—purple or violet in color—were extremely scarce, and therefore sold for high prices. Then the mining of amethysts in large quantities commenced in Brazil, Mexico, and Canada. Now amethyst jewelry can be bought quite cheaply because the gem no longer is very scarce.

Because the precious metals called gold and silver are scarce, they command high prices. That is why they were used for coins, and sometimes still are so used—a subject to be discussed in a later chapter of this book. Gold and silver have some practical uses besides serving as coins, but their high prices are fetched primarily by their scarcity—not chiefly by their usefulness in filling teeth, say.

The goods that we need most may be quite cheap—because they are not scarce. Nobody can get along without water; yet the price of water is very low in America, because water is plentiful. (Nevertheless, water does cost something, and people pay for it through the monthly bills for water, or through the electricity they use for pumping, if they have private wells.)

Or consider all the work that goes into making or distributing a loaf of bread—and yet the cost of a loaf is so small that nearly anyone could afford to eat a loaf daily. The farmer who grows the wheat, the milling firm that grinds the wheat, the trucker who delivers the flour to the bakery, the baker who bakes the loaf, and the delivery man who takes loaves to the shops—these are only some of the people whose labor contributes to the creation of our daily bread. Nevertheless, a loaf of bread is inexpensive, because bread is not scarce and there are many people competing to sell bread to consumers.

Thus, it is scarcity, rather than the amount of labor required to produce a good, that usually determines the value of any good. As economists use the word *value,* it means the high price that ordinarily must be paid for scarce things. To the economist, a valuable good is not necessarily useful or praiseworthy. A thing acquires value because it is scarce—perhaps very scarce; and, therefore, people are prepared to pay a high price for it.

Discuss

21. Can you get something for nothing? What? Wouldn't somebody or other have to pay for the things that you wouldn't have to pay for personally? How might society pay for your "free" goods?

22. Thirty years ago, television sets cost much more in dollars than they do today. During a time when the prices of most goods have increased greatly, apparently the value of television sets has gone down. Can you explain why?

23. What is the most valuable thing that you or your parents own? What makes it valuable? If you were to trade that thing for something else (swapping it, that is, without using money), what could you get in exchange that would be of approximately equal value?

24. Siberian tigers are very scarce animals, an "endangered species." Suppose that an uncle who kept a private zoo should leave you by his last will and testament one healthy Siberian tiger. Would that animal have a high value? To whom? If you kept the tiger, would it be useful to you?

From what we have just said about value and scarcity, you can see that economists are reasonable and logical people—or try to be. Economics is not a guessing game. To understand how economists think logically, we shall turn in the next chapter to the laws of economics.

    This book is not about economics only. You will find in it a good deal of information about political systems and about geography. For governments always have influenced greatly most economic matters: that is why economics originally was called *political economy.* And to understand economics well, it is necessary to know something about the different kinds of goods produced in various regions and countries and about international trade.

    This book also contains some economic history and some political history, especially of recent times. To understand how economies work today, we need to know their background: how economies developed and how economic systems have succeeded or failed in the past. As the philosopher George Santayana put it, people who ignore history are condemned to repeat it. They make the same mistakes, including economic mistakes, over and over again.

    All your life you are going to be involved in economic decisions. This book may help you to make sound decisions.

CHAPTER 2

Economists and Economic Laws

Chapter 2

Economists and Economic Laws

- First Principles of Economics
- The Mercantilists
- The Physiocrats
- The Wealth of Nations
- Ways to Prosperity
- The Limits of Economics

First Principles of Economics

All fields of study have certain *laws,* or general rules, which scholars in that particular discipline recognize as the first principles of their branch of knowledge. These laws are not the sort passed by a legislature or enforced by a court; instead, they are basic truths within a particular discipline. Physicists, for instance, speak of the *law of gravity* and the *laws of thermodynamics.*

Economists similarly speak of the **laws of economics,** meaning the general rules or principles of producing, distributing, and consuming goods. Most of these economic laws are concepts developed by economists during the past three centuries.

Are there some economic laws that apply to all economic systems, everywhere, in all ages? In the Soviet Union or Communist China, do the same economic laws operate that are at work within America's market economy?

Yes, *most economists believe that certain general economic principles are true of every economy, whatever form of government may prevail in a country, or whatever culture a people may inherit.*

Any successful economic system, therefore, must recognize the four factors of production and get them working together. (These factors will be discussed in Chapter 3.) *To produce goods, including services, it is necessary to join natural resources (land and raw materials), labor, capital, and management.* That is a law of economics, regardless of political beliefs. Who owns the land and the raw materials, who directs the labor, who supplies the capital, and who does the managing—why, such matters differ from one society to another. But the law remains that the four factors of production must be joined, if production is to be satisfactory.

When national governments, say, try to ignore the factors of capital and management, production of goods swiftly falls off. Then a government finds it necessary to modify its economic policies. "Experience is a hard master," Benjamin Franklin wrote in the eighteenth century, "but fools will have no other."

On page 27 are set down certain general laws, or principles, of economics that seem to apply in any society. Later in this book there will be discussion of some of these general rules.

Most of these economic laws were not well understood until the latter part of the eighteenth century, or until even more recently, and economists continue to dispute among themselves about the ways these laws operate. Nevertheless, it is difficult to imagine any society or economic system to which these economic principles do not apply. Although there still exist some very simple subsistence economies in which people have not yet reached the economic stage that requires money, the great bulk of the world's population in the twentieth century lives under economic systems in which the preceding ten rules are true—whether those systems are called *capitalist* or *socialist* or *communist* or by some other label.

Some Principles of Economics

1. Human wants for goods always require effort, or work.

2. People have more wants than they can satisfy.

3. Every society is limited by nature in its capacity to produce goods.

4. Individuals and societies try to produce goods as efficiently as possible.

5. Societies try to work (use their labor) in the most productive ways.

6. Better tools, or capital goods, result in increased production.

7. To acquire capital, or tools of production, individuals and societies must save, postponing immediate consumption.

8. When certain goods are very scarce, they become more valuable in terms of other goods.

9. Division of labor, or specialization, usually results in increased production.[1]

10. Economies with division of labor (specialization) require some form of money to make the exchange of goods easier.

Discuss

1. Can you explain the difference between a law of economics and a law passed by Congress or a state legislature?

2. What do we mean when we say that "every society is limited *by nature* in its capacity to produce goods"? (Think of some goods that cannot very well be produced in your state or region because of the limitations of nature.)

3. Do you ever postpone consumption so that you can acquire capital goods (tools)?

---

1. **Specialization:** the concentrating of one's efforts in a particular activity or a specific field. In economics, this may mean that a product is the result of the work of many specialized workers, each doing the particular task at which he is most skilled.

Before we study any of the laws of economics, we need to understand how the science of economics was developed two centuries ago. So first we look at the economic concepts of two eighteenth-century schools of economic thought: the *Mercantilists* and the *Physiocrats*. They lead us to the ideas of the most famous of all economists, Adam Smith.

The Mercantilists

From early in the sixteenth century until nearly the close of the eighteenth century, the principal states of Europe followed the set of economic policies called **mercantilism.** The aim of this economic system was to make the state strong economically. A government backed by great national wealth might maintain large, well-equipped armies and fleets, thus becoming a major power in the affairs of nations.

To grow rich and powerful—so the statesmen called Mercantilists *believed—a state should accumulate as much gold and silver as possible.* This might be accomplished by building up a country's foreign trade and by encouraging its manufacturing industries. The Mercantilists held that a great state should have a dense population, concentrated in large manufacturing towns. To achieve these aims and to develop these methods, the Mercantilists argued, the state should carry on an elaborate regulation of the country's economy. Through taxes on imports, granting of monopolies, subsidies to industry, and other means, the state might build up a huge reserve of precious metals.

Thus, European governments, under the influence of mercantilistic ideas, established colonies overseas from which they expected to obtain raw materials for their factories at home, and perhaps gold and silver from new mines. Mercantilistic governments labored to attain a **favorable balance of trade:** that is, they thought that a country should sell abroad goods of greater value than the goods it buys from abroad. (Thus a country would take in more money than it would pay out.) *In short, the* **mercantile system** *was a plan intended to control a country's* *economy in ways that would give the state greater tax revenues and greater power in the world.*

This mercantile system became fully developed in the seventeenth century. England, the Netherlands, France, Spain, and the other powerful states of Western Europe all adopted mercantilistic economic and political policies. The British government expected the English colonies in America to send raw materials to Britain and to buy British manufactured goods in return. This system frequently was highly profitable for economic interests within the "mother country." One example: Glasgow became in the eighteenth century the largest and most prosperous city in Scotland through importing, processing, and distributing Virginia's annual tobacco crop.

Discuss

4. Look up the word *mercantile* in a dictionary. Can you see how the word *merchant* is related to the idea of a mercantile system?

5. Who would be richer in goods—a person who owned a large, fertile farm with up-to-date equipment and producing large crops, or a person who had ten million dollars in gold coin locked in a safe and never spent any of it?

6. Was the mercantile system popular with most people in the American colonies during the 1760s and 1770s? What advantages and disadvantages did the mercantilistic policies of the British government present for the Thirteen Colonies? (Recollect what you learned in your study of American history.)

The Physiocrats

About the middle of the eighteenth century, some merchants, financiers, and scholars in France began to publish severe criticisms of the mercantile system. At first these critics called themselves simply *the Economists*. They were the first group to try to create a science of production, distribution, and consumption.

A young member of this group, Pierre Samuel du Pont de Nemours, published in 1768 a book entitled *Physiocracy.*[2] Presently

2. The book's title means "the rule of nature."

these French economists began to call themselves *the Physiocrats*. They meant by their title that they hoped to establish a "natural" economy, as opposed to "unnatural" or "artificial" mercantilism.

The mercantile system of the European states had been based on false principles, the Physiocrats argued. The following list outlines their chief beliefs.

Ideas of the Physiocrats

1. Everything in human society is controlled by certain natural laws; scientific study can discover these laws.
2. Individuals ought to decide what is best for themselves; what is best for the individual is best for society.
3. Free economic competition will lower prices and prevent excessive profits.
4. Society's real wealth comes from the land, through agriculture and mining; manufactures are useful but not the basic source of wealth.
5. Freedom of labor is a natural condition; slavery, serfdom, and governmental direction are unnatural.
6. Free trade should exist within a country, and also international trade should be free of heavy taxes. [3]
7. Governmental interference with the economy should be strictly limited.

Out of these physiocratic ideas came the beginning of what is now called **classical economics:** that is, the basic ideas of modern economic science.

The Physiocrats exerted considerable influence at the court of King Louis XVI, just before the French Revolution, which began in 1789. Du Pont and his friends were in power for a brief period during that revolution itself. Also, physiocratic teachings, particularly about agriculture and free trade, much influenced Thomas Jefferson and the

---

3. **Free trade:** exchange of goods without much taxation or regulation by the state. Economists emphasize particularly international free trade, with each country producing the goods which that country is best suited to produce and exchanging those goods for the products of other countries.

Republican party (or Republican-Democratic party) in America at the end of the eighteenth century and the beginning of the nineteenth century.

Discuss   7. Thomas Jefferson owned large plantations in Virginia, and most of his close friends were planters. Can you suggest one reason why Jefferson found himself agreeing with Du Pont and the other Physiocrats?

8. Do you think that the Physiocrats were correct when they argued that free labor is more productive than the labor of slaves, serfs, or prisoners? Why or why not? Where in the world today is unfree labor still used?

9. In opposition to the Mercantilists, the Physiocrats insisted that gold and silver are not the true sources of a nation's wealth. Money, they said, is merely a medium of exchange: a country may have plenty of gold and silver, and yet that country's people may be miserably poor. Can this be true? Why or why not?

We still study the Physiocrats, because it was they who saw the errors of the Mercantilists and made economics a scholarly branch of knowledge. Within the lifetime of the leading Physiocrats, nevertheless, there appeared in a different country an economist whom the Physiocrats recognized as greater than themselves. He was **Adam Smith,** a Scot, *the founder of modern economics.*

The Wealth of Nations

In the year 1726, a three-year-old boy named Adam Smith was playing by a large stone under a yew tree, a few miles from the Scottish fishing town of Kirkcaldy. Along came a band of gypsies and kidnapped the child. Adam's uncle, however, pursued the gypsies into a wood and rescued his little nephew. If the gypsies had succeeded in carrying off young Adam and had made him one of their band, the famous book called *The Wealth of Nations* never would have been written. And possibly the science of economics then would have been developed more slowly, or might have grown in a different way.

However that may be, actually the rescued Adam Smith grew up happily enough. After studying for ten years at the University of Glasgow and at Oxford University, he eventually became a professor of moral philosophy. In 1759, he published an important book, *The Theory of Moral Sentiments*, which strongly influenced the American leader John Adams, among other famous men of that time.

During most of the year 1766, Smith lived at Paris, where he spent much time with the Physiocrats, especially Pierre Samuel du Pont. Later, Smith wrote that the system of the Physiocrats, "with all its imperfections," was nevertheless "the nearest approximation to truth that had yet been published on the principles of that science." Ten years after his residence in Paris, Smith would remedy those "imperfections" of the French economists.

Returning to Scotland, Smith lived for ten years with his mother at Kirkcaldy, happily writing his *Inquiry into the Nature and Causes of the Wealth of Nations*. The book was published in 1776, the year of America's Declaration of Independence. Leading men of the time promptly praised the book as a work of original genius. Ever since 1776, **The Wealth of Nations** has been studied by everybody seriously interested in economics.

Smith's interest in economics began when he thought about the decline of the nail-making industry in his native town of Kirkcaldy. About the middle of the eighteenth century, Scottish shipbuilders began using iron nails in ships, rather than the wooden pegs previously used. Nails were made by hand in Kirkcaldy, and, for a short time, the nail-makers of that town held almost a monopoly of this profitable business.

But the old way of forming nails by hand required much time and labor. To make each nail, one workman had to use a long "fore hammer" while another workman used an ordinary hammer, the two working together. The cost of this labor of two skilled men meant that the price of nails remained high.

Then, at the Carron ironworks some twenty-five miles to the west of Kirkcaldy, an improved method for nail making was developed. The Carron works manufactured improved iron rods in furnaces and turned the rods into nails with much less labor. The nail trade at Kirkcaldy fell away to nothing, while Carron became a major industrial center.

Why did the Carron ironworks succeed and the nail makers of Kirkcaldy fail? Smith found the answer to that question: the **division of labor,** or specialization, in manufacturing. At Kirkcaldy, the old process for making nails had required too much labor and had been too slow for efficient production. But at Carron, the ironworkers had discovered ways of dividing the process of nail making into a series of stages, so that they did not need two skilled workers to turn out a single nail. Smith had read about the division of labor in earlier books, among them the French *Encyclopedia*. He now applied this concept of the division of labor to economic failure in his own town.

Led by his reflections on the division of labor to analyze the factors of production, Smith decided that labor was the most important of the four factors. All the wealth of a nation has to be produced by intelligent labor, Smith concluded. Out of these ideas grew his powerful book. Smith wrote clearly, including many practical examples in his chapters. *The Wealth of Nations* **has been in print from 1776 to the present day.**

Throughout his life, Dr. Adam Smith remained so interested in the division of labor that on one occasion he came near to being destroyed by it. When Charles Townshend, an eminent English politician, visited Glasgow, Dr. Smith took him to see a tannery where an efficient division of labor had been adopted. The London *Times*, years later, described what had happened at the tannery:

> They were standing on a plank which had been laid across the tanning pit; the Doctor, who was talking warmly on his favorite subject, the division of labor, forgetting the precarious ground on which he stood, plunged headlong into the nauseous pool. He was dragged out, stripped, and carried

with blankets, and conveyed home on a sedan chair, where, having recovered of the shock of this unexpected cold bath, he complained bitterly that he must leave life with all his affairs in the greatest disorder; which was considered an affectation, as his transactions had been few and his fortune was nothing.

As this account suggests, Smith sometimes was an absent-minded professor. Like most professors, he did not grow rich.

Yet Adam Smith did vastly increase the wealth of nations. His ideas, when applied to the Industrial Revolution that had begun during his own lifetime, resulted in a tremendous increase of production, distribution, and consumption. His arguments swept away many erroneous public economic policies; his book was especially valuable to statesmen responsible for public finance. William Pitt, the leader of the Tory party in Britain, declared a few years after Smith's death that Smith's ideas about increasing a nation's capital "furnish the best solution of every question connected with the history of commerce, and with the system of political economy." Charles James Fox, the leader of the Whig party, also praised *The Wealth of Nations* heartily.

Alexander Hamilton, the first Secretary of the Treasury of the United States, based his principal financial reports upon *The Wealth of Nations.* Hamilton's political opponents also turned to Smith's book for some of their chief arguments. Even Marxist economists, nowadays, have to acknowledge Adam Smith as a great thinker who discovered economic truths.

What is this "wealth of nations" that Adam Smith described? Why, it is the *accumulated capital* (producer goods) made possible by much intelligent work and much **saving** (postponed consumption). A nation's wealth does not consist of heaps of gold and silver, really; nor of luxurious consumer goods. *A nation that saves to build up the tools of production will prosper; a nation that spends unwisely and sinks into debt will experience poverty.*

Smith's principles, or laws, of economics will have some part in every one of the remaining chapters of this book. Many developments have occurred in economics since Smith wrote, but it was Smith's book that commenced and encouraged these developments.

Someone might say, "Why do we bother to study Adam Smith and the other early economists? Today we know more than they knew."

A wise economist would reply, "True, we know more about economics today than Smith did in 1776. But Smith and the other great economists are the substance of what we know."

Discuss

10. The American War for Independence broke out only a year before Smith published *The Wealth of Nations*. Can you see any connection between Smith's ideas and the ideas of the Patriot leaders?

11. Today, the countries enjoying the greatest wealth *per capita* (per head, per person) are certain Arab states. Is this because of their division of labor and their intelligent use of the factors of production? Or is there some other reason for their national wealth?

12. Adam Smith was a professor of moral philosophy for several years. Is there any connection between the study of morals and the study of economics? Can there be moral economic systems and immoral economic systems? Can you suggest examples of economic policies or systems that seem to improve moral habits? And other policies that seem contrary to good moral principles?

Ways to Prosperity

Economists think of themselves as practical scholars whose study of economics has a practical object or purpose. That aim, or purpose, is to increase the amount of *wealth* possessed by the people of a nation—or perhaps the wealth of the whole world. That is why Adam Smith entitled his famous book *The Wealth of Nations*.

To the economist, this word **wealth** means *all things that have value: all money, property, capital goods, consumer goods*. We say that a wealthy person or a wealthy nation is prosperous. The word **prosperity,** to economists, means *economic success, or the condition of enjoying many goods, including services*.

So economists are scholars whose practical intention is to teach us how to increase the prosperity of a group of people, or of a nation, or perhaps of the world. This book is an attempt to show you how prosperity may be achieved.

The purpose of all economic systems is to increase the amount of wealth—that is, to achieve prosperity. But not all economic systems are equally successful in working toward this aim or end. In later chapters we will point out why some economic methods succeed and why others fail.

The typical economist has more to say about scarcity than about prosperity. For that reason, economics has been called "the dismal science." Often the economist seems to be looking at the dark side of things, fretting about inefficiency and poverty. Perhaps the economist tends to be gloomy because he is aware that *most economic systems of the past failed to produce enough goods to provide adequately for the food, shelter, warmth, and health of much of a nation's population.* The economist knows, too, that many economies of the twentieth century are feeble and badly managed.

So, rather than talking about "achieving prosperity," very commonly economists use such phrases as "diminishing scarcity." So far as America is concerned, that is a somewhat negative way of looking at our economic situation. *The American economy, since the end of the eighteenth century, has done more than diminish scarcity: it has created plenty, in many ways.* Many of the goods that were scarce in the United States in the year 1790 are plentiful in the United States today—even though America's population is about fifty-five times greater today than it was in the year of the first census. Essential goods, to satisfy genuine needs, are not scarce in the America of our time.

Yet actually the phrases "achieving prosperity" and, "diminishing scarcity" mean the same thing. *Economists try to show us how to become prosperous: that is, how to overcome scarcity.* But economists, like politicians and many other people, often disagree about the best means for achieving prosperity or diminishing scarcity. Below we list various ways that have been followed in various countries and at various times to increase the wealth or to diminish the poverty of a nation—or, at least, to increase the prosperity of some element of the population. To put the matter another way, *the following methods are conceivable ways of satisfying economic needs.*

1. **Produce more goods from existing resources.** A simple instance of this method would be to turn out more cotton goods from an existing cotton mill by using the looms (capital goods) more hours in a day—thus producing more cotton cloth (consumer goods) from existing machines. (Of course this practice would require more labor, in the form of two or three "shifts" in factory operation.)

2. **Increase the amount of resources used in the production of goods.** For example, the scarcity of copper pipes might be reduced if miners were to discover a previously unknown source of copper ore in southern Africa and were to mine this vein of copper to supply customers with raw copper (and eventually copper pipe) in America and Europe.

3. **Find *new* resources to satisfy existing wants.** The invention of new formulas for making plastic products that could be substituted for certain scarce metals would illustrate this way of increasing wealth.

4. **Make goods already being produced more useful in satisfying wants.** An instance of this method would be a program to show consumers how to reduce the amount of fuel used in their homes or places of business by insulation that diminishes waste of energy.

5. **Redistribute among the population the goods that are being produced already.** Thus, a Marxist government might take away goods from property-owning people who are relatively well off and give those confiscated goods to propertyless people who are relatively poor.

6. **Simply reduce people's wants.** Often in wartime, governments ration food so that most citizens must eat less than they did before; at other times, some authority persuades consumers to reduce their consumption of energy by turning down their thermostats and enduring

lower temperatures in winter. (Or this latter result may be achieved simply by the increase of the price of electricity and fuels.)

All these methods for dealing with wealth and poverty have been tried more than once, with varying degrees of success. It should be noted that except for the fifth and sixth ways, harder and more intelligent *work* is required to achieve prosperity or to reduce scarcity. *Goods can be produced only through some amount of human* **labor**—*handwork, brainwork, or a combination of both kinds of work.*

So we emphasize work in the following chapters of this book. Countries with few natural resources, like Switzerland or Japan, may become highly prosperous because their people work willingly and intelligently. On the other hand, a country with large natural resources may be poor because its people do not know how to apply their work intelligently to those resources.

The highly productive economy of modern times was developed by ingenious people—that is, by persons good at inventing, good at planning, good at making things. *So long as ingenious people have opportunity to do their work in freedom, an economy prospers. But when a society discourages ingenious people, or restrains and burdens them unduly, or persecutes them—why, then prosperity fades away, and scarcity prevails again.* Just that has happened repeatedly in the course of history. **The true source of prosperity is diligent work directed by ingenious intelligence.**

Discuss

13. What one of the six methods for satisfying economic needs do you prefer? What one do you find least desirable? Why?

14. Why don't governments abolish scarcity by making sure everybody has the same income, so that all citizens might buy whatever they need or want? Do you see anything impractical about this proposal? If so, suggest why it might not work well.

15. Adam Smith wrote that "nobody ever saw a dog make a fair and deliberate exchange of one bone for another with another dog." Can you think of creatures, other than human beings, that have economic systems? (Think of saving, systematic work, capital goods, consumer goods, intelligence.)

16. Can you suggest occupations in which knowledge of economics might help a person to earn a good living?

17. Why don't we leave the study of economics to professional economists and politicians, and just get on with the practical business of making money for ourselves? Give reasons for your answer.

The Limits of Economics

Economics is not a religion. Nor is it a political system. Nor is it a sure recipe for happiness. Economics is simply the study of producing, distributing, and consuming goods.

Most people desire economic prosperity for themselves and their families. As the great moralist Samuel Johnson remarked in the eighteenth century, people who talk about the pleasures of poverty have had no experience of real poverty. Nevertheless, there is much more to a good life than wealth.

There is nothing morally wrong with being poor, so long as one's poverty is not caused by indolence and evil habits. Neither is there anything morally wrong with being rich, so long as one's wealth is acquired honestly. The fact that God does not frown upon material wealth is proved by His blessing upon two well-known Old Testament characters, Abraham and Job. The Lord saw fit to bless each one abundantly, even by the world's standards.

But simply acquiring goods ought not to be the whole purpose of anyone's life. The person who thinks of nothing but making money may benefit other people through his productivity; but he injures himself: he never develops into a full human being. As a popular song of half a century ago put it, "The world belongs to everyone; the best things in life are free." Jesus taught that the aim of life is not mere getting and spending, but rather to "lay up treasure in heaven."

If human beings did not produce, distribute, and consume, the human race would cease to exist. *Because economic activity is necessary to our survival, economics is a valuable study. And yet what economists can teach us is limited.* Economic science does not tell us about the life of spirit, the life of art, or the mysteries of the physical universe. It does not offer us wisdom in anything except the art of increasing the wealth of nations. ***To point out the way to material prosperity: that is the limited, though very useful, aim of economics. That limitation needs to be remembered as you make your way through this book.***

All the goods that keep you alive have been produced by an economic system which rewards intelligent work. Without a vigorous economy, the existence of all of us would be like that of the vast majority of humans throughout the course of history: "poor, nasty, brutish, and short," as a seventeenth-century philosopher put it.

So bear it in mind that we all need to know more than economics; and we all need to be something more, as human beings, than simply producers and consumers. Yet bear it in mind also that unless a good many people understand economics fairly well, the nation may fall into poverty and confusion. The study of economics deserves your attention.

CHAPTER 3

The Factors of Production

NATURAL RESOURCES

LABOR

CAPITAL

MANAGEMENT

THE FACTORS OF PRODUCTION

Chapter 3

The Factors of Production

- •Prosperity does Not Grow on Trees
- •The Factor of Natural Resources
- •The Factor of Labor
- •The Factor of Capital
- •The Factor of Management

Prosperity Does Not Grow on Trees

How do all the world's capital goods and consumer goods get produced? How do we succeed in relieving scarcity?

Why, the production of goods is the result of intelligent use of certain *resources.* Different sorts of resources have to be brought together in this process of turning out goods. Economists call these resources the **factors of production.** There are four such factors:

1. Natural Resources
2. Labor
3. Capital
4. Management

These four factors of production are scarce, even in the most prosperous regions: that is, a demand exists everywhere for more raw materials, more helping hands, more producer goods, better economic direction.

Some countries or economic regions lack sufficient raw materials: they may be deficient in minerals, crops, forests, and even sufficient water. Some have not accumulated capital. Others, with scanty population, do not have sufficient labor available. Yet others have not developed able management. Even when the more prosperous regions of the world are fairly well supplied with all four factors of production, and even when economies have developed efficient forms of production, the demand for more goods tends to outrun the supply. As economists put it, even in the most prosperous economy, "there are still unmet demands and uses to which scarce factors could be put."

Economists, historians, and anthropologists tell us that until man in a given society learns how to combine the four factors of production, most of the people in the society remain extremely poor. They seem to live from day to day, never knowing whether they will have anything to eat the next day. For economic prosperity does not "grow on trees": instead, prosperity (or even a very simple economy that provides just barely enough food and clothing and shelter to maintain life) is the result of intelligent use of the factors of production.

When any producer—a family unit, a firm, a great corporation, a whole society—neglects any one of the factors of production, that producer's prosperity is in danger. For *economic success, on a large scale or a small scale, depends upon some intelligent combination of the four factors.*

The Factor of Natural Resources

The first resource necessary for the production of goods is land and raw materials (usually called **natural resources**). Most enterprises have to erect or lease buildings—which means that they must occupy land. And nearly all enterprises must use some raw materials if they are to produce goods. (If a producer sells only services, rather than material things, he may need few or no raw materials.)

A region may have many natural resources, and yet the people who live there may be poor—if they lack the other three factors of production.

Until late in the eighteenth century, land was a bigger factor in the more advanced economies than it is today because the vast majority of the population in every country was engaged in agriculture—until the Industrial Revolution that commenced in England about 1750.[1] And whether one cultivates crops or grazes animals, agriculture requires much land. "Keep your land, and your land will keep you," a saying ran.

Since the Industrial Revolution, in industrially developed countries, the majority of the population have come to work in manufacturing, commerce, or the service industries. Therefore, the relative importance of land has diminished somewhat in such developed countries.

But land still is a costly resource. At the centers of great American cities, the land on which a tall office building is erected may cost several million dollars—even though the site is only a fraction of an acre in extent.

What any particular piece of land costs is determined by the scarcity of land in a particular area. A small field in densely cultivated Holland or Belgium might cost several times as much as a large (but abandoned) farm in upper New England, say. Land is cheap only in regions where the population is scanty and there exist few profitable uses to which land might be put.

Land is a kind of raw material: that is, land becomes valuable only if human resources are applied to it. To make land useful, it must be built upon, or be planted with crops, or have animals grazing upon it, or (if trees grow there) be harvested by foresters.

But ordinarily when we say **raw materials,** we mean some *substances that can be made into goods.* Land itself may supply such raw materials: for instance, a deposit of clay may be used as the raw material for manufacturing brick or pottery. Or the land may be quarried, where there is rock, to supply stone for buildings.

Raw materials in the ordinary sense, nevertheless, are distinct from land. These raw materials may be grouped in several different categories.

---

1. **Industrial Revolution:** the period during the eighteenth century in which steam-powered machinery was first used for production.

Raw materials may be derived from *animal* substances—for example, wool from sheep or hides from cattle, horses, and swine. Milk, tallow, and bone meal (used for fertilizer) are all raw materials from animal sources.

They may be *vegetal*—derived from plants: for example, cotton, flax, and cereal grains. Some raw materials that we mine or pump from beneath the earth's surface may have been vegetal originally, but now are classified as mineral deposits: petroleum, natural gas, and coal, the fossil fuels.

Raw materials may also be *mineral*, extracted from below the surface, such as the precious metals or uranium (a metal used for nuclear fission). Some minerals were mined in very early times: copper, lead, iron, tin, silver, gold. Gold was found near the Garden of Eden (Gen. 2:11,12), and Tubal-cain, just six generations after his ancestor Cain, was "an instructor of every artificer in brass and iron" (Gen. 4:22).

Even water is a raw material used in the manufacture of all sorts of goods. The potters of the early cultures needed steady streams of water for their potters' wheels in order to produce bowls and bottles. Modern manufacturing is possible only when there exist adequate supplies of the raw material called water.

Discuss

1. Why are the fossil fuels an indispensable form of raw material for developed industrial countries?

2. Some parts of the world that formerly were poor have grown prosperous (or less poor, at least) because they possess natural resources for which there is an urgent demand in the industrialized countries. Can you name five countries or regions that have been enriched by extracting such raw materials?

The Factor of Labor

To produce goods, *intelligent work* is required. This work may be either mainly physical or mainly mental. Economists use the term **labor** to signify both types of work.

"We must find our happiness in work, or not at all," wrote a famous American scholar, Irving Babbitt. He meant that unless we do something satisfying and productive with our lives, soon or late we grow bored and miserable. Also we grow poor. For **unless the large majority of people work with hand and brain, intelligently and regularly, consumer goods become so scarce that a society may not survive.** And if not enough work is done to make or repair capital goods, no adequate quantity of consumer goods can be turned out.

The Bible teaches that prosperity comes mainly as a result of hard work, or diligent labor:

> **He becometh poor that dealeth with a slack hand: but the hand of the diligent maketh rich.** —Prov. 10:4

> **Wealth gotten by vanity shall be diminished: but he that gathereth by labour shall increase.** —Prov. 13:11

Other such references in the book of Proverbs alone are as follows: Prov. 6:6–11; 12:24, 27; 13:4; 14:23; 15:19; 19:24; 20:4, 13; 21:5, 25–26; 22:13, 29; 23:20–21; 24:30–34; 26:13–16; 27:18, 23–27; 28:19. Thus it is no accident that Jewish and Christian cultures, those influenced by the Bible, have been among the most prosperous cultures in history.

Nearly everything we need is produced by human labor. Even South Seas islanders, who can get part of their food by picking coconuts and fruit, must work to catch fish, build huts, and make simple clothing. The islanders must make boats, fishing nets and spears, cooking utensils, and many other articles. When Adam and Eve were thrust out of the Garden of Eden, Jehovah told Adam, "In the sweat of thy face shalt thou eat bread, till thou return unto the ground." This is a way of saying that all people must labor to keep body and soul together here on earth.

To the economist, *labor* means personal service, whether physical or mental. Thus defined, labor usually is the largest item of cost for any big economic enterprise.[2] When we buy goods, ordinarily the cost

2. **Enterprise:** a bold undertaking or attempt; in economics, a commercial or industrial undertaking.

of the labor used in producing those goods forms the major share of the price we pay (though there are exceptions to that general rule). *As a factor of production, labor looms big indeed. That is why inventors and industrialists always are trying to invest in new forms of labor-saving machinery.*

In a market economy, labor enjoys freedom: that is, people who sell their services to employers are free to work for any particular employer who will hire them or to choose not to work for that employer.[3] They are free to bargain with employers about how much they are to be paid, what hours they will work, and under what conditions they will work. Working people may bargain individually for themselves, or they may bargain collectively, through membership in free labor unions.

Usually the labor of free men and women is more produc-tive than the labor of slaves, serfs, or other unfree people. Free men and women know that they are laboring for their own advantage, primarily, and not merely for the advantage of some individual master or of some huge organization that directs them against their will. Also, free men and women ordinarily are more cheerful and energetic than are people forced to work.

In America, we take it for granted that working people (except for imprisoned criminals) are free politically and free economically. Yet the slavery of most laborers was taken for granted in ancient times, and serfdom survived in much of Europe until the latter half of the eighteenth century—in Russia, until the latter half of the nineteenth century. In much of Africa, forced labor under the threat of the *kurbash* or the *sjambok* (whips) survived into the twentieth century. Complete freedom of labor is a modern development, and extends only to portions of the world. Another term for unfree labor is *servile labor. And right up to the present time, much of the world's labor remains servile.*

For in totalist (totalitarian) states with a thoroughgoing command

---

3. **Market economy:** one in which prices and wages are determined by competition in the market.

4. **Command economy:** one in which prices and wages are determined by political authority, and in which government directs the economy in other ways.

economy, "direction of labor" is the common pattern.[4] Under a systematic command economy, men and women are assigned to work by some political authority, according to the totalist state's needs; and wages are fixed by some governmental agency. Free labor unions are forbidden in totalist command economies like those of the Soviet Union, China, Vietnam, and other Communist states.[5] In Poland, during recent years, the big free union called Solidarity was broken by the government. Unions may survive in name in such economies, as they did in Germany under the Nazis, but in name only: they are totally directed by the government. Also, totalist regimes often maintain huge prisons or concentration camps in which political prisoners and people convicted of criminal offenses are compelled to labor without wages under the most miserable conditions.

Freedom of labor is not peculiar to the industrial economies of "free market" countries: most or all laborers may be free enough in certain simple agricultural economies, past or present. *But in the economically developed countries of our time, freedom of labor is the usual pattern in market economies, and direction of labor the usual pattern in command economies.*

Labor is most efficiently productive in economies that offer substantial rewards for good work. It was so with the Pilgrims of Massachusetts Bay, and it is so today conspicuously in such countries as Japan, the Federal Republic of Germany (West Germany), Switzerland, The Netherlands, Belgium, Canada, and the United States, all countries with market economies. Labor is efficient also in some mixed economies with freedom of labor, most notably that of Sweden.[6] Wages generally are lower, and efficiency of production is less, in systems with command economies. There exist political causes, as well as economic

---

5. **State:** an organized political community, usually with a definite territory, not ruled by some higher political authority. States have governments; but the state is permanent, while governments change from time to time. Germany, Britain, France, Brazil, and Egypt, to name a few, are examples of states. In the United States of America, the word state usually means one of the fifty states that make up the federal Union.

6. **Mixed economy:** one that retains some features of the competitive market economy, but also has features of the command economy and sometimes has partial ownership of the means of production by the state.

causes, for the relatively low productivity of command economies in today's world. But the freedom to bargain with their employers possessed by working people in market economies and some mixed economies is a major reason for prosperity in such systems.

The wages and the salaries paid for labor have risen steadily and often swiftly during the twentieth century, especially in the market economies, principally because of the increase of skilled labor as contrasted with unskilled labor. For skilled labor requires training and careful workmanship. Because skilled labor is far more productive than unskilled labor, the man or woman with some skill deserves and obtains a monetary reward in market economies. Before the industrial era, most workers "followed the plow"—that is, they engaged in routine agricultural labors that required relatively little training or active intelligence. Today, both in manufacturing and in agriculture, skill and personal competence are required for successful production; and because production of goods and services is higher, wages and salaries are proportionately higher.

Labor without natural resources, capital, and management would do no more than barely support human life, at best. But without the all-important factor of labor, the other three factors of production would be ineffectual.

Discuss

3. When you purchase a loaf of bread, whose labor are you paying for?

4. If the labor of free persons is more productive than servile labor, why did slavery and serfdom endure for many centuries? Why do totalist states engage in stern direction of labor?

5. Not everybody relishes work. About one man, a neighbor may say, "He's not afraid of work: he can lie down right beside it." Can you offer some reasons why a considerable part of the human race does the minimum of labor? (Think about human nature, early habits, lack of training, lack of incentives, and other causes.)

The Factor of Capital

Goods used to produce other goods, you will remember, are called *capital goods*, or **capital.** This capital may consist of machines, buildings, simple tools, vehicles for transporting goods, or anything else that is used in production and distribution. Often we refer to money as capital, because money will buy the capital goods needed for production. Thus, when we speak of capital that a person owns, we may be thinking of his bank deposits.

But to an economist, *capital* means producer goods. Bank deposits, stocks, bonds, and insurance policies are capital in this sense: they are documents proving that their holder owns shares in some sort of productive enterprise.[7] (The only capital goods of some companies may be desks, typewriters, and office supplies. But those objects, too, are capital, because they are used to produce services.)

Discuss

6. Is a person's house usually capital? If not, why not? Can you think of ways in which a person's house, or part of it, might be called part of its owner's capital?

7. Do carpenters, masons, and plumbers who are self-employed—that is, who do jobs by themselves and do not receive wages from an employer—own capital goods? What sort of goods?

8. Suppose you decided to open a gas station. What capital goods would you need to conduct your business? If you wished to improve or enlarge your station but lacked cash enough to pay for the work, where might you get additional capital?

Anyone who owns producer goods or owns a share in some business that produces goods, is a **capitalist**—even if that person's capital is small and simple. Anyone who owns stocks or bonds, keeps money in a bank, or has a life insurance policy, can be called a capitalist. For such an investment usually means that the investor's savings are

---

7. **Stock:** the capital of a company or corporation, divided into transferable shares at uniform amount. **Bond:** certificate issued by government or company, promising to pay back a certain amount of money borrowed.

used by companies that produce goods. Thus, in the United States, many millions of people are capitalists, owning some share in capital goods.

No matter what sort of government a country has, capital is a necessary factor of production. Quite as much capital is required for building a factory in Soviet Russia as in the United States. In that sense, **all countries with much industrial development are "capitalist" countries:** for in the civilized societies of the twentieth century, technology and mass production require huge investments of capital. In North America, countries of western Europe, and some other lands, most of that necessary capital is furnished by private individuals. In the Soviet Union, Communist China, and other socialist countries, most of that necessary capital is supplied by the political state. Economists call economic systems in which the government owns most of the capital *state capitalism.*

During the nineteenth and twentieth centuries, revolutionaries have denounced capitalism as an unjust and oppressive social system. But actually *capitalism is not a social system, or a political system, or a philosophy, or a religion.* **Capitalism** *is merely an economic structure for getting together the capital necessary to operate large-scale productive enterprises.* But capitalism takes on different forms under differing political systems. The capitalism all about us in the United States is **private** capitalism: the owners of the capital are millions of private individuals. The capitalism of the Soviet Union and similar countries is **state capitalism:** the owner of the capital is the all-powerful centralized political apparatus called the collectivist state.

Discuss

9. Suppose that a farmer named Solomon Grundy owns four hundred acres of land, large barns and other storage facilities, plows and combines, four tractors, and bank deposits. Is Mr. Grundy a capitalist?

10. Suppose that a business executive named Samantha Swenson is paid a salary of a hundred thousand dollars a year for directing a chain of restaurants. She lives simply, gives away most of her income to charities, travels much at her own expense, and

does not believe in saving. "You can't take it with you," she says; so she does not invest, not even in regular life insurance. Is Miss Swenson a capitalist?

11. Do you think there is more personal freedom under state capitalism or under private capitalism? Give reasons for your answer.

When we use the word *capital* nowadays, often we tend to think of tremendous factories, complicated machines, and big business. But actually *capital* also includes many small and relatively simple things. No one of us could survive for more than a few days without access to certain kinds of capital. The Australian aborigine or the pygmy of the Kalahari Desert needs some capital, simple tools, in order to survive.

Robinson Crusoe, Capitalist

To understand this point, we turn to the first great novel in the English language, *Robinson Crusoe*. This famous story, based in part on the real adventures of a Scottish sailor named Alexander Selkirk, was written by Daniel Defoe near the beginning of the eighteenth century. An adventurous merchant, Robinson Crusoe, is shipwrecked on a desolate island off the coast of South America. All his companions have been drowned in a storm.

Crusoe struggles ashore with "nothing about me but a knife, a tobacco-pipe, and a little tobacco in a box." His broken ship is stranded about a mile offshore. Wading and swimming, Crusoe manages to board the vessel and carry to land goods he needs. Here is part of Crusoe's own description of his successful search, after he has climbed into the forecastle of the ship.

Here I found that the ship was bulged, and had a great deal of water in her hold, but that she lay so on the side of a bank of hard sand, or rather earth, that her stern lay lifted up upon the bank, and her head low almost to the water. By this means all her quarter was free, and all that was in that part was dry; for you may be sure my first work was to search and to see what was spoiled and what was free. And first I found that all the ship's provisions were dry and untouched by the water; and being very well disposed to eat, I went to the bread-room and filled my pockets with biscuit, and eat it as I went about other things, for I had no time to lose. Now I wanted nothing but a boat, to furnish me with many things which I foresaw would be very necessary to me.

Having made a rough raft, Crusoe prepares to get ashore whatever may be useful to him for surviving alone on a wild island.

I first got three of the seamen's chests, which I had broken open and emptied, and lowered them down upon my raft. The first of these I filled with provisions, viz., bread, rice, three Dutch cheeses, five pieces of dried goat's flesh, which we lived much upon, and a little remainder of European corn, which had been laid by for some fowls which we brought to sea with us, but the fowls were killed. There had been some barley and wheat together, but, to my great disappointment, I found afterwards that the rats had eaten or spoiled it all.

Crusoe finds enough clothes "for present use," but is still more eager to get hold of tools:

It was after long searching that I found out the carpenter's chest, which was indeed a very useful prize to me, and much more valuable than a ship-loading of gold would have been at that time. I got it down to my raft, even whole as it was, without losing time to look into it, for I knew in general what it contained.

My next care was for some ammunition and arms; there were two very good fowling-pieces in the great cabin, and two pistols; these I secured first, with some powder-horns, and a small bag of shot, and two old rusty swords. I knew there were three barrels of powder in the ship, but knew not where our gunner had stowed them; but with much search I found them, two of them dry and good, the third had taken water; these two I got to my raft with the arms. And now I thought myself pretty well freighted, and began to think how I should get to shore with them, having neither sail, oar, or rudder; and the least capful of wind would have overset all my navigation.

Crusoe does contrive to land his cargo safely. The following day he returns to the wrecked ship for more salvage.

I brought away several things very useful to me; as, first, in the carpenter's stores I found two or three bags full of nails and spikes, a great screw-jack, a dozen or two of hatchets, and above all, that most useful thing called a grindstone. All these I secured, together with several things belonging to the gunner, particularly two or three iron crows, and two barrels of musket bullets, seven muskets, and another fowling-piece, with some small quantity of powder more; a large bag full of small-shot, and a great roll of sheet lead; but this last was so heavy, I could not hoist it over the ship's side. Besides these things, I took all the men's clothes that I could find, and a spare fore-top sail, a hammock, and some bedding; and with this I loaded my second raft, and brought them all safe on shore, to my very great comfort.

Later Crusoe takes from the ship ropes, twine, canvas, a hogshead of bread, . . . a box of sugar, a barrel of flour, two cables, a hawser, much ironwork, razors, scissors, knives and forks, and "about thirty-six pounds value in money, some European coin, some Brazil, some pieces of eight, some gold, some silver."

I smiled to myself at the sight of this money. "O drug!" said I aloud, "what art thou good for? Thou are not worth to me, no, not the taking off of the ground; one of those knives is worth all this heap. I have no manner of use for thee; even remain where thou art, and go to the bottom as a creature whose life is not worth saving."

Nevertheless, Crusoe does take the money ashore. Before the wreck is broken up by a second storm, he gets out of the vessel pens, ink, paper, compasses, mathematical instruments, perspectives (telescopes), charts, books of navigation, three Bibles, prayer-books, several other books, a dog, and two cats. To his sorrow, he is left without any spade, pick-ax, shovel, needles, pins, or thread. As matters turn out for him, Crusoe remains on his desert island for more than twenty-eight years. Except for things he is able to make for himself, all that time he gets no more goods but some clothes from drowned sailors and coins from another wreck.

Discuss

12. Of the things Crusoe salvaged from the wreck of his own ship, what ones should be listed as capital goods (producer goods) and what as consumer goods?

13. Why did Crusoe sneer at the money he found? It would have been capital for him in England, his homeland. Why wasn't it capital on a desert island?

The world generally is in a situation rather like Crusoe's. Capital goods always are in short supply, and in many countries the majority of people survive by using their simple and scanty capital to produce a very slender supply of consumer goods. They have what we call a **subsistence economy**—an economic system that provides just enough to keep a society alive. In countries today like Bangladesh or Ethiopia, from time to time the subsistence economy breaks down because of droughts, floods, wars, or other disasters. And then many thousands of people starve.

Throughout human history, most people have been poor. A principal cause of their poverty has been a lack of capital goods to produce consumer goods. Capital goods, we need to remember, can be created only through intelligent labor: that is, planning the work we do. As a factor of production, capital is of equal importance with raw materials and labor.

Discuss

14. In countries with subsistence economies, why don't the governments provide poor people with adequate food, clothing, and shelter?

15. In countries like Bangladesh and Ethiopia, why don't starving people use credit cards to buy what they need? If they need more capital, why don't they go to a bank and borrow enough money to buy adequate capital goods?

Because capital always and everywhere is hard to obtain, people who own capital are paid for the use of their capital. In developed countries, most of the owners of capital do not work in the businesses that use their capital. They are not paid wages or salaries by the factories or commercial firms that hire their capital goods or their money. Instead, investors of capital are paid money called *dividends* on the stock they own in the business or *interest* on the money they have lent to the business. Most investors have capital of their own because they, or their families, have saved money from their earnings (instead of spending all their earnings for consumer goods) and have used their savings to buy capital goods or to build up bank accounts.

Discuss

16. If a law were passed to forbid paying interest on investments or declaring stock dividends, what would happen to the supply of capital? Would thrifty people keep on depositing their money in banks or buying stock in industrial firms? If not, where would agriculture and commerce and industry then obtain capital?

17. Suppose Abraham Mankewitz invests ten thousand dollars in a company manufacturing cameras. He neither works in the business as an employee nor manages the factory. At the end of the year, he is paid nine hundred dollars in a stock dividend. Some young employees of the company complain that Mankewitz hasn't lifted a finger to help them in the work; yet he is paid more than they earn for a whole month's take-home pay after working forty hours every week. Is it fair that Mr. Mankewitz be paid this money, or unfair? Why?

The owner of land or raw materials is paid for the use of his property, without which there could be no production of goods. The person who does physical or mental work is paid for his labor, without which there could be no production of goods. The person who supplies capital is paid for the use of his savings, without which there could be no production of goods. That accounts for three of the factors of production.

The fourth factor of production is a kind of cleverness or vigorous intelligence—the sort of ability that Robinson Crusoe possessed. Using what scanty capital goods he had, Crusoe managed to survive in a hostile environment for twenty-eight years. That ability made Crusoe a successful international merchant in a later tale written by Defoe.

The Factor of Management

Suppose that you had plenty of land and raw materials, plenty of people to help you by their labor, and plenty of capital in the form of buildings, machines, and cash in a safe. But suppose also that you did not know what to produce, or how to go about production, or how to distribute what you might produce, or who might want it. What would you do in such circumstances?

Why, nothing, probably, for you would be lacking in the imagination and the cleverness that are essential to economic production. You would be unable to decide on any course of action. Then your land would grow up to weeds, and your raw materials would rot or wither. Your helpers would wander off in search of other employment. Your buildings would stand empty and decaying; your machinery would rust. Presumably your money would remain in the safe (supposing nobody stole it), but it would be useless economically because you would not be employing it for production: money doesn't grow unless you invest it in some productive enterprise. Within a few years, if you were to let your factors of production lie idle, you might find yourself as poor as you had once been rich.

That would be the fate of the economy throughout the world if it were not for the fourth factor of production, usually called *management.* As economists use this word, **management** means intelligent directing and supervising of natural and human economic resources. Sometimes economists use the word *ability* to mean the same thing as management. ***Good management combines and uses wisely the factors of land and raw materials, labor, and capital.*** Management, or *executive* ability, is to the economy what the human brain is to the human body. The able manager, economically speaking, knows what to produce, how to produce it, how to distribute what he produces, and who wants his product.

When we say *manager* and *management* in economics, we do not mean simply the woman who manages a dress shop or the man who manages a garage. Those are worthwhile forms of management. (Also they are forms of labor, for unless such managers are also owners of the property, they receive wages or salaries: they are hired for pay.) But when we speak of management as a factor of production, we mean something bigger (and usually riskier) than supervising a small enterprise. We mean *the ability to plan and carry out economic enterprises on a large scale, whether by one person or by a company or corporation.*

The sort of person who undertakes management of economic undertakings on a large scale (or at least on a bold scale, with some danger of losing his investment of money and time) we call the **entrepreneur.** This word, borrowed from the French language, signifies a person in effective control of a business or industrial undertaking. The nearest we can come to an English equivalent for this word is *enterpriser*—somebody with energy and talent enough to start an important *enterprise.*

This entrepreneur, or enterpriser, is a person with *a gift for thinking up new undertakings and getting them accomplished.* Economically, perhaps entrepreneurs think of some new or more efficient methods of production; or perhaps of some superior goods that people will want. Then they contrive to get together the necessary land and natural resources, labor, and capital to make possible production of the intended goods. Having done these things, entrepreneurs must turn out quantities of their products. And they have to develop means for making their products known and for getting them sold to consumers.

If they succeed, entrepreneurs may grow rich. If they fail in any one of these tasks, they may be ruined financially. For *entrepreneurs take high risks.* They will be held responsible if their products turn out to be unsatisfactory, or if they cannot manage their labor force, or if they do not obtain a sufficient supply of raw materials at reasonable prices, or if they cannot persuade enough consumers to buy their products. They have to meet the demand of the market. If they fail to meet that demand, they may be forced out of business. But if it turns out that they have been clever and imaginative and practical, their rewards may be large.

Discuss   18. The economists' term *management* sometimes is called *entrepreneurship.* To be a successful large-scale manager of commerce or manufacturing—that is, an entrepreneur—a certain kind of character seems to be required. What two of the following characteristics or talents are possessed by great entrepreneurs?

1. very cautious, careful, slow methods

2. bold, risky approaches
3. shy, humble manners, never giving offense
4. plenty of imagination
5. easygoing habits, with plenty of leisure for sports, family activities, and civic responsibilities
   19. If you were to set out to become a successful entrepreneur today, what one of the following industries would be a good choice for you? Why?
   1. railroads
   2. satellite receiving dishes
   3. automobile manufacturing

To understand the talents or abilities that a great entrepreneur possesses, let us look at the career of one of America's early "captains of industry": Eleuthère Irénée du Pont, who was born in 1771 and died in 1834. This Du Pont (usually called Irénée, or E. I., du Pont) founded the manufacturing firm of E. I. du Pont de Nemours and Company, which today is one of the biggest industrial corporations in the United States. E. I. du Pont's descendants, who still control their famous family firm, have built upon their ancestor's accomplishments. Some of those descendants have been noted political leaders, diplomats, and military and naval commanders, as well as manufacturers. One of them recently served as governor of the state of Delaware, where E. I. du Pont settled after coming to America.

The Gentleman Who Made Gunpowder for President Jefferson

In 1799—the year when a young Frenchman named E. I. du Pont de Nemours set foot in the New World—the young Republic of the United States was economically underdeveloped. The total capital of the American people was worth about eighteen hundred million dollars, equal to $328 for each human being in the country, including slaves, who owned no property. (Or $418 each, if we count only free white persons.) Agriculture was the only important industry. Many things were manufactured in New England, indeed, but nothing on a large scale. Total exports and imports of the country came to a value of merely seventy-five million dollars.

The biggest city, Philadelphia, had seventy thousand people. In Washington, D.C., the half-finished Capitol and the half-finished White House stood amidst swamps. Wages averaged a dollar a day, but taxes were very low. Foreign visitors called the average American lazy and unenterprising. Travel was slow and difficult. Satisfactory goods, even important ones, were not easy to obtain. Few commercial companies existed. In short, the United States then seemed as unenterprising economically as it was enterprising politically. Although there was unlimited hunting in America, and there had been plenty of fighting until only a few years earlier, even American gunpowder was of poor quality. That fact gave young Du Pont his opportunity for entrepreneurship.

The Du Ponts were a prosperous and influential French family. Irénée's father, Pierre Samuel du Pont de Nemours, was a famous economist and writer. At the age of seventeen, Irénée became the pupil of Lavoisier, a great chemist, chief of the royal powder works. Here young Du Pont learned the science of making gunpowder.

Both the elder and the younger Du Ponts were courageous men, conservative in politics, who hastened to defend the French king against the mob during the French Revolution.[8] Pierre du Pont established a printing business in Paris to oppose the radicals; but this was destroyed by the revolutionaries.[9] The elder Du Pont, a friend and correspondent of Thomas Jefferson, determined to take his family to America, where he expected to found large agricultural, commercial, and industrial undertakings. Jefferson encouraged him. In September 1799, a dozen members of the Du Pont family, led by Pierre, landed at Newport, Rhode Island.

Both Pierre and his elder son, Victor, set up business ventures, but both failed eventually. It was different with Irénée. That young man happened to go hunting with a Colonel Toussard. They bought gunpowder and found it of poor quality. With Toussard's help, Irénée du Pont made a study of gunpowder-making in America. Young Du Pont calculated that even a small powder mill, if efficiently run, could produce better gunpowder, at a lower price, than any available in the United States then—and make a profit of ten thousand dollars a year.

Irénée du Pont became an entrepreneur. He returned to France for

---

8. **Conservative:** a term of modern politics, signifying opposition to radical and sudden change. Conservatives support a country's established constitution and the "permanent things" in a nation's culture.

9. **Radicals:** persons who would uproot or pull down existing social institutions, or who believe in sweeping reforms that would extend to the roots of social order.

three months to obtain machinery and designs. His father's commercial company put up two-thirds of the capital needed to build the improved powder mill. After looking about for a good site, Irénée bought a farm near Wilmington, Delaware, where there formerly had been a cotton mill run by water power. Both Alexander Hamilton and Thomas Jefferson helped in setting up this new business.

In the summer of 1802, Irénée (now barely thirty-one years old), with wife and children, settled in a log cabin on his new farm. He called the place Eleutherian Mills. The remains of his early factories still can be seen there. Like his father, Irénée was mightily interested in agriculture; so, besides manufacturing powder, he grew crops on a large scale and fed and housed his workmen on his land. By 1804, he had good gunpowder ready to sell and the promise from President Jefferson that there would be large orders from the government. For the first six years, his profits averaged seven thousand dollars, despite an explosion that smashed the mill.

By 1811, his year's profit was forty thousand dollars. With associates, E. I. du Pont then built a woolen mill beside the powder factory: the Du Ponts began to expand their operations, which have been expanding ever since.

The United States government, the American Fur Company (which was then opening up the Far West of the United States), and South American countries became Du Pont's best customers. Irénée's advice about industry and agriculture was sought by many people, and he became a director of the Bank of the United States, representing the government on the bank's board. In 1833, when South Carolina threatened to secede from the Union, he refused to fill a South Carolina order for 125,000 pounds of powder.

Like his father before him, Irénée was a highly cultured gentleman, high-strung, energetic, moody—but generous and affectionate. His life was spent amidst dangers and risks. His foresight and imagination led to success at everything he tried.

Even during E. I. du Pont's lifetime, the activities of his company were diversified. Making explosives, which are used in mining and in the building trades as well as for hunting and fighting, remained the company's mainstay for a good while. But the textile mills also prospered. Today, E. I. du Pont and Company manufactures hundreds of different products, from munitions to artificial sponges for household use. It is also a major producer of a variety of fabrics.

Other members of the Du Pont family turned out to be as able entrepreneurs as E. I. du Pont. During the Civil War, the Du Ponts were building mills as far away as California. One of the Du Ponts was a Union admiral during that war; another was a scientific chemist as well as an industrialist.

Several members of the family have been elected to high political office during the past century. The family always has maintained a reputation for good character, intelligence, and sound business principles. By careful planning, they have kept control of their industrial giant within their family structure. Ever since Pierre Samuel du Pont praised the goodness of the agricultural life, the Du Ponts have been active in agriculture as well as in manufacturing. Today the family maintains a great house in Delaware, called Winterthur, with rooms decorated in the styles of various periods; people may go there to study interior decoration, furniture styles, and related artistic matters.

It has been said that the story of many entrepreneurial families is "rags to riches, and back to rags again"—that is, a poor boy rises to wealth through his shrewdness at business; but then his children or his grandchildren waste their inheritance, and the family sinks back into its original poverty. That saying certainly has not been true of the Du Ponts, who have kept their abilities and their wealth for two hundred years.

Discuss

20. E. I. du Pont's powder mill made especially handsome profits in the year 1812. From what you know of American history, can you suggest why that was such a prosperous year for Du Pont?

21. Du Pont set an example of skillful industrial management that native-born Americans might copy—and some of them did. E. I. du Pont was born and educated in France. How did his background give him an advantage over American men of business and industry?

22. Young Du Pont was perhaps the first entrepreneur in the United States to conduct systematic research about the quality of a product and the demand for it. His father was a famous theoretical economist. Can you suggest other connections between economic theory and economic practice? See if you can

find out whether today's big corporations in America spend much time and money in *market research.*[10]

Able entrepreneurs are skillful managers of business or industry, and something more: they are courageous risk-takers. Without such people, the market economy could not function. For the entrepreneur supplies the fourth factor of production: management, or executive ability. *It is the entrepreneur who joins together the four functions and so makes possible large-scale production and distribution.*

---

10. **Market research:** the gathering and studying of data relating to consumer preferences, purchasing power, etc., especially preliminary to introducing a product on the market.

CHAPTER 4

The Laws of Supply and Demand

Chapter 4
The Laws of Supply and Demand

Supply, Demand, and Value-in-Use

The most important thing to understand about economics is the idea of the factors of production. Because of failure to coordinate those factors, nations have lived in poverty, generation upon generation.

The second most important thing to understand about economics is the idea of supply and demand. Because of confused notions of relationships between supply and demand, economic structures have collapsed.

So in this chapter we take up *the fundamental economic principle,* or principles, called *the laws of supply and demand.* A good deal about economic supply and demand has been known for many centuries. But compressing this knowledge into laws, or principles, was the work chiefly of certain nineteenth-century and twentieth-century economists.

Remember that economic laws are not laws enforced by governments. Instead, the laws of supply and demand, like other economic laws, are general economic principles that operate naturally in any economy. They are descriptions of the way in which the supply of any good and the demand for any good are related.

Recall our definitions of *supply* and *demand:*

Supply: the quantity of a good for sale at a certain price. Or, to put it another way, the supply of any good is the amount of that good which sellers are willing to sell at a given price.

Demand: the quantity of a good that people will buy at a certain price. Or, in other words, demand is the willingness and ability of buyers to buy a good at some given price.

To learn how supply and demand are related, we need to understand something about *value.* Why are people willing to pay a price for a certain good? Because it is worth something to them; it has value for them. *A low value causes a low demand; a high value causes a high demand.*

Economists recognize two chief types of value: *value-in-use* and *value-in-exchange.* First we discuss value-in-use.

Many goods have a **value-in-use** for the persons who own them or desire them. These persons wish to consume or to keep a certain good, rather than to sell it again some day. "What is the thing worth to me personally?" is the question buyers ask at a market when they are thinking of whether to buy a particular good. "Can I make use of it?" Value-in-use varies with each consumer's personal wants, for what is very useful to one person may be quite useless to another person. This concept of value-in-use explains decisions about how much individuals want of a particular good.

With all of us, the value we place upon a good varies according to how much of that particular good we already possess. Also, the value of that good for you or me varies with our personal preferences and circumstances.

The Dedham Farmer and the Boston Merchant Bargain

Here is a case. Suppose that in the year 1670, a farmer at Dedham, Massachusetts, near Boston, makes a quantity of pine boards from some of the trees growing on his woodlot. With his wagon, he transports these boards to a dock at Boston harbor, hoping to exchange them for something of use to him. (The boards are not very valuable to him: he has plenty of standing timber on his farm. During the winter months, he has time to cut pine trees and split and plane the wood into boards.)

At the dock, our Dedham farmer meets one of the merchants of Boston, who has a small warehouse by the harbor. This merchant imports goods from England and the West Indies and sells them to the settlers in Massachusetts.

The merchant has just received a shipment of fifty barrels of molasses from Jamaica. Molasses is in demand in Massachusetts. It is eaten on cornmeal mush and used in other New England dishes; also, it can be distilled into rum. (In colonial times, rum distilleries became New England's most profitable industry.) The merchant has bought all this molasses at a reasonable price because of a temporary surplus in Jamaica. But he lacks space to store the fifty barrels, which still are standing on the dock. The merchant needs to enlarge his wooden warehouse.

The Dedham farmer and the Boston merchant strike a bargain. The merchant needs the pile of pine boards to build an addition to his warehouse; the farmer needs the molasses to sweeten his food—and also perhaps to make rum.

They swap their goods, with no money changing hands: for hard money, coin of any sort, is scarce in the Massachusetts of 1670. Both sellers (who are also buyers) have benefited from this exchange by barter. One barrel of molasses seems to the merchant a modest price to pay for a pile of lumber: after all, he has on hand more molasses than he can store. To the farmer, who does not really need his boards, a whole barrel of molasses is a real prize. Both men believe they have done well to trade their goods.

Discuss   1. Suppose that pirates had intercepted several ships carrying molasses from Jamaica to New England, so that our Boston Merchant's barrel was temporarily the whole supply of molasses for sale in Massachusetts Bay Colony. Would the merchant then have asked more payment for his molasses than a pile of boards? Would customers have been willing to pay him something highly valuable in return for his molasses? Why? Explain how this case illustrates the effect of supply upon demand and price.

Actually, both the farmer and the merchant found *value-in-use* through their exchange of goods. They both obtained goods they really could use. But not every market exchange results in such value. If the farmer already had possessed a barrel of molasses, and the merchant already had enough boards, they might not have made an exchange on any terms—not even for hard cash. Let us find out why.

Diminishing Marginal Valuation

If you have a great deal of something, usually you do not want a lot more of the same thing. As economists put it, a good's value-in-use grows smaller if we obtain more and more of that good. The Dedham farmer could make good use of one barrel of molasses, but he might have been puzzled as to what he could do with fifty barrels. The Boston merchant was happy to obtain enough boards to erect a small building, but he might have been overwhelmed if he had received a whole shipload of lumber.

If a friend were to give you a box of chocolates, you might thank him heartily and consume the whole box in a day or two. But if your friend were to give you ten more boxes of chocolates the next day, your eagerness to devour the chocolates would be somewhat diminished. The more we have of a good, in short, the less value any unit of that thing has for us.

Economists call this truth **diminishing marginal valuation** (or, sometimes, *diminishing marginal utility*). The word *marginal* means "on the edge."

Thus, the utility, or usefulness, of any good to any consumer may become marginal: that is, the consumer may have so much of the good already that more of the good would be just on the edge, the margin, of that consumer's wants. When a consumer has a quantity of a certain good, the first few units of that good are highly useful. We may say that they have a high personal valuation. But the more units one gets, the less becomes the personal valuation of each succeeding unit. That is, the marginal value to the owner diminishes. If you already possess ten pounds of chocolates, you are not much inclined to spend money to buy another pound—not right away. For you, any additional supply of chocolates has only diminishing marginal value.

When one makes an exchange in a market, therefore, it is the marginal units of a good that decide one's personal valuation. A person decides to buy or to sell according to his marginal personal valuation of a good. If you had ten pounds of chocolates, you might be inclined to trade your tenth pound for a sandwich, say—even though, ordinarily, good chocolates cost more per pound than do good sandwiches.

Discuss

2. Even money may have diminishing marginal value. Which person is more inclined to work an extra fifteen hours a week for five dollars an hour: Mrs. Harrison, who is already earning four hundred dollars a week, or Miss Topinka, who is earning a hundred and fifty dollars a week? Why?

3. Suppose the Boston merchant had told the Dedham farmer, "Bring me another pile of boards equal to this pile, and I'll trade you another barrel of molasses for them." Might the farmer have been inclined to say no? Why? How does this example illustrate the idea of *diminishing marginal value*, as related to *value-in-use?*

Thus, the demand for any good is affected by the value-in-use that the good has for many possible consumers. Also, the demand is affected by diminishing marginal value. But there is more to the value of most goods than simply whether a consumer can make personal use of them promptly, or whether possible buyers already have a stock of such goods. Most goods do not have to be used up, or consumed, immediately; instead, they can be traded for other goods. So next we are going to discuss the trading value of goods, to see how that kind of value affects demand.

Value-in-Exchange

We have pointed out that value-in-use varies from one person to another, depending on what a consumer means to do with a good and how much he needs it. But there is another type of value, called **value-in-exchange.** This different value is what a particular good would be worth if a person were to exchange that good for some other good. We might call value-in-exchange the *trading value* of any good. Value-in-exchange does not vary from one buyer or seller to another.

Then how is value-in-exchange decided? It is determined in the market, by "what the traffic will bear." In the market, sellers say to possible buyers of the good they wish to trade, "How much will you give me for this?" And buyers ask the sellers, "How much do you want for those goods?" Presently bargains are struck; and the general price resulting from such agreements between buyer and seller is called value-in-exchange. In economics, remember, *market* means the process through which buyers and sellers, meeting together, agree to make a deal—that is, to exchange their goods.

Nowadays we usually express value-in-exchange in terms of money. Value-in-exchange is the same thing today as *price.* By that word **price,** we mean the value that seller and buyer agree upon when the good changes hands. Both seller and buyer ordinarily are satisfied by such an exchange of goods, or else they would not agree on a price.

Now, the pile of boards and the barrel of molasses mentioned earlier in this chapter each had a value-in-exchange, as well as a value-in-use, for the merchant and for the farmer. The merchant could have sold his molasses to someone other than the farmer, and the farmer could have sold his lumber to a different customer. Both merchant and farmer might have carried their respective goods to an open market in the center of Boston to display publicly for sale their molasses and their boards.

The price that merchant and farmer might have obtained for their respective goods in a general market, with many potential sellers and buyers present, would have been the **market price.** And that price would have been their goods' respective value-in-exchange.

For molasses and boards had then, and still have today, their own values-in-exchange. This value varies from one day to another, depending on the supply of those goods and on the current demand for them.

A barrel of molasses does not have to be consumed the same day it is bought. The person who buys it does not have to consume any of it himself: instead, he may sell the barrel of molasses to somebody else, perhaps making a profit on the deal.

Similarly, lumber does not have to be used promptly in construction by the person who buys it. The purchaser may keep it for months until he has need of it, or he may sell it to another customer. (In both cases, of course, the purchaser must expect to pay the cost of storage or warehousing.)

In other words, value-in-exchange may be quite different from a good's value-in-use for a particular person. Value-in-exchange may be either higher or lower than what you or I might wish to pay for something we mean to make use of personally and promptly.

People want many goods, and goods are scarce. The scarcer any good happens to be, the higher will rise the price people are willing to pay for that good. So the traders in the market dicker until they can agree upon a price reflecting the relative scarcity of the goods being exchanged. That agreed-upon price becomes the value-in-exchange (on any particular day) of the two goods.

For instance, suppose that the Boston merchant and the Dedham farmer took their respective goods to an open market. Suppose that both found purchasers who could and did pay money for the goods. (Money was scarce in Massachusetts about 1670, but scarcity does not mean total lack.) Suppose that the merchant was paid twenty shillings in coin for his barrel of molasses: the value-in-exchange of a barrel of molasses that particular day in Boston would have been twenty shillings.[1] Suppose that the farmer was able to sell his boards for fifteen shillings: then the value-in-exchange of a certain quantity of boards would have been fifteen shillings on that particular day in Boston.

Discuss   4. In terms of value-in-exchange, who had the better of the bargain when, in barter, the farmer traded his boards to the

---

1. **Shilling:** a coin used in Great Britain until recent years, worth one-twentieth of an English pound, or twelve pence.

merchant for the barrel of molasses—the merchant or the farmer?

5. If a forest fire had destroyed the woods of eastern Massachusetts about 1670, would the value-in-exchange of lumber have gone up or down?

6. Suppose that a fellow student offers to sell you for eight dollars a new record he had bought at a shop the previous day. (He is short of cash.) You shake your head. "But I paid ten dollars for it just yesterday," he says. You still shake your head. "I don't care much for that singer," you tell him. "That record wouldn't be worth more than a dollar to me."

What kind of value is your fellow student talking about in this bargaining? What different kind of value are you talking about?

7. Suppose an artist offers for sale a huge painting which he has worked on for a full year. He exhibits the picture in an art gallery, asking twenty thousand dollars for it. A visitor to the gallery offers him one thousand dollars. The artist rejects the offer indignantly, saying, "Why, my time alone is worth a lot more than that! And as a work of art, my picture is priceless. It's at least as good as that big French still-life painting that the Art Institute of Chicago paid fifty thousand dollars for just last year."

At the end of the exhibition, nevertheless, the painter has not found any buyer who would pay him twenty thousand dollars. He then persuades the owner of the gallery to buy his big canvas, on speculation, for two thousand dollars. As he puts his check into his billfold, the artist complains bitterly that nobody will pay him a just price for his work.

Do you sympathize with the artist? Is he right in what he says about prices? How is the price of a work of art decided? Would an economist say that the painter was entitled to the twenty thousand dollars he originally asked? Can you think of some way for determining the prices of works of art, or of other goods, different from value-in-exchange or value-in-use?

To put this whole matter very briefly, we can say that *prices are influenced by demand.* If enough people want a particular good, and want it badly, the price of that good will rise: there is strong demand, so the good has a high value-in-exchange. If there exists little demand for the good, its price will fall: it has a low value-in-exchange. At any rate, this is how prices are decided upon in a market economy like that of the United States. And it is a law of economics that demand strongly influences price in any society—though in some economies, governments may attempt to regulate prices (unsuccessfully, in the long run).

Price, Cost of Production, and Scarcity

Our analysis of value-in-use and value-in-exchange has led us closer toward understanding the laws of demand and supply. Another step toward understanding those important concepts is to learn how the *cost of production* and *scarcity* affect demand.

With most goods, the cost of their production and distribution is a major element in their prices. We have seen how the four factors of production enter into the creation of any good. Natural resources, labor, capital, and management are expenses reflected ordinarily in the price of goods.

Yet cost of production and distribution is not the only influence affecting the price of a good. Price is affected also by the scarcity of any good; and sometimes scarcity counts for more than does cost of production and distribution.

All goods, we learned earlier, are scarce in some degree. But just how scarce any good may be depends upon varying circumstances. The supply of a good may happen to decrease or increase quite suddenly; this variation may be true of foodstuffs, the most essential of goods. When a sudden decrease of supply happens, a commodity formerly not difficult to obtain may become very scarce indeed. Then that scarce good will bring a price far higher than before. That price may be much above the cost of production and distribution. If a frost or a blight should wipe out most of California's or Florida's annual orange crop, for instance, the price of oranges would rise greatly—not because the cost of producing oranges had increased, but because the total supply of oranges had vastly diminished. The scarcer a thing seems, the more people desire it, even at a much higher price. With few oranges on sale, the dominant influence upon the price of oranges would be scarcity, not cost of production.

Also, some goods may not be very costly to produce, but people desire them because those particular goods are extremely scarce, even rare, and few people can own them. A "baroque" pearl (one of irregular shape produced naturally by an oyster and found by an oyster fisherman) may bring a price of thousands of dollars if it is big and fine enough; yet the cost of production was merely the day's expenses of the lucky fisherman.

Or a first-class meal in certain fashionable restaurants of New York, Paris, London, or Cairo may cost a hundred dollars; yet the cost of production of the food consumed in that meal may be little greater than the cost of production of the foodstuffs consumed in a roadside franchise restaurant on U.S. Highway 1. The diner at a fashionable restaurant is paying for the services of a successful chef, of course, who collects a good salary; but mostly the diner is paying for the privilege of dining at a famous establishment. Famous restaurants profit from being scarce. Their scarcity and high reputation set the high prices they charge.

When the supply of any desirable thing is scanty, the price is high. When the demand for any desirable thing remains strong, and that thing is scarce, its price is high. In short, there occur many cases in which scanty supply and strong demand are the major influences upon the price of a good—almost regardless of the cost of producing that good.

Conversely, if demand for a good decreases for some reason, ordinarily the price of that good will decrease in proportion—even though the cost of producing the good has not decreased. If a thing becomes less scarce (because fewer people want that good), its value is less.

Thus, both cost of production and scarcity have their part in influencing price. A very successful and famous lawyer conceivably may charge a big corporation a fee of a thousand dollars a day for representing it in an important action at law. What determines this high price for this lawyer's services? Why, cost of production is part of the cause: to obtain a first-rate legal education doubtless cost this lawyer plenty of money before he was admitted to the bar. But, chiefly, the high fee is payment for scarcity: famous and successful lawyers with a high reputation for winning important cases for great corporations are scarce. (Remember that economists regard services, including legal services, as goods. Like material goods, the price of services is influenced often both by cost of production—education, training, business expenses, and the like—and by scarcity.)

Discuss
8. Can you think of any goods that cost relatively little to produce but are high in price?

9. Give some examples of how supply may increase or decrease within an economy.

10. What influences may cause demand to change?

11. The costs of producing learned and skilled people are high. A person might spend ten years and two hundred thousand dollars to qualify as a physician. Today most physicians earn good annual incomes. What would happen if doctors became so plentiful that they could not recover the cost of their production—that is, if their annual earnings, over many years, would not equal what it cost them for medical education? Would more people enter medical schools? How would a diminishing in the number of physicians affect the price of visits to doctors? Why?

We need to remember that the cost of production does not determine the price of all goods all of the time. Often the *shortage* or the *abundance* of goods is a better key to their price (value-in-exchange).

Suppose, for instance, that the owner of a shop selling clothes to young women has in stock twenty Fair Isle sweaters, each priced at forty dollars.[2] (Their actual cost of production at the mill was twenty dollars apiece, say.) Suppose that rather suddenly Fair Isle sweaters go out of fashion; another kind of sweater becomes all the rage. In order to dispose of her old stock and get in the newly fashionable sweaters, the shop's owner finds it necessary to sell her Fair Isle sweaters at the bargain price of nine dollars apiece—actually less than the cost of production, let alone distribution.

---

2. **Fair Isle:** an island in the Shetland Islands group to the north of Scotland, where special patterns of knitwear were developed.

Or suppose, on the contrary, that abruptly Fair Isle sweaters become more fashionable than ever before: demand for them increases overnight. A shortage of those sweaters occurs. The price of such sweaters rises, and the proprietress of the shop finds that she can sell her whole stock of sweaters on hand for fifty dollars apiece, thus making a handsome profit.

We may say that, in the long run, most prices are determined basically by costs of production. But in the short run, in the case of most commodities, scarcity (or the opposite of it, plenty) has much to do with prices.

The Basic Laws of Demand and Supply

Now we are getting to the heart of the matter: the fundamental law of demand, as related to the law of supply. From what we have taken up already in this chapter, you should be able to understand the following statement of the law of demand.

   1. As the price of a good goes up in relation to other goods, demand for that good will fall. Also, it is true that as the price of a good goes down in relation to the prices of other goods, the demand for that particular good will rise.
   2. When the price of a good goes up, suppliers will be encouraged to increase the supply. If supply increases while demand stays the same, the price will tend to fall.

Thus, the price of a good is a signal that sellers (producers) and buyers (consumers) watch. The price level guides their economic decisions.

Or it is possible to compress this law of demand into two sentences:

> *When the price of a good rises in relation to the price of other goods, the demand for that good will fall. When the price of the good falls, then the demand for the good will rise.*

This law of demand can be understood better by the following compressed form of the law of supply:

> *When the price of a good rises in relation to the price of other goods, the supply of that good will tend to increase. When the price of the good falls, then the supply of that particular good will tend to fall.*

To make these economic laws clearer, we can take the example of bicycles. Suppose the price of bicycles goes up sharply. Then fewer people will buy new bicycles: they will repair their old bicycles or get along without bicycles (though some people will continue to buy new bicycles, despite the higher prices). When demand for new bicycles falls off, the price of bicycles will diminish. Then, with lower prices, the demand for bicycles will increase again.

Or we can put it another way, in terms of supply. When the price of bicycles goes up, makers of bicycles will be encouraged to turn out greater production, that being a profitable trade: so supply increases. (Because it takes considerable time to manufacture and distribute new bicycles, or for new firms to enter the bicycle-making business, this increase in the supply of bicycles will not occur immediately.) When plenty of new bicycles come on the market, the price of bicycles will fall, because the larger supply has satisfied the existing demand for bicycles. Then it will be harder to sell new bicycles; so the price will fall, and bicycle manufacturers will reduce their production. When production is reduced, the supply of new bicycles will fall. Supply and demand will have come into balance once more.

Economists use diagrams showing curves of supply and demand to illustrate the ways in which demand and supply interact. Below are examples of these curves, which indicate how much of a particular good consumers are likely to buy at certain prices.

Let us suppose that Mr. Mendoza, a manufacturer of bicycles in San Antonio, is thinking of a campaign to sell his firm's product in Minneapolis and its suburbs. He would like to know the size of the market for bicycles there and what price might be obtained; therefore, he employs a market-research organization to gather information about the demand for bicycles in that urban area and the supply of them—the latter including foreign-made bicycles imported by large wholesalers.

The market-research people soon present Mr. Mendoza with three diagrams that summarize, through demand curves and supply curves, the data they have collected. These diagrams, shown below, suggest on a graduated scale about how much people in Minneapolis would be willing to pay for a new ten-speed bicycle and how many such bicycles manufacturers and wholesalers would be ready to supply at a range of prices.

These are very simple examples of demand and supply curves.

In the first diagram, we see a demand curve. According to that curve, at the price of $300, some five thousand bicycles might be sold next year in the Minneapolis market. At a price of $200, however, ten thousand bicycles might be sold; and at a price of $100, twenty thousand bicycles. As the price rises, demand falls.

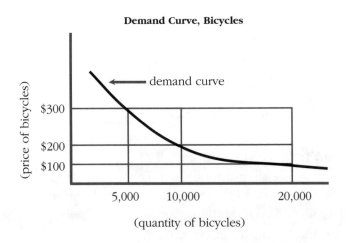

Demand Curve, Bicycles

Also, the market-research firm has calculated for Mendoza the probable supply of ten-speed bicycles, from various manufacturers and importers, which might be made available for sale in the Minneapolis market during the course of the year—that is, how many cycles would be offered for sale at various price ranges. At the price of $100, some five thousand bicycles might be offered for sale. But at a medium price of $200, suppliers of bicycles would put on the market some ten thousand bicycles. At the relatively high price of $300, manufacturers and importers would be ready to supply twenty thousand bicycles. The higher the price, the more ample the supply.

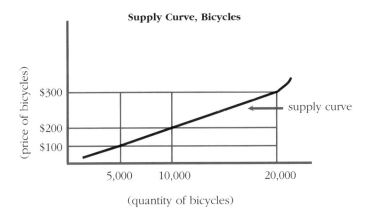

(quantity of bicycles)

Mr. Mendoza is uncertain whether a suggested retail price of $100 for his ten-speed cycles would cover his full costs of production and distribution. He would be happy to sell his bicycles to wholesalers and retailers at a factory price that would permit those dealers to retail the cycles for $300 each; but he wonders whether so relatively high a retail price might not be resisted by potential customers at retail cycle shops— that is, whether the price might not discourage demand. His market researchers then show him the third diagram, in which the curve of demand and the curve of supply intersect.

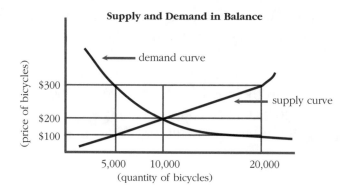

Supply and Demand in Balance

In the third diagram, the two curves meet at the price of $200. Ten thousand customers, it is calculated, would be willing to pay that much for a new ten-speed bicycle. Sellers try to offer prices that will attract the greatest possible number of buyers. So if the researches and computations of the research firm are fairly accurate, the general market price of bicycles in the Minneapolis area will be approximately $200.

Of course, nobody can be sure in advance precisely what demand, supply, and price may be for any particular good at any particular time in the future, but often reasonable estimates may be made. Mr. Mendoza now has some concept of how big the market for his wares may be in Minneapolis and what the market price for cycles may be. He will calculate accordingly whether it would be worth his while to commence a promotional campaign to sell Mendoza bicycles in the Minneapolis region.

If our manufacturer cannot produce a cycle that would sell for a suggested retail price of $200—and leave him some margin of gain— he may as well stay out of the Minneapolis market. What about people who are prepared to pay only $100 or less for new cycles in Minneapolis? Why, they will either have to buy second-hand cycles or go without— unless they are lucky enough to find a dealer who holds a going-out-of-business sale or, for some other reason, offers bicycle bargains for a short period of time. No retailer, in ordinary circumstances, can afford to sell for much less than the general market price: retailers and wholesalers have to pay manufacturers the general factory price. Nobody is in business to lose money.

The diagrams make the point that price is determined when supply and demand come into balance, or equilibrium. If most Minneapolis customers were willing to pay only $100 for a bicycle, not enough bicycles would be offered for sale to satisfy the public's demand. If bicycles were priced at $300, dealers would not find enough customers to buy their existing stocks of cycles. So, as a result of free exchange in the market, some sellers have to reduce the price they would like to charge, and some buyers have to pay more for cycles than they had expected to pay. This is the essential function of the market. All sellers ready to sell cycles for $200 each can dispose of their stock on hand; all buyers ready to pay $200 for cycles can obtain what they want. This is an example of what we call "clearing the market." Of course, sellers who demand higher prices or buyers who cannot or will not pay the market price are excluded from this market.

Discuss

12. Suppose that the price of shrimp at a food market should rise a dollar per pound in the course of one week. Would the demand for shrimp diminish? If people should get into the habit of going without shrimp for lunch or dinner, what then would happen to the price of shrimp?

13. Between 1929 and 1935, during the Great Depression in America, the prices of most goods went sharply down. Because of unemployment and low incomes, most consumers were compelled to reduce their buying of goods. So sellers competed for business by reducing their prices. Can you explain why in terms of the laws of supply and demand?

14. Suppose that over a period of several months, the average price of high-quality pillows stuffed with down should increase by $2.75 per pillow. Would pillow manufacturers therefore tend to increase their output of pillows? If prices of pillows should continue to rise, might new manufacturers enter the business? Why?

Demand and Substitution

Do we have to obey these laws of demand and supply? In recent decades, the prices of most commodities have risen greatly nearly everywhere in the world. Yet, in the more prosperous countries, most people continue to enjoy good food, good clothing, and good lodging. How do they manage to do this?

Why, they substitute less expensive goods for goods that have high prices. Their expenses may not increase very much, because people tend to substitute codfish for steak, say, when the price of steak increases sharply.

Discuss

15. Look at the box "Changing Food Prices." How might a family alter its demand for food if the family's income had remained about the same while prices changed from Price 1 level to Price 2 level? Would the family go hungry under Price 2 conditions in the United States?

Changing Food Prices		
	Price 1	**Price 2**
dinner at a fancy restaurant	$20.00	$40.00
dinner at an ordinary restaurant	6.00	12.00
steak (lb.)	3.75	5.00
pork (lb.)	2.50	3.50
fish (lb.)	1.25	1.75
hamburger (lb.)	1.40	1.80
potatoes (5 lbs.)	1.25	1.50
frozen spinach (lb.)	.90	1.00
cottage cheese (lb.)	1.45	1.70

Changes in demand are made possible by **substitution.** People find some good to replace the good that has become more expensive. When millions of consumers are involved, any change in the price of a good will affect the total demand for that good. For some consumers, any change in price will change their demand, because the price before the change was the same as, or lower than, their personal valuation of the good.

It may be argued that many people do not change their habits of consumption instantly when prices change. That statement is true. Some people enjoy driving so much that they will cut consumption of other goods rather than give up long automobile trips.

Yet the basic economic law of demand remains sound. *For everyone there is a point at which price seems the decisive consideration. There occurs a marginal point at which we alter our economic behavior.*

Discuss

16. Suppose the price of steak should rise to ten dollars a pound. If millions of families should reduce their purchases of steak accordingly, what probably would happen to the price of steak then? Why?

17. Imagine millions of car owners making their personal marginal changes of behavior in gasoline consumption as the price of gasoline changes. Would there be some change in *demand* with every change in price? Why?

In the great majority of cases, demand is *elastic :* that is, if prices go up, people will buy less of a good, thus diminishing demand. As we have seen, they may buy some other good as a substitute and thereby increase demand for the substitute. When the price of natural gas goes up, a good many people in well-wooded country may try to lower their heating bills by putting into their houses stoves that burn firewood. Because the demand for firewood then increases, gradually the price of firewood will rise—but not, perhaps, to the high price of natural gas.

Similarly, if prices go down, demand will increase, ordinarily. An *elastic* thing is something that will expand or contract: demand will expand or contract because of price alterations or other factors. *The availability of substitutes is a major reason why the demand for most goods is elastic.*

But if there are no substitutes for a good, or if, for other reasons, people will pay very high prices—almost any price—for a particular commodity, we say that the demand has become *inelastic*. No matter how high the price of cigarettes goes (mainly because of taxes), many people will continue to buy as many cigarettes as before: their *want* for cigarettes is inelastic, even though those smokers may be aware that cigarettes do them physical harm.

Discuss

18. Can you suggest some other goods for which demand sometimes is inelastic, so far as certain consumers are concerned?

Statutory Laws Cannot Repeal Economic Laws

Congress could pass a statute declaring that the law of gravity was repealed. But even so, if you jumped off a tall building, you still would fall swiftly to the ground and break your bones. Gravity is a natural force or pull over which legislators have no control. The laws of physical science are not enforced by any government. Being part of the natural order of the universe, they enforce themselves.

Similarly, the laws of economics seem to be a permanent part of the human condition. *Governments may tamper with the laws of supply and demand, but they cannot repeal those general principles.*

To understand this truth, consider attempts by governments to fix prices. In recent decades, prices have been rising throughout the world—for reasons we will take up later in this book. Why cannot governments keep prices moderate by simply declaring that they must go no higher? Why cannot some agency of government make a schedule of prices and punish sellers who charge more? This solution to a rise in prices has been attempted many times in history, most notably during wars.

It is quite possible to set up such a governmental agency to regulate prices; but, in the long run, the results are not satisfactory. For such attempted controls upon prices put a stop to the working of the market. Price signals no longer tell producers and consumers how to adjust supply and demand.

If a political agency sets prices below the point at which the producers can make any money, then producers will stop producing, but consumers will still demand the same amount of goods. There will be a shortage of goods.

Shortage is not the same as *scarcity*. Most goods nearly always are scarce. But a **shortage** occurs when demand is much greater than the supply, because the price mechanism is not telling consumers and producers how to act.

When a true shortage happens, consumers must take time to find out where the goods they want may be obtained. Then they may have to stand in line for hours to buy them. Or they may have to wait months or even years, or travel to another region, if they want certain goods. The delay and discontent caused by economic shortages occur most of the time, for most goods, in such collectivist countries as Russia, China, Poland, Cuba, and Vietnam.[3]

Fairly soon, the result of price-fixing by governments is either overproduction or underproduction of certain goods—with resulting serious damage to a country's economy. (If government fixes the prices of a commodity too high, overproduction occurs.) The following fable illustrates on a tiny scale what happens on a huge scale in countries where prices are artificially fixed by political authority.

The High Lord of the Marketplace

In the ancient market town of Altruria is a public market where all exchanges are by barter, Altruria having no coins. The grand marketplace, hard by the guildhall, is watched over by the Altrurian High Lord of the Marketplace, whose power none may defy.

To this market came, one November day, two women from the countryside, Dame Grizel and Dame Sophonisba. The first had apples to exchange; the second, rabbits.

The apple harvest had been wretched that year. Dame Grizel had but thirty bushels of apples to sell. She wanted four rabbits in exchange for a bushel of apples.

Dame Sophonisba declared that this offer was unfair. She asked the

---

3. **Collectivist:** a term to describe economies in which the means of production are owned by the state rather than by individuals or voluntary groups.

High Lord of the Marketplace, whose humble friend she long had been, to intervene.

The High Lord agreed with Sophonisba. He declared that the price of a bushel of apples should be what it had been the previous year: one rabbit.

Grizel went home with all her apples and made applesauce.

Sophonisba went home with all her rabbits and made a great deal of stew. Neither dame enjoyed her food greatly.

The following year, bad weather and insects again reduced the apple harvest. This time, in the marketplace, Dame Sophonisba persuaded the High Lord to force Dame Grizel to sell her scarce apples at a bushel for one rabbit. Grizel did so, most unwillingly. She was hungry that winter and decided that if she continued to grow apples she must starve. Therefore, she cut down her apple trees and sold the wood for fuel. She made up her mind to breed rabbits, for that form of production paid well.

The third year there were no apples at all in the market. But there was an abundant supply of rabbits. Rabbits were very cheap that year.

Discuss

19. Explain why the price controls decreed by the High Lord of the Marketplace resulted in a total lack of apples.

20. If this were a fable of Aesop, it would have a moral at the end. Can you give it a moral?

Supply, Demand, and Rent Controls

Thomas Carlyle, although a bitter opponent of economists and the inventor of the term "the dismal science," had an eye for the essential.[4] He once claimed that to train an economist you had only to buy a parrot and train him to squawk "Supply and Demand, Supply and Demand."

The laws of supply and demand are the bread and butter of economists and still the most useful part of that study. We can illustrate, for example, the problem of price controls with an abstract picture called

---

4. **Thomas Carlyle** (1795–1851): British historian and moralist who sternly criticized the consequences of the Industrial Revolution and was opposed to the fashionable liberal thought of his day.

a supply-and-demand diagram. Let us imagine we are talking about the price and number of apartments for rent in a certain city. Then we wish to understand what effect rent controls might have if imposed by the city council.

First, let us examine the situation in a free market before the city council takes action. A demand curve is shown below:

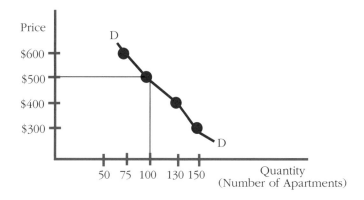

When economists use the term "demand," they mean the amounts of a good that people would like to purchase at different prices. In this graph, we see that if the price were $600 a month, the individuals in the community would choose to rent 75 apartments. But if the price were $300 a month, they would want double that amount, or 150 apartments. But if they need 150 apartments, how can they get along with only 75 if the price were to rise? Very easily, even though oftentimes it is to their discomfort. For example, if they are students, they might find it worthwhile to bunch up four in a single apartment instead of two; if one is an elderly retired widow, she might find it necessary to move back with the children, even though she hates to impose on them.

One final point about demand is that the term refers to the entire curve, not to a particular point on it. For example, when the number of apartments that people want goes from 75 to 150 as the prices fall from $600 to $300, this is not considered a change in demand, but only a change in quantity demanded. A change in demand is shown by the entire curve moving. If it moves to the right, then it is an increase in demand; if it moves to the left, it is a decrease in demand.

At the same time, this city has a supply of apartments which is shown below:

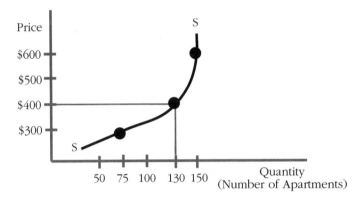

The supply curve, labeled S-S, shows the quantity that the producers are willing to supply at different possible prices. Thus, if the price were $600 a month, there would be 150 apartments supplied. But if the price were $400 a month, then only 130 apartments would be supplied. Does it make sense to assume that a greater quantity will be supplied (notice the difference between the term *supply* and *quantity supplied*) when the rent rises from $400 to $600 a month? In the long run it certainly does, since producers can respond to a higher profit situation by building more apartments. Even in the short run, you might find some people saying that it would make sense to convert that extra room into an efficiency apartment; a little extra money for an old widow in a big house might be very appealing.

Economists are not particularly good in predicting exactly how much increase in supply there might be when the price rises, because they would need to figure out what widows are going to do before they do it, and that is not easy. But they can predict that the quantity supplied would increase because of the careful economizing decisions made by prudent individuals.

Now let us put the supply and demand curves together to see

how price is determined in a free market. Examine the graph below:

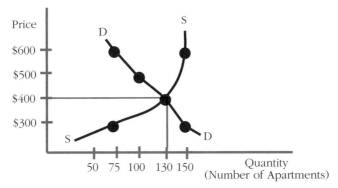

The rent at which the supply equals demand is $400; this is often called the equilibrium, or market-clearing, price. An equilibrium price does not necessarily mean fair or just; it means only that at that price there will not be either shortages or surpluses. In a free market, the market price will be $400 per apartment so long as the underlying factors of demand and supply do not change. This is what economists mean by "other things being equal"; when they want to be fancy, they use the Latin phrase *ceteris paribus*.

We are now in a position to see what will happen if rent controls are imposed. The city council, with the best of intentions, hopes to help the poor pay lower rents. Therefore, they decree that the maximum rent which anyone can pay or charge is $300 per month, instead of the market-clearing price of $400. What are the results?

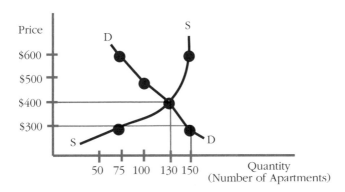

The result is that the city council creates a shortage of 75 apartments. A shortage is defined as the difference between the quantity demanded and the quantity supplied at a particular price. At a rent of $300 per month, people would like to rent 150 units in total, but they can get only 75 units. At the $400 market-clearing price, no shortage exists, even though there is scarcity. *Scarcity is the universal fact that there is not enough of most goods to satisfy all wants.*

A second consequence is that 55 families (the difference between 130 and 75) will actually lose their apartments. Students will have to move back with their families, families will have to double up, and, in general, less desirable accommodations will have to be made. Over time, the shortage will get worse. Suppliers will have little or no incentive to keep up their apartment buildings and make needed repairs. In fact, the situation can get so bad that even economists sympathetic to extensive state interference have recognized that rent control, next to bombing, is the surest way to destroy a city. Some people do gain who are able to maintain their apartments, even though their gains may be eaten away by deterioration as time passes. But the job of the economist is to point out precisely the long-run consequences that people do not immediately see. As Alfred Marshall, a great English economist, once put it, a warm heart must be accompanied by a cool mind.

So it is generally with what we call the laws of economics. It is possible for a government to damage an economy greatly by ignoring or defying those laws, and many governments have done so in the twentieth century. But it is not possible to make a nation prosperous by neglecting some of the factors of production, or forgetting the laws of demand and supply, or pretending that political slogans can be substituted for intelligent work.

CHAPTER 5

The Productive Market Economy

Chapter 5

The Productive Market Economy

- **Signals of the Market**
- **Alternatives to the Test of the Market**
- **Profits and Productivity**

Signals of the Market

All native-born Americans have grown up in a society with a market economy—sometimes called a *free enterprise economy* or a *private enterprise economy.* Most of us take for granted the huge supply of goods, including services, that the market economy of the United States turns out.

In Chapter 1, we defined a *market* as a process by which people exchange goods so that both buyers and sellers can get what they are seeking for themselves. Every human being, especially in a civilized society, is involved in the market to some degree, because everybody has to obtain goods in order to live, and everybody has to give something in exchange for those goods. (Most people exchange their own labor for goods.)

In everyday speech, we may mean by the word *market* a place where goods are bought and sold. Or we may mean a meeting of people who are interested in buying and selling. We talk of various kinds of markets—the stock market, the commodity market, the money market.[1]

---

1. **Stock market:** a center where shares of stock, and also bonds, are bought and sold: for example, the New York Stock Exchange, the London Stock Exchange, and the Paris Bourse. **Commodity market:** in general, a commodity means anything that is bought or sold. But when business people refer to a commodity market, ordinarily they mean buying and selling "primary goods," such as crude petroleum,

There are local markets, big city markets, and regional markets. (Once a market extends beyond the city level, much of the market's business is done by letter, telephone, and other long-distance devices.) Later we will look at some of these different types of markets.

But in this chapter, and usually in this book, when we use the word *market* we mean the process of exchanging goods between sellers and buyers. A market economy obeys the laws of demand and supply discussed in Chapter 4. *Yet it is human beings—producers and consumers, sellers and buyers—who determine what goes on in the market.*

In recent years, huge shopping malls have been constructed on the outskirts of American cities. In every one of the big malls are scores of shops. In every shop are hundreds or thousands of articles for sale. Most of these goods are sold within a few days of being brought into the shop. Every article in every shop is there because sellers have reason to believe that buyers are in the market for that particular good.

Retail centers like shopping malls are only one feature of what we call *the American market*—that is, the exchange of goods within America's economic structure. All the goods enjoyed in the American economy are produced because a demand for them is thought to exist. Certain **signals of the market** cause producers to assume the reality of this demand.

What is meant by this phrase, *signals of the market?* A signal is a sign or a warning conveying information to people a considerable distance away. In a market economy, sellers and buyers usually base their decisions about prices and related matters upon certain signals or indications of changes in the market. Both demand and supply are always changing; so prices, too, are changing all the time. If supply falls, price will rise. Seeing the signal that the price of a good has gone up,

---

cotton, and foodstuffs, which have not required much manufacturing. The most famous commodity market in America is the Chicago Board of Trade, where dealers buy and sell contracts for wheat, corn, oats, and other agricultural products. **Money market:** a set of institutions or arrangements for handling wholesale transactions in money and short-term credit. The money market may be called a system of lending and borrowing. It is carried on chiefly through commercial banks and central banks. One function of the money market is to buy and sell various countries' currencies for international exchange.

producers will try to turn out more of a good. When as a result of more production, the supply of the good has increased—why, prices will fall. Seeing this new signal of falling prices, producers will reduce their production of a good. This is one simple example of signals of the market.

Who demands these many goods? Why, a vast crowd of individuals—the people whom economists call *consumers*. What many people desire, the market produces in great quantity. What few people want, the market economy produces scarcely at all. To put this another way, in a market economy the decisions about what to produce are made by the *test of the market*—sometimes called *the market mechanism*. Consumers send certain signals to producers to suggest what they want and would buy. Bankers, wholesalers, manufacturers, and other people who depend upon the market for their economic decisions are always alert for the market's signals.

The **market mechanism,** or *test of the market,* is a kind of regular, automatic system for communicating information about the exchange of goods. If American consumers want more houses and fewer automobiles than were produced last year, say, consumers will make their new wants known by their *buying decisions* in the market. Producers, eager to learn what consumers wish to buy, will watch for signals (buying decisions) that indicate consumers' preferences. It is as if consumers send out signals that producers receive.

A simple example of this test, or mechanism, of the market is the ordinary grocery store or food market. Weekly, or perhaps daily, the owner or manager of such a shop looks over the goods on his shelves. He finds that some items are not selling well: they remain on his shelves, conspicuously, when he had hoped that they would "move"—that is, be sold promptly. He finds that other items have sold very well indeed: they are out of stock, leaving gaps on his shelves.

Now few customers may have mentioned to the store manager that one type of goods was too high in price or too low in quality for the customers to buy. And no customer may have murmured that another category of goods in the store seemed a good bargain. But the manager can see by a quick glance at his shelves that some goods are profitable to him and that others may cause him a loss. An able manager will order from his supplier more of the goods that sold well, but will refrain from ordering more of the goods that did not sell well. And when a "traveler" (salesperson or agent) comes round to the grocery store to take more orders, the manager probably will tell the traveler that the unpopular goods were unsaleable, making it clear that he wants no more of them.

So signals have been sent from the retail seller (the manager of the grocery store) to the wholesaler who deals in large quantities of groceries. In turn, the wholesaler will pass on the signals to his own sources of supply. Perhaps a certain brand of pickles has sold well. The wholesaler orders a carload lot more of these pickles, in glass jars, from the good-sized company that pickles cucumbers. Encouraged by this and other orders, the pickle producers buy more cucumbers from farmers. In turn, farmers perceive that the market for cucumbers is a healthy one, and so plant more cucumbers in season. (Of course, it takes more than one order from one grocery to produce such results with wholesalers, pickle packers, and farmers. The decisions of producers and distributors are based on many such signals about the price and quality of products, coming from many food markets.)

On the other hand, our grocery store manager may discover that a certain brand of cocoa gathers dust on his shelves even though its price is lower than that of other brands of cocoa. The manager asks some customers who are buying other brands of cocoa if they have tried the lower-priced item. They inform him that they have bought it in the past but don't like its taste, or they say that "it doesn't froth enough."

Then the manager tells the traveler for the wholesaler who supplied that particular brand of cocoa that he won't accept any more of it. The traveler transmits this message back to the wholesaler (sometimes called the *jobber*). If the jobber receives enough such signals, he declines to buy more of that brand from its manufacturer. Then the manufacturer must improve his product or drop cocoa from the line of foodstuffs he produces or perhaps go out of business altogether, having failed the test of the market. Many such signals from a large number of wholesalers would be required, usually, to persuade a major manufacturer to change his product.

Think now of more durable goods, such as automobiles or refrigerators. When demand for any of these durable goods diminishes, as shown by sales or buying decisions, producers of such goods take alarm. They produce smaller quantities of cars, refrigerators, or whatever they have been manufacturing. But when demand for those types of goods increases, as shown by other buying decisions, producers increase the quantities produced.

Discuss

1. Suppose that Henry Courtemanche thinks about insulating his house. He telephones Warm Winter Contractors to inquire about the cost of such work. On learning that he might have to spend six thousand dollars, Mr. Courtemanche tells the firm, "That's too much for me. I'll just nail plastic over my windows." Is Courtemanche sending a market signal? To whom? If hundreds or thousands of decisions similar to Courtemanche's are made in one city, what happens to the insulating market?

2. Suppose that Ola Swenson enters a bookshop near her apartment house, intending to buy an illustrated art book as a wedding present for a cousin. She finds that the shop stocks only popular paperbacks. Annoyed, she departs, telling the proprietor, "If you carried really good books, you'd have more customers." Is Miss Swenson sending a market signal? To whom? In what sense is she "casting a vote"?

3. Suppose that you ask for a box of clothespins at a small hardware store. The old man behind the counter tells you, "Youngster, we used to carry clothespins, but people were always asking for them! We couldn't keep them in stock, what with all that demand, and it was a nuisance always having to order more from the maker. So we don't bother to sell them any more."

Is the clerk responsive to market signals and customers' wants? What buying decision might you be induced to make as a result of his reply?

In a market economy, it is the consumers—you and I, everybody who buys goods—who determine what goods are to be produced, and in what quantity. In effect, through their buying decisions, the mass of consumers tell producers to produce the sort of goods, and in the proper quantity, that can be readily sold. This is the way of a competitive "free enterprise" economy.

Alternatives to the Test of the Market

But not all societies use this test of the market—that is, consumers' preferences—as their means for deciding what goods should be produced. *Most of the world's population today, indeed, has no experience of a true market economy on a large scale.*

One alternative to the market economy's method of making decisions about production is what we may call *decision by tradition*. This method is characteristic of societies with a very simple economy. Such a society's wants may be relatively unchanging: perhaps rice, fish, and vegetables for food; earthenware pots; some cloth; a few simple tools; a one-room hut for a family. In such societies, production scarcely changes from one year or one decade to the next. If the society's population increases or decreases, then the need for production will alter accordingly. But in this simple society, producers generally are aware that consumers' wants are limited, and can plan their simple production with those limited wants in mind. The rice grower knows how much rice he will need for his family and about how much he can sell to other people. The fisherman understands how large a catch is needed to satisfy the limited demand of his village.

Ordinarily, such societies are very poor by American standards, and they may be terribly troubled by natural disasters like floods and droughts. Our present point about them is this: in such traditional societies, there is not much need for anyone to make important economic decisions.

At the other extreme of economic organization is the **command economy,** also called the *planned economy* or *directed economy*. This economic structure usually is governed by a socialist or communist political organization—or at least by a centralized government with power to compel people to obey its economic decrees. In a command economy, decisions as to what shall be produced are made by the central government, without much regard for consumers' preferences.

Countries with free political systems sometimes establish command economies in time of war or some other emergency. But ordinarily it is **authoritarian** or **totalist** governments that set up systems of state economic planning (command economies).[2] Such dictatorial governments arrange "Five-Year Plans" (as in the Soviet Union) or other large-scale, long-range plans for production, distribution, and consumption of goods. Production goals and quotas are often determined by a central ministry of economic planning.

We will have more to say about command economies in Chapter 11. Just now we are contrasting methods of decision-making in market economies and in command economies. In the market economy, decisions about what to produce are made by a multitude of consumers—perhaps by millions of people—without much reference to the political authority. In the command economy, decisions about what to produce are made by a few planners who have the support of the central political authority.

Although there exists some sort of market in primitive societies with a very simple economy and in totalist societies with a command economy, clearly the exchange of goods in those different types of societies differs much from the free choices of the market economy that we know in America.

In either a market economy or a command economy, it is necessary to have some means for deciding what goods to produce, and in what quantities. In America, the consumers decide for most purposes. In countries with a command economy, the central political authority decides for most purposes. Yet the American government's policies affect a good many production decisions in the United States. And even in socialist or communist countries, there usually remains a small

---

2. **Authoritarian government:** one possessing great power, which citizens are compelled to obey.

private sector—that is, a portion of the economy that is carried on by private individuals—which makes decisions about its own limited private production.

In a market economy, the interaction of demand and supply determines what shall be produced, and in what quantity. In a command economy, a central authority determines what the four factors of production shall be used for, and how much of every good shall be produced. (Often, however, in a command economy the economic planning goes wrong, so that too little or too much of a commodity is produced.)

In a market economy, the distribution of goods is decided by consumers: that is, people spend their money to buy what they want. In a command economy, the central authority determines (directly or indirectly) what goods will be made available and to whom.

In a market economy, prices of goods are decided by the working of the laws of supply and demand. In a command economy, prices are fixed by central authority. (This control results very frequently in difficulties of production and supply, as we suggested in Chapter 4.)

In a market economy, people are persuaded to produce goods by the hope of profiting personally. In a command economy, people are required to produce goods in order to receive wages set by central authority.

There are more differences between the market economy and the command economy; some of those we will discuss later. *There is much more personal freedom in societies with market economies, and usually the production of goods is much greater in market economies.*

Discuss

4. If government should issue an order forbidding certain people to buy and sell in markets, what would happen to those people? What choices would remain to them? Can you think of a time in the future when this situation may occur?

5. Do you know of any individuals or groups of people in today's world who get along with very simple markets or with no markets at all? (Think of the geography you have studied.)

6. Why do we need markets? Why couldn't our government

simply build central warehouses, issue ration coupons or tickets to all people, and have citizens pick up the goods they want at the warehouses? Explain your answer.

7. Suppose you browse about secondhand furniture stores, looking for a well-made old desk. The least costly desk that you find in any shop has a marked price of seventy dollars. "I don't want to pay more than forty or fifty dollars," you tell the shop's manager. "Why are you asking seventy? How did you settle on that price?"

The shop's manager replies, with a grin, "It's the test of the market."

What does he mean? Why doesn't he please you by letting you have the desk for forty dollars? Under what circumstances might he change his mind?

8. Suppose you were on a hunting expedition in the southern Sudan and came to a remote little village with a subsistence economy. Suppose that you and your friends of the hunting party wanted omelets for breakfast and so inquired where you might buy four dozen eggs. What success do you think you would have? What would happen to the price of eggs in that village? If foreign hunters and tourists should establish a custom of stopping at that particular Sudanese village, might a market economy develop there? Explain.

9. Suppose that you are touring the Communist-governed country of Bulgaria. You are told that cameras might be bought in a state-owned department store in Sofia, the capital, for the equivalent of thirty American dollars. On asking at the department store, you are informed that the supply of bargain cameras has been exhausted: "We got ten cameras from Central Supply last week, but all were sold within an hour."

You inquire when the next shipment from the state warehouse will arrive; the clerk shrugs.

"Next week, perhaps?"

The clerk shrugs again: "Who can say?"

"When the next shipment does come, will the price be the same?" you ask.

"No, that was a special offer: the next lot will be ten times as much in your money." Whispering, the clerk then offers to change dollars for you at black-market rates.[3]

Why does consumer demand seem to have little effect upon

---

3. **Black market:** any exchange of goods that is forbidden by public authority. In a black market, prices are determined by demand and supply, not by governmental regulation.

the supply and price of cameras in Bulgaria? Why does the state department store offer a special bargain in cameras for a brief time? (You cannot know the reason for sure, but perhaps you can offer some suggestions.) How may such an offer be connected with state political policy? Why might there be a black market in dollars in a country with a command economy?

10. In a command economy, if a consumer wished to make a signal that she did not like the price or the quality of a certain commodity, what might she do? In the United States, if you disapproved of a good's price or quality, what sort of signals might you make? Would you go to a different store? In Bulgaria or in the Soviet Union, would a consumer go to a different store?

Profits and Productivity

Everybody who sells or buys in the market hopes to profit—in the sense that he wishes to exchange his goods or his money for something of greater value to himself. When people talk about the **profit motive,** they mean this hope of gaining something by an exchange of goods.

It is this profit motive that keeps the market operating. Also, *the profit motive is one of the major differences between a market economy and a command economy.* Sellers and buyers would not engage in exchange—not many of them, anyway—if they expected to gain nothing. It is the profit motive that induces most hard-working people to produce. It is the profit motive that persuades men and women to save and invest, plant and reap.

In the popular sense, the word *profit* seems to mean any sort of economic gain—any reward for labor or cleverness. But the economist means something more precise when he uses the word *profit*.

Can we say that in a manufacturing business, all the money a firm takes in (after paying for raw materials and labor) is profit? That, or something like it, is an opinion held by many people.

But the economist tells us that profit is something much narrower and rarer than gross earnings minus the cost of materials and labor. So let us try to look at profit as economists use that term.

Economists say that **profit** is *the excess of the price paid by the buyer over the total costs of the good to the seller.* Profit is made through exchange in the market. The seller makes profit by selling his goods for more than they cost him.

Does this definition mean that if Titus Groane bought a topcoat for fifty dollars from a wholesale clothing firm and sold it at Groane's Haberdashery for a hundred dollars, he made fifty dollars, or a profit of 100 percent?

No, it doesn't mean that at all, even though many people may mistakenly think it does. To put it another way, economists say that profit is the surplus of income over **outgo** (or expenses). This definition of profit often is called **accounting profit**—that is, the profit shown on a firm's account books, outgo having been deducted from income.

This term *outgo* is somewhat deceptive; it includes many items you may not think of immediately.

Economists say that profit is the excess of the price paid by the buyer over the total costs of the good to the seller. But they are quick to add that costs are not simply monetary payments. For the economist, costs are **opportunity costs,** which means the value of these resources in their next best alternative. Thus, ultimately, costs for the economist are based on personal choice by individual decision makers in much the same way as usefulness influences demand.

In other words, profit as defined by the accountant or the tax authorities is only a first step to gathering the information that individual entrepreneurs really need for making their decisions. To show the difference between the concepts, let us take an example.

Suppose Mr. Henry Smith goes into the tree business. He formerly worked for General Motors at a salary of $30,000 a year. He sells $10,000 of GM stock to provide himself the capital to get his business started. In his first year of business, he buys $4,000 worth of saplings and pays his workers $3,000. All other expenses amount to $2,000. At the end of the year, he has sold the saplings for $12,000. How much profit has he made? Is it simply the $3,000 which results from the difference between his total receipts and his total money costs? Unfortunately for Mr. Smith, we have not accurately calculated the costs.

The opportunity costs of his labor are $30,000. This is what he could have earned if he had used his labor elsewhere in its next best alternative. He could have been a shoe salesman at $14,000 a year, but that is not the value of his next best alternative. Also, the money tied up in the business could have been earning dividends from GM in the amount of $1,000 a year. This is the opportunity cost of his use of capital. When you put all these things together, you can see that it is highly likely that Mr. Smith is not earning a profit at all, but making a loss by going into the tree business. If he does not expect the figures to change over the near future, he will decide to go back to work for GM.

To show how the concept of costs is ultimately subjective (that is, personal) and reflects the value of alternatives foregone, let us take a simpler example. Assume that you are thinking of going to the basketball game on a Thursday night. The cost of a ticket is two dollars, and the expected refreshments will cost one dollar. You say to yourself, "The amount of enjoyment I will get from the game is surely more than three dollars." But then you begin to think of the costs which are not measured in money. For example, the opportunity costs may be lost study time for the science exam. If you fail that, you may be grounded for several weeks. The value of that alternative foregone may be greater than the pleasure derived from going to the game. You therefore stay home and study. Now you can begin to understand why economics is called "the dismal science."

The following list suggests how outgo usually equals income— and why true profit is unusual. Profit, actually, is what remains to a firm or an entrepreneur after *all* the expenses of a business have been paid— including opportunity costs.

Items of Outgo in Production and Distribution

- cost of raw materials and land
- cost of labor
- interest on invested capital
- wage of management
- taxes
- insurance
- transportation expenses
- cost of utilities
- interest on short-term business loans
- casualty losses (fire, flood damage, etc.)
- depreciation and maintenance
- security measures
- advertising
- goodwill contributions
- lawyers' and bookkeepers' fees
- obsolescence (becoming out of date) of inventory
- robbery, extortion, and pilferage
- payment for risk-taking
- cost of changes in social and economic environment

It costs the manufacturer or the merchant a great deal of money just to stay in business, you can see. Many people in industry or commerce fancy that they have made a profit over the years, when actually they have done no better than break even. One item that some small-business people fail to take into account is the *wage of management*. This wage is what it would cost to hire managers to run a business. If the owner or owners of the business do the managing themselves, without paying salaries to hired managers, then the owners are entitled to this wage of management. But often the owners confuse this wage with their fancied profit. In reality, as a good accountant might tell them, such owners may not have made a profit over many years; they simply have paid into their own hands the wage of management.

Profits are rare in a truly competitive market economy. But modern industrial economies are not perfectly competitive, as we shall see later in this book. Some firms do make profits, though most businesses merely get back, from year to year, their costs of doing business.

Discuss

11. Explain why there is more risk in putting money into a business enterprise than in depositing it in a savings bank.

12. Why do businesses bother to pay for insurance? Wouldn't it be more sensible for them just to put aside some savings in a bank? Explain your answer.

13. People sometimes say that profits made by "middlemen," such as retail and wholesale merchants, are unjustified. Do you agree? What services do middlemen perform?

14. A well-known economist wrote that there are risks even in a command economy, and that state planning in such economic systems also has to balance profit against loss. The economist summed up, "The only way in which state planning can abolish profits is by preventing change, so that wants can be foreseen without uncertainty."

Explain, if you can, in your own words, what this economist means. Could a state policy of preventing all change be successful? Why or why not?

All the same, virtually all entrepreneurs earnestly try to make a profit. And even the most cautious and easygoing manufacturers and merchants expect to obtain from their business at least an annual income that will include the cost of their materials, the wages of the labor they employ, interest on their invested capital, and other essential items of expense. Not all of them succeed. Every year, for one reason or another, thousands of American businesses fall bankrupt—among them some very big businesses.[4]

To understand something about profit and loss, we are going to look at a representative small business—a shop that is imaginary, but which has many real counterparts.

The Great Expectations Bookshop

Rosemarie Molnar, vice-president of the Businesswomen's Association of the middlewestern city of Megalopolis, owns and operates the Great

---

4. **Bankrupt:** declared legally unable to pay debts—that is, financially ruined.

Expectations Bookshop. This long-established store is situated next door to the huge, vacant stone building that used to be Megalopolis' central railroad station, when passenger trains still ran.

Mrs. Molnar and her husband fled from Hungary in 1956, after the defeat of the Hungarian rising against Russian domination. Both the Molnars had university degrees and were able to obtain employment in the United States. After her husband's death in an automobile accident, Mrs. Molnar invested their savings and her life-insurance payment in the purchase of the Great Expectations Bookshop from its elderly proprietor.

Loving good books, Rosemarie Molnar reads fluently in several languages. At the back of the ground floor of her bookshop, she has a kitchen, so that she can serve coffee or tea to preferred and leisurely customers. Her bookshop is a center for local people with literary interests. On the ground floor, she has a stock of new books and "publishers' remainders"—that is, recent books sold off by their publishers for a fraction of their original price. Upstairs she has a tremendous stock of secondhand books, some of them scarce and valuable.

When Mrs. Molnar bought the bookshop, the streets near the railway station attracted many more shoppers than come there nowadays. At least half the retail business that once occurred downtown now has shifted to shopping malls in the suburbs. What is still more ominous for the Great Expectations Bookshop, in those shopping malls have appeared several new franchise bookstores. These new stores carry a stock of books less varied than Mrs. Molnar's, but they advertise much more than she can afford to. Also, it is easier for shoppers to park at the malls than on Front Street, near the old railway station. So Mrs. Molnar's business is not what it was fifteen years ago.

Let us make ourselves invisible and pay a call on Mrs. Molnar. It is ten o'clock at night, and Mrs. Molnar is in her little office at the bookshop, trying to put her financial records in order. She knows it to be somewhat unsafe to work there at night, for two burglaries have occurred at Great Expectations during the past year—not to mention a daylight armed robbery. But she is so busy in the shop all day, every day except Sunday, that she has to spend at least two nights a week in office tasks.

Rosemarie Molnar is believed to be a successful businesswoman. People say that she does more than half a million dollars' worth of business every year. This is true; or, more precisely, her gross receipts last year totaled

Does Great Expectations Bookshop make a handsome profit? Most people who buy books there assume so. Mrs. Molnar, who dresses well, is known to give nearly three thousand dollars a year to St. Stephen's Church, and smaller sums to various charities.

She has a good deal of money invested in her stock and in her well-varnished bookcases and tables. She estimates the capital assets of the shop (most of the value being in the books) at $400,000. But she's not sure of that sum: many of her "new" books are depreciating in value.[5]   During the past year she may have ordered too many new books and may have paid more than she should have paid for two large private libraries of old books. She is somewhat overstocked. Business is slow at present, but Rosemarie Molnar hopes that this condition is merely, or mostly, a seasonal business slump. Great Expectations is a well-appointed shop, with a handsome front and attractive display windows. Yet the building is old, with a roof in need of renewal. Mrs. Molnar herself is not growing younger.

Although Mrs. Molnar has an accounting service do the shop's regular bookkeeping, she knows a good deal about accounting practice herself. Tonight, unassisted, she is trying to find out just how profitable her shop was during the previous year.

She begins with her total annual receipts: $502,700. From this income she must deduct many items of business expense.

First of all, she must subtract the cost of the goods she bought last year. New books and old books purchased for resale, plus the purchase of some stationery for her shop's sideline stationery department, cost her a total of $320,600. She already has sold most of the stock she acquired during the past year; still, she perceives that she was too optimistic in her buying. She is going to be stuck for some months, or even years, with an overstock of recent books that crowd her shelves. Well, take away $320,600 from the total income of $502,700. That leaves Rosemarie Molnar with a remaining business income of $182,100—quite a drop.

Mrs. Molnar is helped in her shop by her invalid daughter, Ann, who lives at home and is paid the minimum wage for what work she is able to do—chiefly answering the telephone and wrapping parcels to be mailed. Also, Mrs. Molnar employs two full-time clerks: one a rather slow-moving retired teacher of literature, the other a bubbly, energetic girl of Cuban parentage. There are usually several part-time clerks, especially during the Christmas season—most

---

5. **To depreciate:** to diminish in market value.

of them college students. Mrs. Molnar pays a janitor to come half days, five days a week. And since the robbery of the shop's cash register nine months ago, she has hired an armed security guard—not around the clock, for she can't afford that, but during business hours. Altogether, Mrs. Molnar's expenses for labor have been approximately $58,000 (including fringe benefits). That leaves remaining, out of Great Expectations' income, the sum of $124,100.

Mrs. Molnar owns the business, but not the building in which her bookshop is lodged. Her rent is a thousand dollars a month for two entire floors of the nineteenth-century building. She has to pay her own utilities. Were it not that Mrs. Molnar sends her rent check very promptly, every month, to the realtor who manages the property, the building's owners might be inclined to raise the rent. But she still can set down the figure of $12,000, counting herself lucky, for the year's cost of rent. That reduces her business income to $112,100.

Business taxes cost Mrs. Molnar $5,400. (This sum includes Social Security taxes on her employees' wages, federal and state unemployment-fund taxes, and certain municipal and state small-business taxes.) Interest she had to pay on a business loan from her bank amounted to $7,000. Insurance cost her $6,000; she feels fortunate to be able to obtain fire insurance at all, because Front Street is becoming a high-risk area for insurance firms because of robberies and arson. Professional fees paid to her lawyer and her accountants amounted to almost $3,000. Heating, air-conditioning, lighting, and water gave her a total utilities bill of some $4,800 for the year. The telephone bill was $1,300. Postage and shipping amounted to slightly more than $2,000. Her advertising bill came to merely $1,100; she wishes that she could have spent far more for this, to compete with the bookstores in the malls.

Having subtracted these eight items of outgo (totaling $30,600) from what remained of her business income, Rosemarie Molnar discovers that she has left the sum of $81,500.

From this balance she must subtract depreciation of her inventory—that is, the cost of the declining value of her stock of books and the gradual wearing out of her bookcases and other shop furniture. The "book" value of her inventory she has estimated at $400,000. Figure 5 percent annual depreciation of her stock and equipment: On $400,000, 5 percent is $20,000. To calculate her profit or loss, this sum must be taken away from her business income for the year. That leaves Mrs. Molnar with $61,500.

Next she must allow for interest on investment—that is, the amount of interest she could have earned by investing her capital in some other enterprise than her bookshop. Put her capital at $400,000; suppose that she could have obtained interest on this sum at the rate of 10 percent if she had invested in the common stock of some vigorous corporation. Then she would have received $40,000 in interest or dividends. Subtract that amount from the income from the bookshop: she is left with $21,500.

Now for her wage of management. Mrs. Molnar feels confident that if she would accept a post as manager of a big franchise bookshop (and twice she has been offered just that), she could get a salary of perhaps $35,000. Or if she were to hire a full-time manager for the Great Expectations Bookshop, she would have to pay approximately that amount in salary. So it seems reasonable to count her wage of management (what she saves by running her business herself, working hard for long hours) as $35,000. She makes no allowance, however, for what economists call payment for risk—even though her book business has become physically risky (what with robberies) as well as financially risky.

It's just as well she doesn't bother to deduct payment for risk from her balance sheet: such a deduction would be of no help. For if she subtracts her $35,000 wage of management from her remainder of business income, already reduced to $21,500—why, she gets a negative figure, minus $13,500.

Is that Mrs. Molnar's annual profit—that small sum? No: it is Mrs. Molnar's *loss* for the past year. Having finished her calculations, Rosemarie Molnar sits for some minutes with her head between her hands. Then she joins Ann in the kitchen for a melancholy cup of tea.

"My dear," she says to her daughter, "Great Expectations may last as long as I do. But I doubt it."

Discuss

15. After Mrs. Molnar deducted from income all the cash outgo from her bookshop, she had $81,500 left over. So what did she have to complain about? Didn't she make a good profit? Explain your answer.

16. Mrs. Molnar's balance sheet would show a small profit instead of a small loss if she were to discharge one of her full-time clerks and hire no replacement. Would that be a good idea? Why or why not?

17. Suppose that Rosemarie Molnar, going out of business, were to take a job as manager of a big bookshop in a shopping mall for $35,000 salary. Suppose she were to sell the Great Ex-

pectations Bookshop for its "book" (or inventory) value of $400,000. Suppose she were to invest that capital for an annual return of 10 percent. What would Mrs. Molnar's annual income be then? Would she be better off financially or not? If she would be better off, might she have any reason for not selling her Great Expectations Bookshop?

18. It is said that many people who run their own independent business would have bigger incomes if they took jobs for wages or salaries with some reliable employer. Also, they might obtain various "fringe benefits," like medical insurance and vacation pay, if they were to work for large firms. If this is true, why are so many men and women still running their own businesses? Why would still more people like to have their own place of business and independent occupation?

19. Can you suggest why the business of the Great Expectations Bookshop seems to be declining—or why the shop doesn't make a profit, anyway? Can you think of some businesses, including factories, in your own neighborhood, town, or city, that have declined or failed for similar reasons?

The economic problems of our Great Expectations Bookshop are not unusual. Most independent businesses do not make a profit, most years (as the term profit is strictly defined by economists). Their owners may or may not make a good living out of such a business, but the economic return they receive ordinarily consists of interest upon their invested capital, plus their wage of management—not what the economists call profit.

The fact that most businesses do not make a true profit is a benefit to consumers. That is, in a market economy, prices for the consumer are kept low because *competition* among sellers (producers) makes profits rare. (We will discuss competition in the next chapter.) The prices that consumers pay for many commodities reflect only the costs of production and distribution; the consumer does not provide a profit for the producer or the distributor.

Yet some entrepreneurs do succeed in making genuine profits, and big profits—through favorable circumstances or through their entrepreneurial abilities. So we turn now to another supposal. Suppose that there is a man named George Spanos, who makes a profit in . . .

Planktonburgers

On the surface of the oceans float billions of tiny plants and animals called *plankton*. These masses of living creatures are fed upon by whales, herring, and other sea creatures. Most of the different species of plankton are invisible to the human eye.

Some kinds of plankton can be eaten by human beings. Plankton amounts to the biggest source of protein in all the world. If only most plankton somehow could be converted into food for humans, the perpetual human want for food might be considerably relieved everywhere in the world.

Now suppose that a young man is hard at work upon a plan for converting plankton into a substance that can be introduced into every kitchen. This aspiring entrepreneur is George Spanos, who has lived all his life in Santa Barbara, California. He is no scientist himself, but he has had an amateur interest in marine biology ever since he was a small boy. Spanos has inherited some capital from his father, a successful restaurateur; and he is even more interested in making money than in sea creatures.

Having read in magazines about the possibilities of plankton as a source of protein, Spanos asks himself, in 1984, "Can't I do something about this?" He gets together the reports of governmental agencies and scientific societies concerning plankton. Presently he invests nearly all his own capital in additional research, engaging the famous research firm of Arthur D. Little and Company to carry on studies for him. He contrives to obtain a grant from the United States government to help him with his heavy expenses.

After three years of study, Spanos decides that it is practicable to convert most plankton into an edible (and tasty) substance. He then turns to the problem of designing a ship that can collect plankton—and that also can carry on at sea the first stage of turning the tiny creatures into food. It takes him three years to make a satisfactory design. He then contracts with Japanese shipbuilders to construct a fleet of ten large "planktoncraft"—floating fisheries and factories.

Or rather, the firm of Spanos Aquatic Foods, Ltd., a multinational corporation, arranges to have this fleet built. Mr. Spanos is president of this firm. The cost of his research alone has run into millions of dollars. To obtain more capital, he has gone to German and Japanese investors and to several large American banks. Clearly, this Aquatic Foods is a risky project; investors at first are difficult to persuade.

But George Spanos, full of enthusiasm, is a talented salesman. When

114

he requires still more money than Japanese, German, and American sources of capital are willing to supply, he turns to Arab investors, with their fortunes founded upon oil wells. He convinces the Arabs that it is their duty toward humankind, as well as a source of profit to themselves, to back his protein plan. The scientific research is completed; the ships are built and put into service.

Ten years after the birth of Spanos's idea, tremendous quantities of plankton have been collected and processed. Frozen plankton is being sold in the biggest supermarkets and the smallest rural groceries. The Soviet and Chinese governments contract for millions of pounds of plankton concentrate.

But throughout the world, the general public is suspicious of this new sea stuff. Is it really as good as beefsteak? An association of fast-food establishments that sell either hamburgers or tacos buys space in newspapers to suggest that plankton may disagree with the human stomach.

At this, Spanos launches an international advertising campaign to persuade the public of the dietary advantages and delightful flavor of plankton. In defiance of the vendors of hamburgers and tacos, he opens, throughout the United States and Canada, franchise fast-food restaurants with the name "Toilers of the Sea." Within a few months, both the advertising and the franchise houses are triumphant. Planktonburger's cost per pound is far less than the cost of hamburger or even of tacos. It begins to appear that the planktonburger will supplant the hamburger everywhere in America.

George Spanos has secured international patents on his techniques for converting plankton into food, on his special gathering-and-preparing ships, and on means for preserving and fast-freezing plankton that have been developed in his laboratories. For some years, Spanos Aquatic Foods will be the only firm able to manufacture and sell edible plankton. In that multinational corporation lie the possibilities of "wealth beyond the dreams of avarice."

By 1999, Spanos is decorated by the president of France for "noble foresight to the high benefit of all humanity." The governments of Chile, the Ivory Coast, and Iceland also confer honors upon this entrepreneur.

Also by 1999, Spanos's firm has paid off the immense debts (at high interest rates) it assumed in its early years. The gross income of Spanos Aquatic Foods exceeds three billion dollars—with sales expected to double within three years.

In 1985, friends had said of Spanos's scheme, "George is going to lose his shirt in that crazy fish business; he ought to stick to his dad's hash-house." But by 1999, Spanos counts up his winnings in this risky undertaking. After allowing for all costs (including the wage of management, interest on capital invested, and even the factor of risk), Spanos has made a pure profit, personally, in 1999 alone, of $7,453,000. (A substantial part of this sum, nevertheless, must go to the United States government for personal income tax.) George Spanos expects to become, within a very few years, one of the wealthiest men in the history of free enterprise.

Our friend George Spanos is imaginary. As yet there has not really been developed a satisfactory method for converting plankton into food for the mass market. But it remains conceivable that research and development may work out such techniques within our own lifetimes—particularly under the pressure of increasing population throughout most of the world.

Real cases of development and marketing of new food products by entrepreneurs have occurred fairly frequently in recent decades— though not on the scale of the imaginary George Spanos's imaginary planktonburgers. For instance, in 1984 there appeared on the streets of New York City a brand-new frozen dessert, Tofutti, sold from carts by vendors. This product was the result of a good many years of endeavor by David Mintz, owner of a kosher restaurant in Brooklyn. The principal ingredient in the new dessert is tofu, a substance derived from soybean curd. Tofutti tastes like ice cream but is not a dairy product and, therefore, contains no cholesterol and no lactose, substances harmful to the health of some people. Mr. Mintz planned to produce and market Tofutti flavored with many different fruits and nuts; he began with five flavors. The research for the new food was conducted in his own office and his restaurant kitchen. Within a year, Tofutti became widely popular from coast to coast; so Mr. Mintz, once a small entrepreneur abruptly became an entrepreneur on a large scale.

The *New York Times* of June 20, 1984, reported that David Mintz was developing a "revolutionary" Tofutti shake to compete with milk shakes. "Ovens are being brought in so that he can perfect a meatless hamburger that tastes like the real thing. This tofu visionary foresees a time when tofuburger franchises replace McDonald's and Burger King; and a time of tofu TV dinners."

Discuss

20. What international problems might arise from large-scale "harvesting" of plankton in the oceans? What countries might be the most eager to get large supplies of this new foodstuff? Would those countries be strong enough to enforce their claim to priority in the distribution of planktonburgers?

21. Do you think it fair that George Spanos should make so big a profit in addition to return on his investment, his wage of management, etc.? Why or why not? What did Spanos do to entitle him to a grand reward?

22. Governments issue *patents* to scientists and inventors who develop new techniques. Such patents entitle the inventors to a monopoly of the manufacture and sale of a new device or technology for a period of years. Spanos obtained such patents on his process for making plankton into food for human beings. If he had not been granted patents, would Spanos probably have made so large a profit? In what other ways would a private enterprise like Spanos's be helped by governments?

Both the small retail shop and the multinational corporation operate because of the profit motive. Nevertheless, the profit motive is not the only reason that entrepreneurs (big or small) are in business. Our imaginary friend Rosemarie Molnar keeps her bookshop not simply because she hopes for a profit, but also because she loves books and hopes to encourage people to acquire them. Our imaginary friend George Spanos makes food out of plankton not solely because he means to grow rich, but also because he enjoys the adventure—and the opportunity to feed people throughout the world.

If the profit motive were forbidden, and if no market economy existed, still there would occur some production of goods in society. But it seems certain that under such circumstances, economic productivity would be far lower than it is in our present culture. And it is doubtful whether, in the long run, such a reduced economy could sustain a high civilization.

It has been said that if you mean to make a donkey carry a load for you, you must give him either the carrot or the stick. The carrot is the reward for doing work; the stick is the punishment for not doing work. This hard truth can be applied to human beings also. In economic systems, the carrot is the prospect of profit. The stick is the prospect of the punishment called slavery. The former of these alternatives is the method of the market economy. The stick is the method, in ancient times or modern, of the command economy.

CHAPTER 6

The Good That Competition Does

Chapter 6
The Good That Competition Does

- Healthy Competition, Ancient and Modern
- How Competition Works Practically in the Market
- Imperfect Competition
- Oligopoly and Monopoly
- Monopoly versus the Market

Healthy Competition, Ancient and Modern

Competition means a contest for some prize, honor, or advantage. We compete in sports, in studies, in popularity. **Economic competition** is a contest among producers (sellers) and among consumers (buyers).

In a market economy, healthy competition improves the quality of goods and lowers their prices. Among producers, a huge contest is always going on. The object of this contest is to attract consumers who will buy products. *The way to attract consumers is to offer them goods that are lower in price, or higher in quality (or both), than the goods offered by other producers.*

Also, a huge contest is always going on among consumers. For the buyers of goods are hunting for bargains: that is, they are trying to find the things they want at lower prices than many consumers pay. Or perhaps they are looking for goods of better quality than the goods most consumers are able to obtain.

This healthy competition in the selling and buying of goods is a major reason why countries with a market economy are prosperous. Yet is this competition helpful to the men and women who seem to be losers? In any contest, some people win, and others lose. What about the people who are not successful at selling or at buying? What about the people who may be physically handicapped, or those who are slow, or those who simply don't work hard—the losers in the economic race? Is economic competition good for them, too?

Yes. In the long run, competition helps those who lose the economic race as well as the people who succeed in the contest. For one result of competition is better goods at lower prices for *everybody*. If a worker is paid only the minimum wage required by law (and so is relatively poor), still such a person is better off in an economy with products of good quality at low prices. *It is better to be relatively poor in such an efficient economy than to be absolutely poor in an inefficient economy with goods of low quality at high prices.*

Also, a society with an efficient economy can afford to help its poorer citizens economically through voluntary charities or governmental assistance. *Competition, in short, makes possible a better standard of living for everyone in a prosperous society.*

Throughout the centuries, societies that lacked economic competition usually did not produce adequate goods, including services. Competition in selling and buying usually has been a mark of prosperous societies.

Discuss

1. Have you ever engaged in competition? In what sort of contest? Do you think that competition is enjoyable for its own sake? Why or why not?

2. Suppose that Felicia Schwartz takes a job as a typist, but turns out to be slow at typing, making many mistakes. Her employer discharges Felicia at the end of three months. Later, she finds another job as a dentist's receptionist. She has failed as a typist. Why is she better off in a competitive economy (which rewards good typists and discharges poor ones) than she would be in a very simple agricultural economy that does not have much competition?

You can see that there are advantages in healthy competition. Yet there exist forms of competition that are unhealthy: competition that is selfish, deceptive, or violent.

Hesiod on Competition

More than eight hundred years before Christ was born, there lived in a rural region of Greece a poor farmer named Hesiod, who was a poet—and a wise man. In his long poem *Works and Days*, Hesiod declared that there are two different kinds of competition, or "strife." The evil sort of competition produces deception, fierce quarrels, and war. But the good kind of competition has been put into human nature by God. This good competition is meant for the improvement of mankind. Healthy competition leads people to work hard and produce good things—to grow good crops, to write good poems.

When we see other men and women succeeding in their work, Hesiod pointed out, we strive to succeed as they do. This contest, or competition, rooted in human nature from the beginning of the human race, results in high achievement. Here is the way Hesiod expressed this ancient truth in his poetry:

> *The needy idler sees the rich, and hastes*
> *Himself to guide the plough, and plant the wastes,*
> *Ordering his household: thus the neighbor speeds*
> *To wealth, and neighbor emulous succeeds.*
> *That strife is good for men: incensed to zeal,*
> *Potter with potter turns the glowing wheel;*
> *Smiths beat their anvils; beggars envious throng,*
> *And bards provoke to jealousy of song.*

In other words, nearly everybody wishes to be as well off as his neighbor. So farmers improve their land when they see other farmers doing well. Makers of pottery compete to turn out more and better pots. Blacksmiths engage in a contest to turn out articles of iron, satisfying demand. Even beggars would like to sing songs as popular as those of successful poets.

Discuss

> 3. What does Hesiod mean by his phrase "neighbor emulous succeeds"? (In a good dictionary, look up the words *emulation* and *emulous*.)

The market economy sometimes is called the *competitive economy*. A major reason that America's economic system has been so productive is the long-established American desire to "get ahead"—to become as well off as the people next door. Hesiod's verses suggest that this same motive was strong among the Greeks near the dawn of their history.

Dr. Samuel Johnson, who compiled the first great dictionary of the English language, tells us that "a man is seldom more innocently occupied than when he is engaged in making money." Economic competition is a contest in money making. By comparison with the fierce competition of war or the desperate competition of power politics, economic competition is innocent enough.

Discuss

> 4. Hesiod was cheated out of his inheritance by his brother Perses, who bribed judges to award the whole of their father's little estate to himself. Here is an instance of the "evil competition" that Hesiod condemned. Can you suggest other examples of unfair competition?
>
> 5. Irving Babbitt, a famous American literary critic, writes that "There is something in the nature of things that calls for a real victory and a real defeat. Competition is necessary to rouse man from his native indolence; without it life loses its zest and savor." Can you explain in your own words what Babbitt meant? Would there be much pleasure in life if nobody had to compete for anything?

Not all individuals nor all communities are competitive. A peaceful life with little competition sometimes may be more satisfying, though commonly less prosperous economically. In America, religious groups like the Amish and other "Plain People" abstain from competition and from most modern labor-saving devices. There have long existed religious orders, particularly among Catholics and Buddhists, devoted to a life of poverty and prayer and good works, which do not engage in competition. And in various parts of the world, there survive old-fashioned economic systems in which competition has only a small part. (One example is life in the Hebrides, or Western Isles, off the coast of Scotland, where most remaining inhabitants are small crofters—that is, they cultivate small plots of land and live very simply by fishing and tending their tiny farms. Such an existence supplies little in the way of cash income, but it provides modest comfort and a tranquil life.)

So it is possible to be happy without much competition—although rarely is it possible to have abundant goods and services without competition, unless one inherits a good deal of capital. Economists, being concerned with production of goods, do not have much to say about alternatives to competition.

How Competition Works Practically in the Market

Were there no competition, no market could exist for the exchange of goods. The market is the economic sports stadium, so to speak, in which sellers compete with other sellers and buyers compete with other buyers. If there were no economic contests, there could be no economic stadium.

Both buyers and sellers are competing for the prize called prosperity. Out of these two sets of competitors emerges the market price of any good. In Chapter 4, on demand and supply, we discussed this process of competition in the market.

In a free market, open competition is supposed to exist. Under the conditions of **open competition** (sometimes called *unrestricted competition*), there will be many sellers willing to sell a good and many buyers willing to buy that good. In this market with open competition, no one seller or buyer (or group of sellers or buyers) will have enough influence on the market to affect the price or the quality of the goods traded there.

In short, in an unrestricted market, price and quality will be determined by many bargains among sellers and buyers. In this open market, nobody will interfere in any way with the freedom of sellers and buyers to bargain among themselves. This freedom will result in lower prices and higher quality—or, to speak more accurately, *open competition tends to turn out the highest quality of goods for the price people are willing to pay.*

To understand what open competition is, let us take an example from Spain today.

The Melon Market at El Escorial

In the market square of the old town of El Escorial, sellers of melons gather during the summer months. These vendors are peasant women from the surrounding sunburnt countryside who have grown the melons themselves. They sit close together on the pavement of the market square, each with her heap of melons beside her.

To these melon vendors come the consumers—the people of El Escorial. These local buyers inspect the fruit for ripeness and juiciness. One woman selling may ask a certain price for a half-dozen melons; a housewife bargaining with her may offer to pay a few *pesetas* less for those melons. Eventually these two women may strike a bargain. Or possibly the intending buyer may move on to a different vendor in hope of lower prices or better melons.

By the time the sun begins to set over the mountains, most of the melons have been sold. Some vendors in the plaza begin to offer their remaining stock at a reduced price, for such goods spoil quickly. Most of the vendors will be back the following morning with fresh melons to offer.

For the day, the local demand for melons has been satisfied. The supply available at the market, if not wholly exhausted, at least has been reduced to the melons of inferior quality. No vendor has made a great deal of money by the day's business: competition was too keen for that. Nevertheless, those women who were really good at growing and selling melons have made more money in their competition than have the other vendors. The market has been cleared under conditions of open competition.

This market at El Escorial, like similar outdoor markets at

hundreds of other towns in southern Europe, is a simple illustration of free competition. In most American cities, one still finds large farmers' markets that are nearly as good examples of competition among buyers and sellers. But most forms of competition are more complicated in the twentieth century.

To see how competition works in one industry of the huge national American market for goods, we can take an example from the fabrics trade. Let us look at a firm manufacturing and distributing bedspreads. The bedspread trade remains highly competitive today in the United States, and every year a considerable number of firms in this business fail in their competition and are forced into bankruptcy. They have not been efficient enough to cover their costs of production and distribution. Other bedspread firms, nevertheless, seem to thrive.

Thistle River Industries

One of the better-known firms in the bedspread trade, let us suppose, is called Thistle River Industries. This company makes its own bedspreads, buying its cloth chiefly from mills in the southern states or from textile manufacturers in Taiwan or Hong Kong. (For the most part, this "Thistle River" example is taken from a real existing firm with a similar name, owned by an entrepreneur with a similar name.)

Thistle River owns a mill in Indiana where cloth is sewn into bedspreads: several hundred women and men work at its sewing machines. But the firm's sales offices are in New York City, in the "garment district" of Manhattan, which for more than a century has been America's chief center of the fabrics trades. Thistle River sells its bedspreads to the more fashionable department stores, to some specialty shops, and to interior decorators. The firm operates a few retail shops of its own.

Thistle River has been successful in its line of business for a quarter of a century. The firm's prosperity is the work principally of its owner and founder, who personally directs its operations. He is Carl Totter, a big, genial man, once a sergeant of Marines, who has a remarkable talent for designing attractive fabrics. He studies old designs and patterns in New York's museums, for one thing, and adapts them for today's market. Also, Mr. Totter is a first-rate salesman.

The market for Carl Totter's products is not confined to some sunny plaza, for Thistle River bedspreads are sold in every state in the Union—with some sales to Europe, too. Thistle River has a rather complicated system for getting its goods on the market. Mr. Totter employs more than twenty regional salespeople who go from city to city seeking buyers in department stores and specialty shops or showing samples to interior decorators. Also, in several cities, Thistle River spreads can be bought at small, fashionable shops selling nothing else: these are shops either owned by Thistle River or else licensed by Thistle River with an "exclusive franchise" for the sale of Thistle River spreads locally.

Thistle River's line is advertised, often in color, in magazines read by well-to-do people and interior decorators. The bill for advertising is one of the largest items in Thistle River's budget. Annually, the firm issues a handsome, illustrated catalog which is so attractive that Mr. Totter is able to sell it for a dollar a copy.

Thistle River's gross sales amount to millions of dollars every year, and Mr. Totter makes a very good living from his business. He keeps a fashionable apartment on Central Park, in Manhattan—with Thistle River spreads on all the beds. He buys books and paintings, has built a country house in Long Island, and owns a yacht, several horses, and a farm. He travels abroad often, with wife and children.

Yet Thistle River Industries never will make Mr. Totter immensely rich. Why not? Because of competition.

For Thistle River is only one of hundreds of firms that manufacture and distribute bedspreads for the national market. All those other firms are trying to outsell Thistle River. They may not be able to offer customers better quality than Thistle River's line of spreads, but certainly they often offer lower prices.

Potential buyers may be attracted by Thistle River's catalogs and advertising. Yet when some of these buyers find that the average price of Thistle River's products is at least 20 percent higher than that of Firm X or Firm Y—well, the charming design of a Thistle River bedspread is challenged by the relative cheapness of its competitors. Many or most people are more influenced by price than by the "prestige name" or "designer label" of a consumer good. Thistle River, after all, will do only a small part of the selling of bedspreads that occurs in the vast national market during the course of twelve months. Nobody really has to buy the spreads so cleverly designed by Mr. Totter. Customers with a good deal of money or with refined taste will buy Thistle River spreads. But even in terms of design and quality of fabrics,

Thistle River has competing firms. This competition will tend to keep prices relatively low in the bedspread trade—and so to prevent Mr. Totter, or any other manufacturer, from making large profits, year after year.

How is it, then, that Mr. Totter enjoys so high a standard of living? Probably because he deserves, and gets, a large wage of management. That is, he is so good a designer and so energetic a business executive that he earns money through his personal efforts rather than through clear profits of the firm he owns. Were he to work for a salary from some huge industrial or commercial firm, presumably he could demand a salary as large as what he now earns for himself, if not a larger one.

In short, the bedspread trade, like the melon market in El Escorial, is highly competitive. Consumers can choose from hundreds of patterns and types of spreads at a considerable range of quality and price, manufactured and distributed by scores or even hundreds of competing firms. No one bedspread maker (or group of bedspread makers) has enough influence to affect the price or quality of the bedspread market. Prices therefore tend to be low, and quality (or at least a choice of different levels of quality) tends to be high in the bedspread market nationwide.

Discuss   6. If you intended to buy a new bedspread, where would you look? What sort of stores might you visit? How might you select a spread without going to any shop? Show how "shopping around" by potential buyers promotes competition.

7. Suppose that Cosmopolitan Multifabrics, Inc., should offer to buy Thistle River Industries from Mr. Totter. The officers of Cosmopolitan Multifabrics see that Totter is doing a good business. His firm's only visible assets, nevertheless, are a rather old sewing factory in Indiana, a New York showroom, a few small shops in rented premises, and a stock on hand of bedspreads and cloth. They offer Mr. Totter a million dollars for Thistle River's assets—including the firm's name. But if Mr. Totter will join Cosmopolitan Multifabrics as an executive vice-president and manage for them their new subsidiary of Thistle River, they will pay him two million dollars for his business plus an annual salary of $190,000. Why the big difference in these two offers? How does the second offer to Mr. Totter suggest that there is com-

petition in the sale of services as well as in the sale of material goods?

8. Suppose that Thistle River has been selling one of its better bedspreads for a "suggested price" of two hundred dollars retail. (That is, the price would be two hundred dollars in Thistle River's own specialty shops, and Mr. Totter would try to persuade department stores, interior decorators, and other retail outlets to charge the price of two hundred dollars for that particular spread.) Suppose also that Firm X, a major competitor with Thistle River, should offer a spread almost identical in appearance and quality at the price of one hundred twenty-five dollars, retail. Customers probably then would buy the spreads of Firm X, leaving Thistle River with a large overstock of unsold bedspreads of this type. What would Thistle River probably do in order to market its unsold goods? How would such action prove that competition is beneficial to the public?

9. Suppose that Firm X should take over much of the business formerly done by Thistle River so that Mr. Totter's firm were in danger of bankruptcy. Suppose that Mr. Totter then should complain to his New York state senator about "unfair competition" and should ask for passage of a state law setting minimum prices for bedspreads so that no bedspread manufacturer would go out of business. Would such a statute be good for the people of New York state? Why or why not?

The bedspread trade is very competitive—yet *not perfectly* competitive. Carl Totter influences buyers' choices through his advertising, for instance—not simply through price and quality. He has to pay minimum wages to his employees, according to federal and state laws— which he would not have to do under theoretical conditions of perfect competition, as economists define perfect competition. In some other ways, the vast American market for fabric goods like bedspreads is not so unrestrictedly competitive as the simple melon market in El Escorial. Nevertheless, the manufacture and selling of bedspreads in the United States is a good example of healthy competition among sellers and among buyers.

Imperfect Competition

Economists say that competition is *imperfect* when the number of producers (sellers) is limited, so that any one producer may form some idea of what his competitors are likely to charge in prices. When competition is imperfect, those prices tend to be higher, and often quality of the product is lower. Or if there are only a few possible consumers (buyers) for a good, competition is called imperfect: then buyers may get together to settle on the price they are willing to pay producers.

Many businesses are not so competitive as our example of the bedspread trade. Imperfect competition often exists in industries that require a great deal of capital, causing those industries, therefore, to have only a few producers.

The American automobile industry often is mentioned as an example of imperfect competition. Sixty years ago, there existed many more automobile manufacturers in the United States than there are today. In recent years, there have been only three or four major car-making firms in the United States, plus some other more specialized companies that make particular types of vehicles.

Costs of manufacturing automobiles have risen greatly during the past sixty years. The cost of labor in automobile factories is the biggest item in this increase. When costs of production increase, prices tend to rise, perhaps sharply. Some producers, unable to sell their goods at higher prices, may have to go out of business.

For when prices increase, people purchase fewer cars—or buy cars less frequently. So for the past decade, American automobile manufacturers have found it harder and harder to sell their cars. When the quantity of cars demanded by consumers diminishes, new producers seldom enter the market. Therefore, only a few American producers of automobiles remain in business—though they still compete with one another.

As prices of American cars have increased, competition has grown from a different source of supply: automobiles imported from Germany, Japan, and Italy, chiefly. Manufacturers in those countries still can turn out cars at lower cost. Despite the expense of shipping cars overseas, European and Japanese firms often can sell automobiles at prices less than those of cars produced in the United States. This competition makes it harder for American manufacturers to sell their products. So as American production of cars goes down with the diminishing of demand, unemployment in the American automobile industry results.

Competition among American automobile manufacturers is imperfect, because only a few firms still exist. Those firms all have about the same costs of operation, and they know about what their competitors' prices will be. Yet the automobile market in America remains competitive—because of the imported cars from foreign manufacturers.

There is a competitive *international market* in cars. Adam Smith emphasized that international *free trade* keeps competition vigorous. He meant that governments should not impose high taxes upon goods imported from other countries. For competition from abroad tends to keep prices low and quality high. High import taxes are a restraint of trade. (In Britain, taxes on imported goods are called *duties;* in the United States, such taxes are called *tariffs.*) If a government establishes high taxes (tariffs) on many agricultural products or manufactured goods—why, sometimes that policy may protect the country's agriculture and industry from foreign competition. But *the result is higher prices for consumers within any country that sets high tariffs.*

Were it not for the competition of foreign car manufacturers, the prices of automobiles in America would be higher than they are already. The automobile market still is competitive, but it is not perfectly competitive. American manufacturers of cars continue to compete with one another, and European and Japanese manufacturers add to the competition. Yet this competition is not so keen as that of the bedspread trade, say.

If prices of both American and imported cars are high, why don't new producers enter the automobile-making business in the United States? Because of the amount of capital required. Billions of dollars in capital would be needed to build up an automobile firm on the scale of General Motors, Ford, Chrysler, or the German, Italian, and Japanese car manufacturers. Also, a great deal of money and time would have to be spent in training a large labor force to work in new automobile factories. For such reasons, the automobile-making business cannot be so competitive as the bedspread-making business (which does not require a tremendous amount of capital for starting a new firm). The automobile industry probably will remain an example of imperfect competition.

Is anything wrong with imperfect competition? If goods still can be supplied to consumers under imperfect competition, why worry? But governments do worry. In any market economy, the government makes some effort to prevent competition from being reduced to a few firms.

There is a legal term to describe any attempt by producers to reduce competition. That term is **combination in restraint of trade.** In the public interest, governments try to keep markets competitive. This is not always an easy task, for, as Adam Smith pointed out, when men of business are gathered together, often they begin to talk with one another about ways to reduce competition. Why? Because *if producers all could agree to charge the same price to consumers, then they could set their price high—and make large profits.*

Public authorities oppose such combinations in restraint of trade, in order to protect consumers against high prices and to keep a country's economy efficient. *In any market economy, imperfect competition is less satisfactory than is the open competition of many sellers and buyers. Yet imperfect competition is better than no competition at all.*

Discuss

10. Suppose that all the bedspread-making firms in the country were bought up by Cosmopolitan Multifabrics and two or three other very large corporations. What would happen, at least temporarily, to competition? What would tend to happen to

prices? How about variety of choice for consumers? How might more active competition in the bedspread trade, before long, be restored? Is it improbable that merely three or four firms might come to control production and distribution of bedspreads in America? Explain your answer.

11. The grocery business in America still is highly competitive. Food prices are lower in the United States than in any other large country, and a wider variety of foods is available to most people than anywhere else. Yet there are fewer food stores, per head of population, than there were in the United States sixty years ago. Much of the food retailing business has been taken over by large chains. Would you say that we now have imperfect competition in food distribution? Why or why not?

12. In 1926, the price of a Ford Model T was merely $280. Today the price of the cheapest automobile in America is more than twenty times that sum. There were more automobile firms in business in 1926 than there are today. Does the higher price of cars result chiefly from the reduction in the number of firms—that is, from the loss of competition?

13. Suggest three businesses or industries that seem very competitive today. Suggest three that seem to have only imperfect competition.

Oligopoly and Monopoly

When some industry or business is dominated by a very few firms, economists call such a condition **oligopoly.** Under oligopoly, there is very imperfect competition.

When some industry or business is dominated by just one firm, economists call such domination **monopoly.** Under monopoly, there is no competition at all.

Economists recognize that some oligopolies and monopolies are *natural.* For under certain circumstances and in certain industries, it may not be possible or efficient to have many competing firms.

Transportation of passengers and goods by aircraft is a kind of natural oligopoly. Airlines compete for business, but the number of large airlines is limited. A vast amount of capital is required to finance an airline. Landing space at airports is limited. If fifty little airlines tried to operate out of a small city's airport, confusion would result—or perhaps something worse than confusion. So air space and some other conditions of air transportation are regulated by governments. The number of airlines serving any one place varies from time to time, but the number always is limited. Competition is imperfect in air transportation—and in rail transportation, for that matter.

Under oligopoly, considerable competition still may be carried on among the few firms engaged in the trade or industry. But an oligopoly can turn into a combination in restraint of trade, increasing prices and perhaps lowering quality of goods, including services. For when only a few firms are involved, the owners or managers of those firms might agree to charge the same prices and offer only the same sort of services—at the expense of consumers. So governmental regulating agencies watch closely any industry in which there are few producers.

Also, there is such a thing as a **natural monopoly.** In most cities or regions of the United States, there is only one electric company, one distributor of natural gas through pipelines, one water company (although, here and there, competition exists in even such economic enterprises) because it would be technologically difficult to have parallel competing electric cables, gas pipelines, water mains, and telephone lines. Also, there may not be enough business in an area to pay the costs of operating more than one **public utility** of this sort.

With these natural monopolies, usually some governmental agency regulates the prices of the goods provided by the monopoly. In some American cities, and in many other countries, the government itself carries on these economic natural monopolies.

In various eras, governments have established monopolies as a means of collecting money for their treasuries. In France, before the French Revolution, the royal government kept a monopoly of salt, from which it extracted much revenue. Various European countries today have state monopolies of the sale of tobacco. Various American states, since the 1930s, have made the sale of intoxicating beverages a state monopoly. And in the communist lands today, nearly every form of industry and business is a state monopoly.

What is wrong with a monopoly? Why, if a producer has little or no competition, that firm can charge consumers "what the traffic will bear"—that is, the highest possible price that buyers will pay to satisfy their wants. Such a monopolistic producer could set high prices, lower the quality of his product, and still sell his goods—because customers could buy from nobody else. So monopolists may make huge profits at consumers' expense.

Discuss

> 14. Suppose that you were a farmer in the African country of Uganda, growing coffee for export. Suppose that the dictator of Uganda should declare the coffee market of the country to be a state monopoly. You still could grow coffee, but you could sell it only to one governmental agency. Do you think that you might get a better price for your coffee that way? Why or why not? Why might the dictator decide to establish such a monopoly?
>
> 15. With what natural monopolies does your family do business? If one of those monopolies should double its prices suddenly, what could your family do about the matter?

Monopoly versus the Market

Except for natural monopolies operated or regulated by government, no industry or branch of commerce in America today is dominated by a monopoly. Imperfect competition exists in various industries, and there are some oligopolies—but no monopolies.

One reason for this absence of monopolies is action by the federal government against combinations in restraint of trade. The Department of Justice frequently prosecutes, under the **antitrust laws,** individuals or firms charged with trying to reduce competition. But such action at law is not always effectual, because enforcement of the antitrust laws is difficult.

A more important reason for the American freedom from monopolies is the operation of the free market itself. If one firm temporarily gains control of most or all of the supply of a good, soon competing firms will enter that business. These new competitors will offer lower prices and better quality in order to win customers away from the monopolist. If, for example, one chair-making firm should somehow manage to buy up all other chair-making companies, establish a monopoly of the chair market, and sell its chairs only at high prices—why, in short order, new chair-making companies would be organized and would readily find a market for their lower-priced chairs. Thus competition would be restored by the process of the open market.

Or should some great corporation secure a monopoly of raw materials of some sort—of coal, say—consumers gradually would find substitutes for the high-priced coal of the monopoly. They might turn to fuel oil, to natural gas, to firewood, to peat (in some regions), or to electrical heating. These substitutes might be costly, but they might cost less than coal if all the coal mines were owned by a monopoly. Then, in the long run, the firm owning all the coal would have to bring its prices down to the level of other fuels.

Something of this sort happened during the 1970s when the Arab states and other countries producing petroleum greatly raised their oil prices. Americans affected by these price increases found other sources of supply for oil, reduced their consumption of gasoline and fuel oil, and obtained some substitutes for petroleum. Before long the foreign producers of oil were left with an oil "glut"—that is, more unsold barrels of oil than they knew what to do with. Then they had to reduce the price of their oil.

In this fashion, the market tends to find its own remedies for monopoly. *Where no free exchange of goods exists, monopolies endure, because they are supported by the force of the government or operated by the government itself.*

Would a monopoly of labor be possible? If every employed person in America were compelled to belong to one national labor union, then the officers of that union could create a monopoly of labor. They could set wages and hours of work and working conditions pretty much as they might choose.

But nothing like such a national monopoly of labor ever has existed in the United States. In many states, *right-to-work laws* keep the labor market more or less competitive.[1] Under federal laws, the *closed shop*[2] is forbidden in labor contracts:[3] which means that no union can legally tell employers what people they can or cannot hire. Sometimes, however, labor unions may be so powerful that it would be very difficult for employers to operate a business without contracting with a particular union. Such a condition can result in greatly increasing labor costs, and so increasing prices.

Labor is an economic commodity, to be bought and sold. Therefore, we have competition in labor as well as in raw materials, capital, and management. *Individuals compete with one another for good jobs. Employers compete with one another to find first-rate labor (either physical labor or mental labor).*

Labor unions have become a tool by which a group of working people may bargain in this sort of competition. This is called **collective bargaining.** Just as governments take certain measures to preserve competition among sellers and among buyers, so governments take certain other measures to preserve competition in the labor market. But in the United States, the governmental restraints upon labor unions are far less severe than are the controls exercised in much of the world.

Discuss

16. Suppose that some great corporation should buy up all the sugar imported to the United States, and (having a monopoly) should raise the price of sugar to twenty dollars a pound. If the government did not interfere, how would the mechanism of the free market deal with this monopoly? Would new dealers in sugar

---

1. **Right-to-work law:** a statute providing that a person does not have to be a member of the union in order to be employed. Such laws have been enacted in several states of the Union.

2. **Closed shop:** the policy by which any worker in a particular firm or organization must be a member of a labor union in order to obtain and retain employment. Usually this policy means that an employer must accept the union "hiring hall": that is, the union selects new employees when the employer needs more labor.

3. **Contract:** an agreement, either written or oral, between two persons or groups; either party to the contract promises to do something for the other party. In economics, usually a contract is an agreement to buy or sell.

spring up? Would people find substitutes for cane sugar? If so, what substitutes would be possible?

17. In order to gain a real monopoly of cane sugar in the United States, the monopolists would have to control the sugar cane crop in the regions where cane is grown. From your knowledge of geography, can you suggest what countries or regions would be involved?

18. The federal government holds a monopoly of certain services. Private organizations and state governments are not permitted to engage in those services or activities. Can you name three or four such services or activities?

19. Suppose that the printers' union at a daily newspaper should go on strike, telling the newspaper company's president, "We won't lift a finger to get out the paper until you give us a 10 percent raise in wages." Would that be a labor monopoly? Why or why not?

20. Explain how governments create or encourage monopolies by the following devices: patents and copyrights, state-owned stores, tariffs, postal services.

From colonial times to the present, most Americans have disliked monopolies and have approved competition. In 1832, Henry Clay, one of the most famous men ever to sit in the United States Senate, told his fellow senators:

By competition the total amount of the supply is increased, and by increase of the supply a competition in the sale ensues, and this enables the consumer to buy at lower rates. Of all human powers operating on the affairs of mankind, none is greater than that of competition.

Perhaps Senator Clay exaggerated somewhat. For love is a greater power than competition, and so is fear. But certainly competition has moved mountains, and has driven the wolf from many a door.

CHAPTER 7

Efficiency of Production

Chapter 7
Efficiency of Production

- • Measuring Efficiency
- • Real Cost and Efficiency
- • Efficiency and the Division of Labor
- • Overspecialization
- • Geographic Specialization
- • Efficiency and Comparative Advantage
- • Scale of Production as a Source of Efficiency
- • Intelligence and Imagination as Causes of Efficiency

Measuring Efficiency

The market economy is efficient—more efficient than any other economic arrangement ever has been. A major cause of this superior efficiency is healthy competition. Now what do we mean by *efficiency?*

Dictionaries define **efficiency** as productiveness, or the power of producing intended results. When people get good results from what they do, they can be called *efficient* people.

In economics, efficiency means the same thing as *productivity.* When economists use the term *efficiency*, they mean getting the largest possible *output* of goods from a given *input* of the factors of production. An efficient producer turns out plenty of goods from a limited amount of raw materials, labor, capital, and management.

Goods can be produced in various ways—some of those ways efficient. An efficient producer may keep his input constant (unchanging) and obtain from his input the maximum output. Or an efficient producer may keep his output constant but reduce his input (cost of production) to the minimum. *Really efficient producers turn out goods of high quality at relatively low prices.* To judge whether a method of production is efficient, we need to know these things:

1. The **output**: how much is produced;
2. The **input**: the total cost (in time or money) needed to produce the good.

The efficiency of one method of production may be compared with the efficiency of another method of production. Or the efficiency of a producer at one time may be compared with that producer's efficiency at another time. Economists call this **comparative efficiency**.

To understand this concept, let us take the example of producing tomatoes. We can compare the efficiency of three methods of growing tomatoes. We need to look at the input required for each method and the output obtained by each method. The figures used in the box below are imaginary—that is, they are only a rough comparison of the degrees of efficiency of the three different methods. These methods are growing tomatoes in a small garden, growing them on a large farm, and growing them in a large greenhouse.

Three Ways of Producing Tomatoes

Method	Input (Cost of Production)	Output (Amount of Production)	Cost per pound
1. small garden	$200 (rent of land seeds spades, poles, fertilizer, pesticide labor of one person)	500 pounds of tomatoes	40 cents
2. big farm	$40,000 (rent of land seeds fertilizer, pesticide tractor, plow labor of 15 persons in season, manager)	200,000 pounds of tomatoes	20 cents
3. big greenhouse	$48,000 (rent of land upkeep of greenhouse tools fertilizer, pesticide labor of 5 persons all year, manager)	200,000 pounds of tomatoes	24 cents

Discuss

1. If the production cost of tomatoes grown on a large farm is less than the cost of those grown in a small garden, why do people bother to grow their own tomatoes? What costs may people diminish or eliminate by growing some of their own food? May people grow tomatoes and other things for reasons that are not wholly economic?

2. In this example, the input required for growing tomatoes in a large greenhouse is two hundred forty times as great as the input required for growing them in a small garden. Can you explain why, nevertheless, it is comparatively more efficient to grow tomatoes in the greenhouse?

3. If large farms can produce tomatoes for a cost somewhat less than that of greenhouse production, how do the truck gardeners who grow tomatoes in greenhouses manage to stay in business?

4. Might it be an efficient operation to build an orangery (a greenhouse for orange trees) in a northern city, so avoiding costs of transportation from California or Florida? Why or why not?

You can see that the comparative efficiency of the farm method is somewhat greater than the efficiency of the greenhouse method. Comparatively, both farm and greenhouse methods are far more efficient than is the garden method. How do we figure that? We divide the input by the output. The same method of calculating comparative efficiency can be applied to any form of production—from household chores to the most complicated kinds of manufacturing.

Real Cost and Efficiency

Remember that the most efficient means of production, roughly speaking, is the method that produces the most or the best goods at the lowest cost. Every producer tries to find out what the lowest *real cost* of a particular product may be, so as to produce with the greatest possible efficiency. The most efficient producer wins in the economic contest that we call competition.

But it may be difficult in many branches of industry and

commerce to discover the lowest real cost of any particular sort of production. To find out the lowest real cost, we have to consider the four factors of production: natural resources, labor, capital, and management.

Any producer seeking to find the real cost must study the relative cost of each of these factors in his line of production. Having looked at these four factors, the producer may decide to spend less upon one factor or more upon another factor. He tries to arrange the combination of factors that would give him the lowest real cost of production.

Any producer must examine, for instance, the comparative costs of labor and capital. In some forms of production, costs may be reduced by a larger investment in machinery (capital). In other forms of production, costs may be reduced by hiring more employees (labor). These choices are suggested in the box below.

Comparative Costs of Capital and Labor

	Case 1	Case 2
Annual cost of machine doing the work of ten persons	$250,000	$110,000
Annual cost of wages of ten employees	$140,000	$140,000

Discuss

5. Of the two cases in the box above, in which one would it be more efficient to invest capital goods (machinery)? In which case would it seem better to employ more working people, rather than to buy new machinery?

6. Look back at the box "Three Ways of Producing Tomatoes" on page 144. In each way of producing, identify the factors of production. What way of production has the lowest real cost— the one that uses the least land and the least capital per unit of output?

7. In countries with large populations but little modern industry, usually the cost of labor is relatively low. Are entrepreneurs likely to invest heavily in new machines in such countries?

The factor of land also must be taken into account by producers. Where land is plentiful, naturally its cost is low. Where land is scarce, its price is high. But where there is plenty of land, there may be few people—which makes the cost of labor high. Or raw materials may be scarce in cheap-land territory; or little capital may be available there. The producer has to balance one factor against other factors to estimate the lowest real cost.

In one form of production, management may be the most important factor of the four. This is especially true of the **service industries,** which do not produce material things.[1] In such a business, the factor of land may be unimportant; few or no raw materials may be needed; and capital may consist chiefly of an office and business machines. One way of reducing real costs in the service industries may be to diminish the first factor of production by finding inexpensive office space. On the other hand, sometimes handsome offices in a fashionable office building are needed to attract good customers or clients. And perhaps the best form of investment for such a firm would be to pay large salaries to very competent managers.

Discuss   8. Some big corporations—in the oil industry, the automobile business, chemical manufacturing, and other forms of production—pay salaries of hundreds of thousands of dollars to a number of their high executives. Can you explain what corporate executives mean when they argue that large salaries increase efficiency? To what factor of production are they referring? If some person should offer to serve as president of a hotel chain for a salary of merely ten thousand dollars a year, should the directors of the chain hire him promptly in order to reduce real costs by lowering the president's salary from one hundred thousand dollars to ten thousand?

This *allocating of the factors of production* is one important means for increasing economic efficiency by reducing real cost. (To *allocate* means to assign or apportion—to set aside resources for a

---

1. Some examples of service industries or occupations are plumbing repair, free-lance writing, medical treatment, legal advice, real estate sales, dry cleaning, hair dressing, house painting and repair.

particular purpose.) *The able entrepreneur or manager has a talent for judging what proportion of available resources to allocate to each of the four factors of production.* In a competitive economy, if an entrepreneur makes serious errors in such allocation, his real costs will increase. Such mistakes account for many of the business failures that happen in a market economy.

Yet allocating the factors of production, though essential, is only one aspect of the problem of lowering real costs. So we turn now to other means for increasing economic efficiency.

Efficiency and the Division of Labor

Before civilizations existed, people discovered that production was more efficient if work was divided. One person could become a skilled hunter. Another might make arrowheads and tools. Still others could sow seeds for crops. In even very simple economies, such specialization (*division of labor*) resulted in greater efficiency of production.

In industrialized countries of the twentieth century, specialization has been carried farther than in any previous age. The mass production of today's factories makes necessary sharp division of labor into many separate tasks. On the assembly line of an automobile factory, for instance, one worker may operate a machine setting wheels upon axles; another worker may tighten certain nuts; another one may supervise the installation of windshields; and so on, to scores or even hundreds of separate, specialized tasks.

Similarly, men and women are trained for highly specialized professions in our society. Physicians and surgeons ordinarily tend to specialize in some particular branch of the medical arts. Lawyers increasingly take up some particular branch of the legal profession.

Adam Smith on Pinmaking

Adam Smith's book *The Wealth of Nations*, written not long after the beginning of the First Industrial Revolution, contained three chapters analyzing the division of labor. The first example that Smith offered was the straight-pin industry. The following passage from Smith's book remains a good explanation of economic specialization. Of the pinmaker's trade, Smith wrote,

> A workman not educated to this business (which division of labor has rendered a difficult trade), nor acquainted with the use of the machinery employed in it (to the invention of which the same division of labor has probably given occasion), could scarce, perhaps, with his utmost industry, make one pin in a day, and certainly could not make twenty. But in the way in which this business is now carried on, not only the whole work is a peculiar trade, but it is divided into a number of branches, of which the greatest part are likewise peculiar trades. One man draws out the wire, another straights it, a third cuts it, and a fourth points it, a fifth grinds it at the top for receiving the head; to make the head requires two or three distinct operations; to put it on, is a peculiar business, to whiten the pins is another; it is even a trade by itself to put them into the paper; and the important business of making a pin is, in this manner, divided into some eighteen distinct operations, which, in some manufactories, are all performed by distinct hands, though in others the same man will sometimes perform two or three of them.

Smith went on to mention a small factory, without very good machinery, in which ten men were employed. They could make about twelve pounds of pins in a day. (There were about four thousand pins in a pound.) Together, the ten men made more than forty-eight thousand pins daily.

> But if they had all wrought separately and independently, and without any of them having been educated to this peculiar business, they certainly could not each of them have made twenty, perhaps not one pin in a day; that is, certainly, not the two hundred and fortieth, perhaps not the four thousand eight hundredth part of what they are at present capable of performing, in consequence of a proper division and combination of their different operations.

At the time Smith was born, Scotland was a poor country. The things we take for granted nowadays were very scarce in Scotland early in the eighteenth century: cups, plates, chairs, mattresses, blankets, knives and forks, sheets, tablecloths, glass for windows, fuel for heating. But the division of labor, new machines, and the increase of trade had made Scotland comparatively prosperous by the time of Smith's death. Even pins had been costly when Smith was born; they were cheap by the time he died. What made the difference? The increase of efficiency of production. The division of labor, Smith wrote, was a principal cause of that efficiency.

Discuss

9. Can you think of some good examples of the division of labor in your own community, state, or region? Do members of your family work in specialized occupations?

10. A paper of pins (for they still are sold stuck into papers, as they were in Smith's day) costs little nowadays: perhaps eighty-five cents for a paper of ninety sharp pins, retail price. What do you suppose that just one pin would cost if there were no division of labor and no pinmaking machines, so that a worker could produce only one to twenty pins by a day's labor?

By the division of labor, individuals specialize in both simple and difficult tasks. Companies specialize in the production of a single commodity or of a limited number of goods. The entire economy of a region or a country may center about one industry—like coffee-growing in Colombia or petroleum-extracting in Saudi Arabia.

This division of labor has come about because often (though not always, in all circumstances, in all occupations) such specialization results in low real cost and high comparative efficiency. Yet there are objections to economic specialization, as well as advantages. (Adam Smith pointed out some of the disadvantages, as well as the advantages.) Points on both sides of the question are suggested in the box on page 151.

The Division of Labor

Advantages	Disadvantages
1. more goods per person	1. boredom of workers
2. inventions encouraged	2. standardization of goods
3. fewer tools needed per worker	3. technological unemployment
4. best use of land and other fixed costs	4. decline of small-scale industry
5. more leisure for workers	5. decline of skilled craftsman
6. greater variety of goods, including services	6. hostility between labor and management in large-scale industry
7. development of specialists	7. possible dislocations of a delicately interdependent economy

Discuss

11. Can you think of some advantages of the division of labor not mentioned in the box above? Or of some other disadvantages?

12. How can standardization of goods be considered a disadvantage? Why is there a tendency toward boredom when doing some work that is highly specialized? How is technological unemployment connected with the division of labor today? Try to explain these disadvantages of specialization.

13. Can you think of some ways to reduce or correct certain disadvantages of specialization? Or of ways to increase the advantages?

Overspecialization

Sometimes the division of labor may be carried too far. The entrepreneur may be so impressed with the efficiencies of the division of labor that he may think that you cannot have enough of a good thing. But in the dividing of labor, as in the eating of chocolate bars, you can have too much of a good thing. Beyond some point of development, specialization may be overspecialization. If this happens, productive efficiency drops rather than increases.

To understand this concept of overspecialization, we can use Adam Smith's example of pinmaking. Suppose that a manufacturer of pins employed eighteen workers, each one performing one specialized task. Suppose that this manufacturer should decide to make the process still more specialized. Therefore, he might have nine more specialized machines made for his factory, and he might hire nine more specialized workers.

Pins produced by this new method would require twenty-seven specialized tasks instead of eighteen tasks. This use of more machines and more employees might cost the manufacturer 50 percent more for machinery (capital) than he had invested in machinery previously. And probably it would cost him 50 percent more for his labor payroll than he had paid in wages previously. Now his total output of pins would be far greater, and possibly he could produce pins of better quality.

But suppose also that within a few months the manufacturer should discover, by looking over his account books, that his increased output had brought him only 25 percent more money in total sales. That might happen because there had been no great additional demand for pins. Or perhaps the cost of his new machines had meant that he had invested too much in the factor of capital. Or possibly the additional cost of wages meant that he had invested too much in the factor of labor. Whatever the reason, it would appear that his real cost of production had risen too high.

The pin manufacturer would have passed the point of efficient specialization in his manufacturing process. His cost of increased specialization would not have been repaid by the money he had received from his increased output of pins. He would have to examine closely his method of production to determine where he had gone wrong. Perhaps he should have increased his specialization only to the extent of two new machines and two more employees. Possibly he could have gained if he had increased to the extent of four machines and four workers, or some other number. Perhaps he should not have increased his specialization at all. Wherever he went wrong, painful experience would teach such an entrepreneur that he had increased, rather than decreased, comparative costs.

Discuss

14. Turn back to the box "The Division of Labor" on page 151. Can you suggest how some of the disadvantages of specialization listed there may lead to inefficiency? Perhaps you know of cases in which the division of labor seems to have been carried too far.

15. What organism in the animal kingdom has the highest degree of economic specialization? Would it be desirable for humans to be this highly specialized? Why or why not?

Geographic Specialization

Trade between regions and between countries is closely connected with the division of labor. One important cause of America's prosperity is the fact that within the immense free-trade area of the United States, geographic specialization leads to a greater abundance of goods at lower prices. And a major reason for the prosperity of the wealthier nations in our time is international trade.

Consider the fact that oranges *can* be grown in both Florida and Iowa. Also wheat *can* be grown in both states. But Florida has an advantage over Iowa in orange production, because Florida's climate is kinder to citrus fruits. Conversely, Iowa has an advantage over Florida in producing wheat, for the Florida climate is not favorable to grains. Therefore, it is to the advantage of everybody concerned that Florida settle for growing oranges, at comparatively low real cost. And it is equally advantageous that Iowa settle for planting wheat, at comparatively low real cost. That is efficient agriculture for both states. Florida and Iowa, as well as the other states, exchange their products in the agricultural market. It would be inefficient for every state to try to grow within its own boundaries every vegetal raw material that the state's people want. Rice would be extremely costly to grow in Michigan, and apple orchards would not flourish in Louisiana.

At best, to produce oranges in Iowa would be *marginal*, economists know. Such orange production would be on the margin of failure every year. Similarly, production of wheat would be marginal, or borderline, in Florida—uncertain as an economic undertaking and unlikely to be profitable.

Florida enjoys an economic advantage in growing oranges, whereas Iowa has an economic advantage in growing wheat. Every region or country produces some particular goods better than it produces other goods. The inhabitants of desert oases may be able to grow figs and dates better than they can produce anything else. Eskimos of the Arctic region can produce for sale, better than anything else, cured sealskins and carved pieces of ivory. On the other hand, the inhabitants of Switzerland would be foolish to try to grow figs and dates; nor can the Swiss hunt seals or find walrus tusks to carve. So the Swiss do well to stick to their profitable banking business and their making of watches and clocks.

Geographic specialization (division of labor among regions and countries) occurs because different areas find it to their advantage to produce different goods—and to exchange their products for those of other areas. This leads us to one of the trickier theories of economists—*comparative advantage.*

Discuss

16. Americans import their coffee from Brazil, Colombia, Kenya, Ethiopia, Java, Yemen, and other distant lands. It is possible to grow large quantities of chickory, a substitute for coffee, in the southern United States. Why don't Americans drink chickory instead of coffee, and so save sending their money abroad? Or why don't Americans grow coffee plants in American greenhouses so that they wouldn't have to import coffee and pay transportation costs? Explain whether it would be economically efficient to stop importing coffee into the United States.

Efficiency and Comparative Advantage

Florida could grow wheat; Iowa could grow oranges. But it is to the **comparative advantage** of either state to stick to growing the crop for which it is better suited. Similarly, it is to the comparative advantage of individuals or firms to produce the goods for which the abilities and resources of those individuals or firms are better suited.

Every individual is better at one particular sort of work than he is at other kinds of work. A dentist might be able to get a job as a driver of a school bus, but probably the dentist is better at dentistry. A bus driver might be able to run a nursery school, but quite possibly the driver is better at driving. The dentist has a comparative advantage at dentistry, the driver a comparative advantage at driving.

A firm manufacturing toothpaste might be able to shift to preparing processed foods, but that, too, depends upon the principle of comparative advantage. A firm of lawyers might be able to spend part of their time as business consultants, but they would have to decide whether their comparative advantage might be in legal practice or in economic analysis.

Here is an imaginary example of comparative advantage. Suppose that Mr. Adams is skilled at making furniture, Mr. Bolan at raising chickens, and Mrs. Corelli at teaching children. It makes sense for each of these people to concentrate on one job. Then they can exchange goods (or services) among the three of them.

In practice, however, production and exchange are not always so neat and simple. Even in this small society of Adams, Bolan, and Corelli, we find that Adams could not only produce the best furniture, but could also raise chickens more efficiently than Mr. Bolan, and teach children better than Mrs. Corelli. Should Adams, being so efficient, do all three jobs?

The economists (and common sense) answer no. Even the person with an absolute advantage of efficiency in all three occupations should specialize in one. But *what* one?

Here we begin to see how the idea of *comparative advantage* is useful. This concept can be understood by studying the following simple table.

Comparative Advantage

	Adams	Bolan	Corelli
Efficiency in furniture making	100	50	60
Efficiency in chicken raising	70	65	50
Efficiency in teaching	80	60	70

In this table we give "grades" to Adams, Bolan, and Corelli according to their comparative efficiency in the three kinds of production.

Adams is *absolutely* the best in all three kinds. But Adams is *comparatively* much better than Bolan and Corelli in furniture making. At that craft, Adams is 50 and 40 points ahead of Bolan and Corelli, respectively. Adams is less far ahead in chicken raising and education. So by the rule or law of comparative advantage, Adams should stick to furniture.

Bolan is better than Corelli at chicken raising, but not so good as Corelli at teaching. So Bolan should stick to chickens, and Corelli to teaching.

By this division of labor, the whole group of three will be better off than under any other arrangement. Labor will be allocated in the most efficient way.

Because of comparative advantage, specialization usually results in greater total productivity. The following table shows how this specialization would work in the case of two manufacturing firms, both producing small electric heaters and large electric fans. (We assume that the fans and the heaters are sold for the same price.)

How Comparative Advantage and Specialization Increase Total Product

1. With the same resources, two firms can produce thus:

Acme Electric Company:	100 fans or 80 heaters
Top Electronics:	50 fans or 60 heaters

2. If the two firms do not specialize in either fans or heaters, we have the following production:

Acme Electric Company:	50 fans and 40 heaters
Top Electronics:	25 fans and 30 heaters
Total product:	75 fans and 70 heaters

3. But if each firm specializes, we have this production:

Acme Electric Company:	100 fans and 0 heaters
Top Electronics:	0 fans and 60 heaters
Total product:	100 fans and 60 heaters

You can see above that Acme Electric Company enjoys an *absolute* advantage in making both fans and heaters: Acme is more efficient in both products than is Top Electronics. But Top does better at making heaters than it does at making fans: Top has a comparative advantage, therefore, in making heaters. If Acme makes only fans and Top makes only heaters, both firms will specialize in producing the good that each can produce most efficiently. And the total product will be bigger than it would be if both firms had kept on producing both fans and heaters.

Discuss

17. Suppose that Jack Sprat and his wife work together picking cherries in their orchard and selling the cherries door-to-

door. Mr. Sprat can pick thirty quarts of cherries in a morning, but Mrs. Sprat, younger and nimbler, can pick fifty quarts in the same amount of time. Suppose that Mr. Sprat usually sells thirty-five quarts of cherries in an afternoon, while Mrs. Sprat sells forty-five. Which one of this couple has an absolute advantage in both aspects of the cherry business?   Does Mr. Sprat have a comparative advantage in anything? Should husband and wife separate the tasks and specialize rather than work together at both picking and selling? Can you think of some reason why they might not decide to specialize?

18. In the preceding group of Adams, Bolan, and Corelli, suppose that Bolan should insist upon making furniture, Corelli should insist upon raising chickens, and Adams should be compelled to teach. What would happen to their total productivity? Would any one of their three occupations or kinds of production then become more efficient than it was before the three of them switched jobs?

19. Suppose that Acme Electric Company and Top Electronics, ignoring the advice of an economist, should decide upon a different sort of specialization than the division of labor suggested in the preceding box. Suppose that Acme should decide to specialize in heaters and Top in fans. What then would happen to the real cost of production in both firms?

Even the person who can work, but is not especially good as a worker, usually is better at some particular occupation than he is at other occupations. Therefore, that person has a *comparative* advantage in working at the occupation at which he is best (or least bad). Similarly, firms, regions, and countries have some *comparative* advantage in producing some sort of goods—even if they do not enjoy an *absolute* advantage at any one line of production when compared with other firms, regions, or countries.

Scale of Production as a Source of Efficiency

Sometimes (though by no means always) economic efficiency may be increased by enlarging the size, or scale, of the business or operation. A good example of the advantages of large-scale enterprise is the American automobile industry.

Consider the Ford Motor Company, one of the best-known industrial firms. Henry Ford, a machinist in Michigan near the end of the nineteenth century, became chief engineer of the Edison Illuminating Company at Detroit. He studied the early automobiles being developed in Germany, Britain, and the United States. By 1899, he knew enough about automobile making and had gotten together enough capital to become a manufacturer himself.

Ford made his first car in a very small machine shop near the heart of Detroit and called his firm the Detroit Automobile Company. Much labor was required to make the early Ford cars: it took nearly three months to assemble one of them. These labor costs made Fords and other early automobiles so expensive that only the wealthy could purchase them.

Henry Ford and Mass Production

Knowing that millions of Americans might buy his automobiles if the price were lower, Henry Ford sought ways to diminish his cost of production. He borrowed four ideas from other men, combining them to form the "American system" of *mass production*. This system that can turn out masses of identical products is based on four features:
  (1) standardized parts;
  (2) division of labor, or specialization;
  (3) automatic conveyance (the assembly line);
  (4) production efficiency.

Mass-production methods required far less labor per automobile than other methods. By 1908, Ford was producing the Model T Ford, a relatively cheap car (very cheap by today's standards), priced at $809. By 1926, with increasing efficiency, the Ford Motor Company was able to reduce the price of its Model T to $280.

Ford centered his mass production at his Rouge Plant, a few miles outside Detroit, which soon became one of the biggest industrial installations in the world. He reinvested his profits in his productive facilities, so increasing output steadily. He bought raw materials and parts on a huge scale at lower costs for each item. In various parts of the country, the Ford Motor Company built assembly plants to reduce costs of transportation.

Ford's moving assembly line for putting cars together, a technique Ford was the first to use, began operation in 1914. In 1900, Ford produced twenty cars. In 1907, he made eight thousand cars. In 1914, he manufactured two hundred fifty thousand cars.

Many other automobile companies arose in the early decades of the twentieth century, and eventually all of the companies that survived adopted the assembly-line method of production. The amount of capital required for successful competition in automobile manufacturing rose steadily higher, and firms that lacked capital or were inefficient began to fail.

Henry Ford was not a scientist, nor did he engage in much research during the earlier part of his career. But he had a keen practical mind and a great talent for organization and production.

Henry Ford did not invent the first "gasoline buggy," but he was the most successful entrepreneur in this new field of industry. The major reason for his immense financial success was his scale of operation. He could turn out two hundred fifty thousand cars at a real cost, per unit, far lower than the real cost, per unit, of manufacturing and selling only twenty cars.

Large-scale production of many goods has become typical of the American economy. One reason for this fact is the vast national market of the United States—with today about two hundred fifty million consumers, all living in one free-trade area with no tariffs or other economic barriers. Only China, the Soviet Union, and India have populations larger than that of the United States; but the typical consumer of those countries has far less money to spend than does the typical American consumer. The American mass market makes possible American mass production.

It needs to be remembered, nevertheless, that not every form of economic activity grows more efficient merely because the scale of operation is enlarged. Also, it is true that an industry or business may grow too big and too centralized for good management. The efficiency of an overgrown, unwieldy enterprise begins to decline. Henry Ford is said to have regretted, late in life, that he had centralized his operations so heavily at his Rouge Plant. Some very big industrial firms in the United States and in Western Europe in the nineteenth and twentieth centuries have grown *too* big for efficient management; therefore, their real costs have increased and their returns on investment have diminished; and eventually such giants have been broken into smaller firms or have gone into bankruptcy.

A point may be reached when a big firm has over-expanded—when its costs of operation have increased, but production and sales have not increased proportionately. At that point, an entrepreneur or a firm needs to take alarm. Either the business or commercial concern ought to stop expanding at that point (and perhaps reduce its operations to a more manageable scale), or else the concern must develop better techniques of management, production, and selling.

Increase of scale, in short, often results in increase of efficiency. But there can also occur foolish and unsuccessful increases of scale, resulting in inefficiency. Besides, some forms of economic activity are more efficient on a small scale than on a large. A small fashionable restaurant serving very good (if high-priced) food, for instance, may be more profitable to its proprietor than would be a very large cafeteria serving ordinary food at low prices to a crowd of customers. This advantage of small scale applies as well to various forms of specialized manufacturing or distribution. It is chiefly in the manufacture and distribution of standardized goods to a mass market that large scale becomes a more efficient means of operation.

Discuss

20. In chapter 5, we considered examples of unprofitable and profitable businesses. We found that Mrs. Molnar of the Great Expectations Bookshop had begun to lose money in her business. If she were to double her inventory of books, hire two more full-time clerks, commence a large-scale advertising campaign in the local mass media, and in other ways operate her bookselling trade on a larger scale—do you think she might turn her present loss into a future profit? Why or why not?

21. Suppose that Mr. Spanos, creator of planktonburgers, had decided to operate on a small scale in the beginning, establishing one Toilers of the Sea restaurant and finding out whether customers would like his new form of food. Do you think that eventually he would have been just as successful by this cautious small-scale business method as he was by his bold borrowing of capital and campaign of advertising?

22. "Think big," some people tell us. "Small is beautiful," others say. Would you prefer to be involved in a small economic enterprise or in a large-scale one? Give several reasons for your preference.

23. Suppose that neither Henry Ford nor any other entrepreneur had moved into mass production of automobiles; that, instead, production of cars had remained small and costly,

so that only a minority of American families ever thought it possible that they might one day possess their own passenger automobile. In what ways would the United States be different if the "transportation revolution" of the gasoline engine had occurred only on a much smaller scale? If you have elderly relatives or friends who remember a time when not many people owned automobiles, ask them to tell you about the different patterns of life in America then—particularly economic differences.

Intelligence and Imagination as Causes of Efficiency

Efficiency, economists say, is a matter of getting greater output from scarce resources. We have seen earlier in this chapter that among the causes of economic efficiency are proper allocation of the factors of production; division of labor, or specialization; and (often) large scale production. Those and other causes of efficiency depend upon the primary source of efficiency: the human spirit.

The fundamental reasons for the success of such famous American entrepreneurs as E. I. du Pont and Henry Ford were shrewdness of intellect, initiative, and a certain power of imagination. Du Pont's gunpowder and Ford's automobiles were produced in large quantity, efficiently, because the entrepreneurs' intelligence was sufficient to plan and execute large-scale efficient operations. Both men perceived what was inefficient about existing methods in their fields of industry and set to work forming better-conceived industrial methods.

Similarly, the efficiency of regions and countries that have succeeded in economic production is caused primarily by the initiative of the average man and woman and by cultural attitudes toward work in such regions or countries. One of the most prosperous lands of the late twentieth century is Switzerland.[2] That mountainous country has

---

2. Swiss per capita income in 1988 was the highest in Europe or America.

few useful natural resources, except for swift mountain streams that provide some electrical power.

But Switzerland does have abundant human resources. The typical citizen of Switzerland is hardworking, thrifty, and law-abiding. An admirable system of public instruction has given a sound education to the great majority of young Swiss. Until recent centuries, the chief industry of Switzerland was war: the young men went abroad as mercenary soldiers. In the nineteenth century, Switzerland gradually developed economically. And in the twentieth century, Swiss watches, precision machinery, and other industrial products have obtained a profitable world market. *It is the efficiency of Swiss managers and Swiss working people that accounts for Switzerland's present economic success.*

Similarly, Japan looms large in the world's economy today, and yet the island country of Japan conspicuously lacks the natural resources possessed by the chief industrial countries of Europe and North America. Japan is deficient in deposits of coal and iron, which are necessary for the making of steel. Yet Japanese steel nowadays can be sold at Detroit, say, for less than the price of comparable American-produced steel. Japanese steel mills must import their iron and coal from abroad, at large expense; and transportation costs of sending their finished product to the interior of the United States are equally high. Moreover, Japanese industrial wages today are approximately as high as American industrial wages—sometimes higher, if we take into account the "fringe benefits" commonly received by Japanese industrial workers.

Then how is it that the Japanese can compete most successfully in international markets for such industrial goods as steel? A major cause of their success appears to be a high level of diligence, intelligence, and imagination among many Japanese, combined with a thorough system of education and training.

No country or region or industry can be efficient if the people who do the work are lacking in mental vigor. And even those regions

and countries seemingly the poorest in resources can become prosperous if their people who do the work make good use of their intelligence
and imagination.

We all have some notion of what the word *intelligence* means.
An intelligent person is one who is mentally alert—someone who
understands. Work stupidly undertaken, without alertness and understanding, usually accomplishes little. *It is intelligent work that creates the
wealth of nations*. Work does not have to be grand or well paid to be
intelligent work. There are intelligent ways of sweeping a room, and
unintelligent ways. Intelligent work is the sort of labor that does not
waste energy to accomplish its purpose. It is work carried on for a
purpose and directed by a willing mind. The great seventeenth-century
English poet George Herbert illustrated this principle well in the
following poem.

The Elixir

Teach me, my God and King,
In all things thee to see,
And what I do in any thing,
To do it as for thee:

Not rudely, as a beast,
To runne into an action;
But still to make thee prepossest,
And give it his perfection.

A man that looks on glasse,
On it may stay his eye;
Or if he pleaseth, through it passe,
And then the heav'n espie.

All may of thee partake:
Nothing can be so mean,
Which with his tincture (for thy sake)
Will not grow bright and clean

A servant with this clause
Makes drudgerie divine:
Who sweeps a room, as for thy laws,
Makes that and th' action fine.

This is the famous stone
That turneth all to gold:
For that which God doth touch and own
Cannot for lesse be told.

Now for the word *imagination,* which is not so well understood by most people as is the word *intelligence.* A dictionary defines imagination as "the action of forming mental images or concepts of what is not actually present to the senses." The truly imaginative person has the power of creating within his own consciousness pictures (so to speak) of concepts that cannot be detected by his eyesight, his hearing, his sense of taste, sense of smell, or sense of touch.

The entrepreneur and the economist need that power called imagination, or inner vision. Both must perceive what does not exist, at the moment, in any material form. The entrepreneur needs to imagine economic developments that have not yet come to pass—and which may seem impossible dreams to most people. The economist needs to imagine intellectual abstractions—theories taking into account many things beyond his own immediate personal experience.

Usually, power of imagination is rarer than ordinary intelligence. That is a principal reason why successful entrepreneurs and famous economists aren't found around every corner.

All the ingenious methods of all the efficiency experts in the world would have no result if there were only stupid and indolent people to use their methods. The oldest known instrument for mathematical calculating is the *abacus,* which consists of a frame stretched with wires upon which balls are manipulated by hand. The new form of mathematical calculating instrument is the improved electronic calculator. The abacus, if operated by an intelligent and skilled person, can be more efficient even today than the latest electronic calculator if that recent invention is operated by a slow, lazy, or inexperienced person.

For at bottom, ***all forms of economic efficiency depend upon human diligence and human determination.*** A country may be potentially rich in natural resources but poor economically because of feeble human resources. The economic system with which we are familiar in the United States is unusually efficient. American prosperity is neither accidental nor surprising. For the American economy, like the American political pattern, was brought into existence by unusually motivated people.

CHAPTER 8

Why Everybody Needs to Save

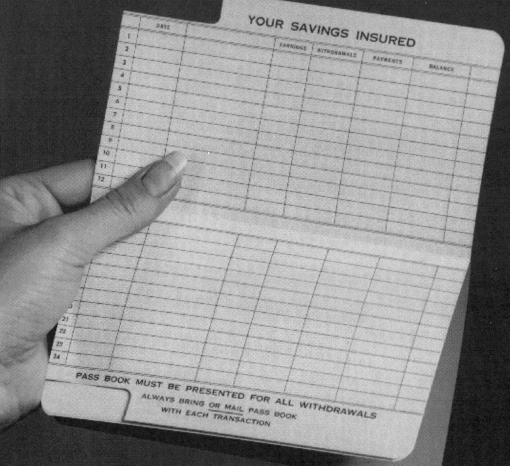

	DATE		EARNINGS	WITHDRAWALS	PAYMENTS	BALANCE
1						
2						
3						
4						
5						
6						
7						
8						
9						
10						
11						
12						

YOUR SAVINGS INSURED

PASS BOOK MUST BE PRESENTED FOR ALL WITHDRAWALS
ALWAYS BRING OR MAIL PASS BOOK
WITH EACH TRANSACTION

Chapter 8
Why Everybody Needs to Save

- • Fables of Saving
- • Scarcity, Money, and the Factors of Production in Old Egypt
- • The Rewards of Abstinence
- • Payment for Risk
- • Wise Saving and Foolish Saving
- • Many Forms of Saving
- • Savings in Stocks and Bonds
- • Investment in Land
- • Compulsory Saving
- • Why Modern Societies Require Huge Amounts of Capital

Fables of Saving

Because Americans in general have been an intelligent people, ever since the seventeenth century there has been much saving in what is now the United States.

If people did not save, there could be no capital (production goods). And were there no capital, most of us would die of starvation or exposure. Any survivors from our civilization would find themselves living—barely living—by the primitive economy of hunting and gathering. And even so, those survivors would have to save part of what food and clothing they could get by their hunting and their gathering, in order to live during seasons when game and wild fruits and berries cannot be found.

Men and women of the early cultures understood well this basic economic truth. In the sixth century before Christ, a slave named Aesop, living in Asia Minor, wrote many moral fables in the Greek language. One of the more famous of Aesop's fables makes the point that everybody must save in preparation for hard times to come. This story may be even older than Aesop's version. Possibly the fable may go back thousands of years before Christ, to ancient Egypt. The following version is translated from the seventeenth-century rendering of the fable by Jean de La Fontaine, a French poet.

The Grasshopper and the Ant

A Grasshopper gay
Sang the summer away,
And found herself poor
By the winter's first roar.
Of meat or of bread,
Not a morsel she had!
So a begging she went,
To her neighbor the ant,
 For the loan of some wheat,
 Which would serve her to eat,
Till the season came round.
 "I will pay you," she saith,
 "On an animal's faith,
Double weight in the pound
Ere the harvest be bound."
 The ant is a friend
 (And here she might mend)
 Little given to lend.
 "How spent you the summer?"
 Quoth she, looking shame
 At the borrowing dame.
"Night and day to each comer
 I sang, if you please."
 "You sang! I'm at ease;
For 'tis plain at a glance,
Now, ma'am, you must dance."

  The humble ant is a favorite creature with fabulists (authors of fables). Leonardo da Vinci, the great artist and engineer of the fifteenth century, wrote a number of fables, most of which have been lost. One of those that have survived, the little story entitled "The Ant and the

Grain of Wheat," tells of a wheat grain that begged an ant not to carry it off to be eaten in the ant hill. The grain promised the ant that if it would dig a little hole and bury the grain, it would return every year—"a hundred of me"—to feed the ant colony. Such is the mystery of life. When the ant returned the following year, "the grain of wheat had grown a new plant laden with seeds, and so kept its promise."

This, too, is a fable of saving, showing how what we call *investment* may pay for itself a hundred times over.

The Bible recognizes the industrious nature of the ant in Proverbs 6:6–8. Here, the sluggard is admonished to consider the ant and learn from her. Without supervision, the ant provides for her needs, including the storing up of supplies for winter. We are also told in Proverbs 30:25 that the ants are not strong, yet they prepare for the cold winter. Because of this, God lists them among the "exceeding wise." To properly communicate the importance of the concept with which we are dealing, God put Proverbs 10:5 in Scripture. "He that gathereth in summer is a wise son, but he that sleepeth in harvest is a son that causeth shame."

Discuss

1. Do you know any human grasshoppers? Or any human ants? Why is the ant's remark "Now, ma'am, you must dance" a deadly prediction?

2. The grasshopper, trying to borrow food from the ant, promised to repay with 100 percent interest by the next harvest: "double weight in the pound." Why didn't the ant advance the loan on such seemingly advantageous terms? (Why are some people such bad risks that nobody will lend to them at any interest rate?)

3. If generous ants lent food to needy grasshoppers, what would become of the race of ants?

4. How does Leonardo's fable suggest the difference between a hunting-and-gathering economy and an agricultural economy?

The two fables above are concerned with the simplest forms of saving—keeping part of the harvest for consumption at a later time, or planting a part of the harvest so that another harvest will follow months later. Now we turn to a more complex kind of saving, also known in the ancient world.

Scarcity, Money, and the Factors of Production in Old Egypt

In the book of Genesis, the ruler of Egypt, Pharaoh, dreams a frightening vision about kine (cows) and ears of corn. Only Joseph, a Hebrew favored by God, is able to interpret the meaning of Pharaoh's dream. He tells the king that his vision predicts the coming of seven years of great plenty for Egypt, with splendid harvests. But that period of plenty shall be followed by seven lean years, resulting in terrible famine.

Convinced that Joseph speaks truth, Pharaoh appoints him governor over all the land. The wise Hebrew fills the king's storehouses in Egyptian cities with much of the grain that is harvested during the seven years of plenty. Then come the seven lean years of crop failure and famine "over all the face of the earth."

From the king's granaries, Joseph is able to feed those Egyptians who can pay for their bread. (In the Old Testament, our word *bread* often means any sort of food, not necessarily baked bread.) People in Canaan and more distant lands, learning that food may be purchased in Egypt, come to Joseph to buy bread at any price.

Pharaoh and his governor Joseph had saved grain while grain was plentiful; no one else had possessed the foresight or the ability to save food in large quantities. But, of course, the supply in the king's granaries is limited. As all other sources of food are exhausted, buyers beg Joseph to sell to them at any price. Joseph, on behalf of Pharaoh, holds a monopoly of grain: that is, he controls the whole remaining supply of the most essential of all goods. Here is the story of what then happened, as told in the King James English translation of Genesis 47.

Joseph the Bread-Seller

And there was no bread in all the land; for the famine was very sore, so that the land of Egypt and all the land of Canaan fainted by reason of the famine.

And Joseph gathered up all the money that was found in the land of Egypt, and in the land of Canaan, for the corn which they bought: and Joseph brought the money into Pharaoh's house.

And when money failed in the land of Egypt, and in the land of Canaan, all the Egyptians came unto Joseph, and said, Give us bread: for why should we die in thy presence? for the money faileth.

And Joseph said, Give your cattle; and I will give you for your cattle, if money fail.

And they brought their cattle unto Joseph: and Joseph gave them bread in exchange for horses, and for the flocks, and for the cattle of the herds, and for the asses: and he fed them with bread for all their cattle for that year.

When that year was ended, they came unto him the second year, and said unto him, We will not hide it from my lord, how that our money is spent; my lord also hath our herds of cattle; there is not ought left in the sight of my lord, but our bodies, and our lands:

Wherefore shall we die before thine eyes, both we and our land? buy us and our land for bread, and we and our land will be servants unto Pharaoh: and give us seed, that we may live, and not die, that the land be not desolate.

And Joseph bought all the land of Egypt for Pharaoh; for the Egyptians sold every man his field, because the famine prevailed over them: so the land became Pharaoh's.

And as for the people, he removed them to cities from one end of the borders of Egypt even to the other end thereof.

Then Joseph said unto the people, Behold, I have bought you this day and your land for Pharaoh: lo, here is seed for you, and ye shall sow the land.

And it shall come to pass in the increase, that ye shall give the fifth part unto Pharaoh, and four parts shall be your own, for seed of the field, and for your food, and for them of your households, and for food for your little ones.

And they said, Thou hast saved our lives: let us find grace in the sight of my lord, and we will be Pharaoh's servants.

Discuss

5. Suppose Pharaoh had ordered that grain should be given away free from his storehouses to all people in need of food. What would have happened then?

6. First the buyers of grain paid Joseph in money; next in cattle; finally by exchanging their fields and themselves for food. Can you suggest why the hungry Egyptians didn't simply borrow more

money to buy grain, instead of sacrificing their cattle and themselves?

7. Having sold their fields and themselves, the Egyptians ceased to be free people and became something else, for which there is an economic and political name. That name is not "slave." Can you give the correct name or term that describes their condition after they agreed to be Pharaoh's servants?

8. Forever after, the Egyptians who had sold their land and themselves were required to pay annually to the ruler of Egypt one fifth of the harvest. Why did not Pharaoh demand payment in money rather than "in kind" (that is, a share of the goods produced)?

9. By the end of the "years of dearth" (the seven lean years), Pharaoh owned all the land in Egypt except the land belonging to the temples. (Pharaoh had given the priests food free of charge, so the priests did not have to sell their land.) How did this economic change increase the power of the central government in Egypt?

The ancient Egyptians who did not save during their seven years of prosperity later had to pay with their money, their real property (land), their personal property (cattle), and their own bodies. Similarly, in the twentieth century, nations and individuals who do not save when they are able must pay heavily later on.

In the old agricultural societies, it was easy enough for everybody to understand that seed must be saved so that the next season crops might be planted. In today's industrial societies, too, most people understand that there must be saving so that tools and equipment may be acquired for production in the near future.

It is a little harder for some people to understand today that there must be very large savings by industrial societies so that research and development may be carried on. Yet *industrial societies must save for the improvement of technology—just as earlier societies had to save to obtain hand tools, looms for weaving, and other productive equipment.* Earlier cultures saved in order to construct water mills, then windmills, then steam engines; for the past century, men have saved to build dynamos for electricity.

Our civilization must save in this age of the computer to provide for a growing population and for new human wants. Robots, like water mills, are paid for out of savings. Unless modern people save, they will find themselves poor.

The research and development needed to improve our industrial economy may cost as much as 10 or 15 percent of the total productivity of an advanced economy. In other words, the United States and other industrial powers need to put aside, as invested savings, 10 to 15 percent of the total national income. In countries with market economies, most of this saving is done by the "private sector"—private corporations, partnerships, and individuals.

That may seem a very large portion of today's production to set aside merely for scientific and technological research and development. But consider that in today's world as many as a million scientists and engineers are working in new fields that are meant to bring about economic growth. Two or three assistants are needed for every scientist or engineer. Twice or thrice as many scientists and engineers could be employed in such research and development—if society could afford to pay them.

In effect, for the next few years there will be several million people engaged in research and development who will be supported by the savings of other people. This will be a sound investment, for those researchers presumably will create better tools and means of production—to everybody's economic benefit. But the expense of this scientific and technological work will require very large savings. Therefore, it is necessary to persuade many people to save substantial portions of their incomes. *In a market economy, people are persuaded to save by being given rewards for saving.*

People and organizations that do save are paid well for their saving, in a time when other people find it necessary to borrow. Pharaoh and Joseph were paid immensely well for their foresight in saving grain. Let us see why savers are entitled to special payments, whether or not those savers have provided any labor to produce goods. (Pharaoh and Joseph certainly did not plant corn personally.)

Today the people who save money (or goods) usually are called investors. The payment for the use of their capital funds, or savings, is called *interest.* Why does investment deserve a reward, or return, called *interest?*

The Rewards of Abstinence

Any person who saves has to give up the opportunity to spend his money, or use his goods, for some other purpose. If you have five dollars, there are pleasant ways for you to spend that sum immediately. Saving is not pleasant for most people. The choice is yours. If you spend the cash now, you obtain immediate satisfaction. If you save the cash, you will get a reward later; you will have postponed your satisfaction, or gratification. (Economists ordinarily use the latter word.)

If you decide to keep your five dollars in reserve, adding more money to it from time to time, with the intention of buying a car eventually—why, you are *abstaining* (or refraining) from immediate consumption. You are keeping yourself away from the pleasure of the latest fashion, the hamburger, and the soft drinks. You are practicing **abstinence**—the act of keeping away from something. Eventually, if your plans go well and you continue to save, you will receive a *reward of abstinence,* in the form of a car.

So it is with the usual **investor,** or *person who saves capital and puts it to good use.* Anyone who saves can expect some return, or payment, if he invests his savings. When we say **invests,** we mean that the saver, or investor, either lends his money (or goods) to somebody else, or that he uses his savings (in money or goods) to produce something more himself. If he invests his money or goods in someone else's enterprise, usually he will be paid a reward (perhaps at the end of a year) that is called *interest* or *dividends.* If he invests his savings in some enterprise of his own, he expects to get a reward equivalent to the interest or dividends he would receive from investment in some other business.

This saver, or investor, is being paid a reward because he has *abstained* from immediate consumption of his income or capital. Here is an example.

Suppose that a woman earns twenty thousand dollars in a year. She might spend all that money upon a good apartment, good food, entertainment, clothes, and travel. But she decides to save 10 percent of her earnings (two thousand dollars a year) and to invest that sum in a savings account in a nearby bank.

Under favorable circumstances, she may receive interest upon her bank deposits at the rate of 10 percent a year. On a deposit of two thousand dollars, she would thus earn a year's interest of two hundred dollars. This interest that she receives is her payment for abstinence.

She could have spent that two thousand dollars on herself immediately, but she did not do so. She put that sum into the bank, enabling some borrower from the bank to make use of her savings as capital for some enterprise. In effect, the borrower from that bank paid to the woman (through her bank) a reward called interest of two hundred dollars. The bank acted as intermediary (go-between) in this case. That is what banks ordinarily do, receiving deposits and making loans, so serving both lenders of money and borrowers of money.

The thrifty woman earned a reward by abstaining for a time from consumption because the borrower, needing the two thousand dollars, expected to pay someone or other for the use of that money. To be persuaded to save, people have to be paid. In this case, the woman who did the saving was paid by some borrower through her bank.

Discuss

10. Suppose that someone you knew only slightly should ask you to lend him five dollars. There are many things on which you could spend five dollars pleasantly. Would you expect this borrower to do more for you than simply give you back the five dollars eventually? Would you lend him the money at all?

11. In Chapter 3, "The Factors of Production," you read about Mr. Mankewitz, who got nine hundred dollars as a stock dividend. In the light of this idea of payment for abstinence, show why it was fair, or unfair, that Mankewitz should be paid that sum without having worked for it.

12. In Chapter 5, Rosemarie Molnar of the Great Expectations

Bookshop sets down forty thousand dollars as her interest on investment. Can you show how that sum represents Mrs. Molnar's payment for abstinence?

Payment for Risk

People who save money or goods and lend them to borrowers have to be paid for something besides abstinence. That other element requiring payment to lenders is *risk*. For it never is quite certain that a lender will get all his capital back again from a borrower. In all civilized countries there exist courts of law that are intended to make debtors pay their creditors. But if a **debtor** (borrower) has spent every cent he borrowed and has no assets of his own, even the order of a judge cannot get the capital back for the **creditor** (lender).

Lenders (investors) therefore take some risk, small or big, when they permit somebody to borrow capital from them. *So part of the interest that borrowers pay to lenders is payment for the chance (risk) of loss that the lender takes.* In other words, the lender's interest in part is payment for abstinence; but also in part it is payment for the risk of loss that any lender runs.

How much the lender (the person who has saved) charges a borrower depends on how much risk to his capital seems to be involved. A lender may charge low interest to a borrower who is a good friend and owns property. He may charge high interest to a borrower he doesn't know well and who does not have assets in the form of a house or stocks and bonds.

Discuss   13. Suppose that a Latin American government applies to a New York bank to borrow five hundred million dollars for ten years. The borrowing government has had financial troubles for many years and is threatened by revolutionaries. Do you think that the bank would set high interest rates or low interest rates if it should decide to lend the money to that government? (Remember that all the money in the bank represents the savings of somebody—indeed, the savings of a great many people.)

14. In many civilized countries, until well into the nineteenth century, people who did not pay their debts could be imprisoned until they had satisfied their creditors—that is, until they had paid back all or part of the savings they had borrowed. Does that treatment seem fair to you? Why or why not? Do you see any difficulty about that way of getting back money for creditors (savers)?

In any society, but especially in modern industrial societies, it is necessary that there be much saving so that capital may be accumulated. *In collectivist nations, most of that saving is directed by the government and enforced by the civil service and the police.* Such a system is called **compulsory saving.** *In the United States and other societies that have a market economy, most saving is voluntary, and people are paid for being savers.*

Abstinence and risk-taking are the services for which savers are paid in a free enterprise economy. The benefit that a market economy derives from much voluntary saving is the accumulation of a vast stock of capital. When much capital has been built up, virtually all people in that society can have their essential needs provided for—even those people who do not bother to save.

Wise Saving and Foolish Saving

In the United States, the majority of men and women do some saving. (American women have more total savings than do American men.) These savings may be only a few dollars tucked away in a book or under a rug "against a rainy day," for use in some emergency. But most people nowadays have more than a few dollars saved. And their savings often are in a better form than cash.

For merely hoarding gold or silver or paper money, without investing such savings in some productive enterprise, is not usually profitable. As the philosopher Aristotle wrote four centuries before Christ, "Money does not breed." He meant that money cannot reproduce itself automatically. To grow, money should be put to good use. (Nevertheless, it is true that during times of inflation or political insecurity, gold may be a good investment, because its value increases under such circumstances.)

This same truth was expressed by Jesus of Nazareth in his Parable of the Talents (Matthew 25:15–30). In this story, Jesus is warning his followers to make good use of their time here on earth. To make his point, Jesus uses an economic example. He begins by saying that a rich man who was about to travel abroad left his capital, in the form of talents (gold coins), with three of his servants to keep for him while he was away. To one servant, the master gave five talents of gold; to another servant, two talents of gold; to the third servant, one talent. Then their master left the country.

The Parable of the Talents

And unto one he gave five talents, to another two, and to another one; to every man according to his several ability; and straightway took his journey.

Then he that had received the five talents went and traded with the same, and made them other five talents.

And likewise he that had received two, he also gained other two.

But he that had received one went and digged in the earth, and hid his lord's money.

After a long time the lord of those servants cometh, and reckoneth with them.

And so he that had received five talents came and brought other five talents, saying, Lord, thou deliveredst unto me five talents: behold, I have gained beside them five talents more.

His lord said unto him, Well done, thou good and faithful servant; thou hast been faithful over a few things, I will make thee ruler over many things: enter thou into the joy of thy lord.

He also that had received two talents came and said, Lord, thou deliveredst unto me two talents: behold, I have gained two other talents beside them.

His lord said unto him, Well done, good and faithful servant; thou hast been faithful over a few things, I will make thee ruler over many things: enter thou into the joy of thy lord.

Then he which had received the one talent came and said, Lord, I knew thee that thou art an hard man, reaping where thou hast not sown, and gathering where thou hast not strawed.

And I was afraid, and went and hid thy talent in the earth: lo, there thou hast that is thine.

His lord answered and said unto him, Thou wicked and slothful servant, thou knewest that I reap where I sowed not, and gather where I have not strawed:

Thou oughtest therefore to have put my money to the exchangers, and then at my coming I should have received mine own with usury.

Take therefore the talent from him, and give it unto him which hath ten talents.

For unto every one that hath shall be given, and he shall have abundance: but from him that hath not shall be taken away even that which he hath.

And cast ye the unprofitable servant into outer darkness: there shall be weeping and gnashing of teeth.

This story from the New Testament is quite as true today as it was during the lifetime of Jesus. In our time, a man might hide ten thousand dollars' worth of gold coins in his cellar for twenty years, say. At the end of that time, he would have merely his original ten thousand dollars' worth of gold—if nobody had stolen it, and if the price of gold had remained unchanged. (In the market, the price of gold, like the price of any other commodity, can go down as well as up.)

But if the same man should invest ten thousand dollars in some sound industrial firm's bonds, for instance, for twenty years, at 8 percent interest, he would be as wise as the first and second servants. If that man should reinvest annually in the same firm the interest paid to him on his investment, he would **compound interest**—that is, earn more interest on the interest paid to him earlier. At the end of twenty years, this investor would have built up his capital to a total of $46,609.57. He would have done even better than did the two servants in the parable.

So the prudent investor does more than hide his money. He may invest his savings in something of economic use to himself, like a house or the tools of his trade. Or he may invest in something that will pay him a return (interest or profit) on his invested savings.

Discuss

15. If all savers put their money in holes in the ground, how would people manage to exchange goods? Could an industrial economy function under such conditions?

16. What does the third servant mean when he says that his master, a "hard man," reaps where he has not sown and gathers where he has not strawed (scattered)? Do you think that this master might be described as an entrepreneur?

17. What does the master mean by saying, "To him who hath shall be given"? Can you apply this saying to the principle of saving? Is the saying true of the man whose interest on his investment of ten thousand dollars was compounded for twenty years?

Many Forms of Saving

Any person with savings has a wide variety of ways to make use of his accumulated capital.

A common and simple form of saving is a **savings account** at a bank. There interest is paid on the saver's deposits. With a savings account, the depositor is expected to leave his funds on deposit for a comparatively long time and to give notice before he withdraws money.

Even more common than the savings account is a **checking account** at a bank. With such an account, the depositor can withdraw his money (by writing checks) whenever he likes. Little or no interest is paid on checking accounts. The depositor's advantage is that the bank guards his money for him, and that he can pay for goods by the safe and simple process of check writing. (In recent years, the old distinction between checking accounts and savings accounts has become somewhat blurred, what with borderline NOW accounts, money-market funds, and other novel forms of bank accounts.)

Another general form of investing savings is **insurance policies:** life insurance, fire insurance, medical insurance, and several other types. The buyer of an insurance policy pays to an insurance company sums called *premiums*, in return for which the person insured is entitled to various cash benefits in case of need. (With life insurance, ordinarily, the heirs of the person insured obtain the benefits.) Now, it would be possible for individuals to do their own saving as insurance against death, fire, bad health, and other risks: that is, any person could put away money in some bank that he could use in such emergencies. But ordinarily it is easier and cheaper for individuals to put part of their savings into insurance policies than to maintain large cash reserves against the chances of death or misfortune. Therefore, many forms of insurance are primarily savings for the people insured—and good investments for them. Some types of insurance policies, particularly what is called regular life insurance, pay interest to their holders.

The insurance companies, in turn, invest the premiums paid to them in a wide range of industrial and commercial undertakings—and sometimes in public utilities, the bonds of governments, and other "safe" or "secure" investments. Much of the capital for the enormous technological developments of the twentieth century has been supplied by big insurance firms—which, like big industrial corporations, have arisen chiefly since the eighteenth century.

A form of saving closely related to insurance is the **pension plan,** generally a financial system intended to provide for people's retirement from work after a fixed term of years (often thirty or forty years). Pensions may be provided by governmental units, by private employers, or by labor unions; sometimes employees contribute to these pension funds, but in other cases employees are not required to participate in this form of saving. In effect, under a pension plan the employers (or perhaps the employers and the employees, jointly) set aside every month or every year, say, a specified sum of money for the eventual retirement of each of the employees. This money is invested in stocks, public or private bonds, or some other form of economic activity. At the end of thirty or forty years (or whatever length of service is required for receiving a particular pension), payments of pension funds are commenced for the benefit of retired former employees.

You can see that these pension funds amount to an important form of saving for persons who receive salaries or wages from an established government, business, or union—or any other long-lasting institution, such as a university or college. The administrators of pension funds, like the administrators of insurance companies, invest their annual receipts from members of the pension plan in some corporation or other form of economic activity that can pay a relatively large and safe return to investors. In recent decades, pension funds (especially the pension funds of labor unions) have grown so large that they have become the largest stockholders in major industrial and commercial enterprises.

Discuss

18. If you had ten thousand dollars in money saved, how much of it would you keep in cash? How much of it would you invest in life insurance, medical insurance, and property insurance? Would you be willing to spend part of your money for a pension plan? Would you maintain a savings account at a bank? Or would you spend most of your money? If so, on what? Explain the reasons for your choices.

19. In countries that are suffering from civil war or revolution and in which the authority of the government is shaken, often people put most of their savings into gold coins, gold bars, or jewelry. In the great Chinese port of Shanghai during the Chinese civil war of the 1940s, a woman shop attendant might wear around her neck and wrists ten thousand dollars' worth of gold ornaments. In such circumstances, why are such forms of investment chosen?

Another general form of saving is investment in one's own house or condominium. The majority of American families live in houses or apartments owned by themselves, rather than rent their living quarters from some landlord. This situation is not true of most other nations. Family home-owning is encouraged by the federal government of the United States: under Internal Revenue Service regulations (established by Congress), homeowners can claim as a deduction on their income tax returns the amount of interest they pay on a house that they are buying. For most heads of American families, their own house is their largest capital investment and form of saving.

For people in a profession or an independent business—doctors, lawyers, shop owners, self-employed craftsmen, and many others—a principal form of saving is investment in their own offices or stores or the tools of their trade. Buildings and equipment used in earning an income can be sold if necessary. So they have a commercial value as well as being immediately useful to their professional or commercial owners.

Savings in Stocks and Bonds

Less personal forms of saving are stocks and bonds, mentioned briefly in earlier chapters of this book. Both **stocks** and **bonds** are investments in some industrial or commercial company or corporation.

A **corporation** is an organization owned by many people. The corporations we know in America today developed out of an earlier form of business organization called the *joint-stock company.* Every owner, or investor in the corporation, receives a share of the corporation's profits (supposing there are any profits). An important feature of the corporation is the *limited liability* of its investors, or stockholders. **Limited liability** means that if the corporation fails or goes bankrupt, the individual stockholders do not personally have to pay the firm's creditors. (This is the major distinction between a corporation and a partnership; for individual partners are liable at law for all the debts of a *partnership.*)

A person can invest in a corporation in several ways. The investor can buy *common stock, preferred stock,* or *bonds.*

A **stockholder** is a person who owns a share in a business but does not own all of the business. A stock company, or corporation, may have only a few stockholders. But most big corporations are owned by thousands of stockholders—some holding large numbers of shares, others owning only a small amount.

Holders of common stock can vote to decide who the officers of a corporation will be. As their reward for investing in a company, common stockholders receive *dividends* in years when the company makes money. (The word *dividend* means something that has been divided up—that is, a division of the firm's profits, a share of the firm's annual return on investments.) There are two kinds of dividends. One is the cash dividend from stock: payment in money. The other is the stock dividend: payment in additional stock in the firm.

In a prosperous year for a company, holders of common stock may receive large dividends. In a year when the company has not prospered, dividends may be small; or there may be no dividends at all.

Holders of preferred stock receive a fixed amount in cash dividends annually: that is, they are guaranteed a return on their investment—supposing the company makes enough money in a year to pay them. The amount of dividends for preferred stock is relatively small; so if the company does remarkably well one year, the holders of preferred stock receive only the amount of the dividend guaranteed to them. All the rest of the year's profits go to the holders of common stock. Usually holders of preferred stock are not permitted to vote at meetings of the company's investors.

Both the common and the preferred stockholders take a risk with the money they invest. Neither may receive any dividends if the company has a bad year. If the company has a good year, the common stockholder stands to make a much higher return on his money than does the preferred stockholder. The common stockholder takes a larger risk; therefore, he receives a larger reward, or "premium for risk."

A **bondholder** is a person who lends money to a company and is guaranteed repayment (and payment of interest) by a document called a *bond*. Ordinarily, a bondholder has no voice in the management of a firm. He is promised by the company a fixed rate of interest on the money he has lent. The bondholder has a right to be paid before either the preferred stockholder or the common stockholder receives dividends. Thus, *bonds are the safest form of investment in a company; but also they are the least profitable form,* since when a firm prospers, they pay the lowest return, at a fixed rate of interest. The less the risk, the less the reward. Sometimes, if a company is failing, bondholders obtain a court order to take over that company and manage it themselves, so as to get as much of the interest owing to them as they can.

Nearly all governments issue bonds, which are sold either to citizens of the country concerned or to foreign investors. *The bond is the chief form of borrowing used by political units*—national, state, county, or city governments. Buying government bonds usually is considered a fairly safe form of investment. But ordinarily, the rate of interest paid on such bonds is less than what an investor could get from an industrial or commercial corporation.

Most stocks and bonds can be sold easily enough to other investors, in the stock market, or stock exchange—although often, if a stockholder or bondholder wants his money in a hurry, he may have to take less than he originally paid for his stocks or bonds. So stocks and bonds are called **liquid investments,** meaning that they flow easily: that is, they can be converted into cash or into other investments without much difficulty.

Investment in Land

Stocks and bonds were not common forms of investment before the eighteenth century. Until then, people invested in individual enterprises, in partnerships, or in land—chiefly in land.

Speculation in land values was common in America from the beginnings of European settlement. The majority of the men who drew up the Constitution of the United States chose land as their preferred form of saving.

Today, land remains a widespread and usually desirable form of saving. It may be agricultural land, forest land, or land for development (for erecting houses or industrial buildings). It may be resort land (beaches, mountain sites, and other spots attractive to vacationers). Even in time of economic depression, land retains at least some value.

An investment in land may be unfortunate, nevertheless, if for a long time the owner derives no income from it. Owning vacant lots in a city often is a dubious investment: for the investor has to pay real-property taxes on his holdings and usually has some costs of maintenance. So over the years, any gain he might make by selling the land tends to be eaten up by the owner's costs during the period when the land is idle.

Discuss

20. The interest paid on bonds issued by the United States government is less than the interest on many other forms of investment. Yet both American citizens and people in other countries annually buy billions of dollars' worth of federal bonds. Give reasons why many people—and especially wealthy people—choose this form of investment.

21. If people earn more interest on savings accounts in banks than they earn on checking accounts, why are checking accounts more numerous in most banks?

22. If you possessed a million dollars in cash, what form of saving would you choose? Why? Would you *diversify* your investments—that is, use more than one form of saving?

23. Suppose you lived in a country like the Soviet Union or Communist China, in which no citizen was permitted to own land, to set up a business (except perhaps a very small one like a shoe-repair shop, a barbershop, or a little cafe), to buy stock in private business or industry, to pass on wealth to his children or other heirs, or to buy gold. Suppose also that all banks had been **nationalized**—that is, taken over by the government. How might you invest your savings in such a society? Would you save?

24. A government official who was known to be a prudent and successful investor once was asked this question: "If you had some money to invest and wanted a good and safe return on it, what would you do with your money?" The official replied promptly, "I'd go to a region where land is fairly cheap, buy land with trees on it, and let the trees grow." The surprised questioner persisted: "But surely there's a better and quicker form of investment than that?" The official smiled: "No, there isn't."

Why did the official think that buying timberland was a safe and profitable form of saving? What are the advantages and the disadvantages of owning forest land? (Think of demand, risk, cost of operations, liquid investments.)

Compulsory Saving

Although we have just now discussed several important types of saving, we have not mentioned the biggest form of saving for many American citizens: the federal Social Security system. The great majority of Americans have claims on this huge fund—the financing of which has become shaky in recent years.

The other forms of saving we have discussed are voluntary. With **voluntary saving,** people can choose for themselves whether to use one or another of those modes of saving, or indeed whether to save at all. But Social Security is a form of compulsory saving: that is, nearly all citizens are required by the government to contribute payments into the Social Security fund, whether or not they like this type of saving.[1]

Social Security is not the only form of compulsory saving in the United States. Most employers are required to pay money into government-supervised funds for unemployment relief—another form of saving for a rainy day. Some states, educational institutions, and large corporations have compulsory pension systems into which employers or employees, or both, must pay.

But there is far less compulsory saving (in proportion to voluntary saving) in the United States than in most other principal nations of the twentieth century. In the collectivist countries, of which the Soviet Union and Communist China are the biggest examples, voluntary saving is small and often discouraged. Instead, the governments of such countries insist upon large-scale state saving. The average citizen of a collectivist society is left little income to save for himself and few chances to invest any private savings.

---

1. Some economists and others say that Social Security should not be described as a form of compulsory saving. Certainly its payments are compulsory; but Social Security does not meet a strict definition of the term "saving." For the federal government does not invest the collected Social Security taxes in economically productive enterprises, but promptly spends those revenues for current general purposes. And not all people who pay Social Security taxes receive insurance benefits: those who die before the age of sixty-two, for instance, do not obtain old-age retirement benefits unless earlier they have obtained payments for being disabled.

Nevertheless, even in a totalist country the government usually leaves some place for individual savings. In most such countries it is possible for citizens to buy bonds, but these are the government's bonds, and so private savings simply go back into the collectivist economy. Also, it is possible for a collectivist government to cancel such bonds when it likes or to refuse to pay interest on its bond issues—as has happened more than once in the Soviet Union.

Thus America's Social Security system is just one kind of compulsory saving. This American form of social insurance was not enacted until 1935. In return for making payments to the government, citizens are insured to some extent against poverty in old age, medical expenses in later years, the cost of crippling personal injuries, loss of parents in one's childhood, and other risks. *The federal government uses the immense sums annually paid into the Social Security system for the government's current expenditures.*

To pay for these insurance benefits, everyone in the United States who earns a wage or a salary (except for some public employees) must contribute a proportion of his income to Social Security. Every employer must match the payment made by every employee. *Many Americans pay more in Social Security taxes than they pay in federal and state income taxes.*

Economists and legislators argue every year about the weaknesses of the Social Security system—particularly about whether its financial structure can endure without radical reform. Certainly it has become a severe financial burden for the economy, though this burden is less heavy in the United States than in Britain, Sweden, and other countries that have similar systems of social insurance.

Discuss

25. Why does payment to Social Security have to be compulsory? Could it be made voluntary? Formerly, self-employed people did not have to contribute to Social Security if they wished not to participate. Why, do you suppose, have self-employed people been compelled to pay Social Security taxes in recent decades?

26. Americans over sixty-five years of age who cease to work

for pay become entitled to retirement benefits from the Social Security system. But other Americans equally old who continue working until they reach the age of seventy receive no such benefits until after their seventieth birthday. Indeed, they have to keep making Social Security payments for the benefit of other people. Why? Does this situation seem fair to you?

27. The central government of the Soviet Union undertakes huge construction projects extending over thousands of miles, such as the laying of pipelines for natural gas all the way to Western Europe and the building of canals and waterways in central Asia. How does the Soviet government obtain capital for such undertakings, when there are no private banks or insurance companies to borrow from?

Why Modern Societies Require Huge Amounts of Capital

If we were to total up all forms of saving in the twentieth century—both voluntary saving and compulsory saving—throughout the world, we would find that saving looms larger than it did in any previous century of human experience. Why so?

The answer is this: today's industrial economies require much more capital investment than any earlier society, with a simpler economy, ever needed. Gigantic industrial plants, airlines, rail systems, ocean freighters, department stores and shopping plazas, housing projects, military and naval establishments, and all the other material developments of twentieth-century life are far more costly than the economic apparatus of any previous civilization.

Therefore, much more saving is needed to build and maintain this huge economic "plant." For efficient large-scale production of goods, much capital must be found. And all capital, remember, comes from one source: savings.

The tendency of many individuals is to spend promptly everything that they earn. But for most such people there arrives, before long, a day of reckoning when necessities have to be paid for. Such people find themselves in the situation of the grasshopper that had sung away its summer.

If such spenders still have decent credit ratings, they may be able to borrow in an emergency to meet essential expenses.[2] Borrowing means that they must restrict consumption and postpone expenditure in the future. If they have poor credit ratings, such thoughtless spenders will have to tighten their belts or seek public assistance. Once upon a time, they might have found themselves in jail for debt.

Most governments, too, tend to spend immediately the whole of their revenues—which are chiefly their receipts from taxes. Thus, often governments find it necessary to borrow money where they can find it. Such policies frequently lead to the economic phenomenon called *inflation*—a subject we will discuss later. Inflation of the currency discourages people from private saving.

When less saving occurs, there must be less investment in capital goods. When investment in capital goods diminishes, the means for producing all goods are reduced. When facilities for producing goods are weakened, few goods for consumers can be supplied. And then everybody (or nearly everybody) begins to suffer economically, because there are no longer enough essential goods available to satisfy most people's urgent needs—let alone most people's wants.

Any person's prosperity and any nation's prosperity must be founded upon thrifty habits. A major cause of personal and family poverty is lack of knowledge of how to save something out of income. A major cause of political instability and widespread national poverty is unsound public policy that does not encourage people to save.

Discuss   28. In some regions of central Africa, little saving has occurred for many centuries. So capital is not accumulated. There is only enough production of consumer goods to provide for the bare

---

2. Banks and other lending institutions ordinarily assess a person's financial stability before granting a loan of money. In many cases, a customer who is known to have repaid a loan promptly and on time in past transactions will be given a good credit rating. In other words, the lending institution regards the customer as a good risk. On the other hand, a person who has failed to make repayments on time in the past will be regarded by the lending institution as a bad risk and will be unlikely to receive a loan.

subsistence of most people. A cause of this poverty is the social custom of sharing all consumer goods immediately among all the members of a tribe, clan, or system of extended families. When, for instance, one household or family reaps a good harvest because of favorable climatic conditions during the growing season, relatives may come from many miles around to share in the consumption of the "surplus" of food harvested by the fortunate family. The relatives stay with their hosts until all the food has been eaten; they then go home again. Thus, the family which has enjoyed the fine harvest is left with no food that can be preserved or sold for cash. Temporary prosperity is followed promptly by unpleasant poverty. Can you explain how this generous sharing does harm, in the long run, to all members of the extended family or clan? Can you suggest what might be done to remedy this cycle of alternating want and plenty?

29. During the 1920s, after the Bolshevik Revolution of 1917–18 had established a Communist regime in Russia, millions of Ukrainian peasants managed to save some of their production and became relatively prosperous. These successful peasants were called kulaks—a term of abuse. In 1931, saying that the kulaks were making themselves capitalists, the Soviet government seized their land and deported them to Soviet Asia, never to return. Agricultural production in the Ukrainian homeland promptly and ruinously declined, and widespread starvation resulted.

Can you explain how this disaster was related to ignorance of the necessity for saving and to misunderstanding of the factor of production called capital?

The voluntary saving of a market economy keeps a people free, as well as fed. The Egyptians' failure to save for themselves made them all the serfs of Pharaoh. The seizure of the Russian peasants' savings made them all the serfs of the Communist dictatorship. Economic freedom and political freedom are closely related. *Without saving, there can be no security and little liberty.*

CHAPTER 9

What Money Is Good For

What Money Is Good For

The Difficulty of Getting Along without Money

Money is a mixed blessing. We can employ money in evil ways as well as in good ways. But every civilization has found it necessary to employ some kind of money.

What we call the market, you will remember, is the process by which sellers and buyers exchange goods. Big, efficient markets of the twentieth-century kind are possible only because money is in use generally. Large-scale savings and healthy competition also depend upon the existence of money.

For money is the *medium of exchange*. When we say this, we mean that sellers and buyers use money when they are exchanging goods—instead of swapping one object or service for some other object or service. As one of the larger dictionaries puts it, money is "any article of value which is generally accepted as a medium of exchange." The word *medium* signifies "means" or "agent." So a **medium of exchange** is a means or way for exchanging goods.

For instance, a consumer who buys a milkshake priced at one

dollar usually pays for his shake with a dollar bill or two half-dollar coins or four quarters or smaller change—forms of money used as a medium of exchange. It would be awkward to have to pay for a milkshake by offering several tomatoes or fifteen minutes' labor at dishwashing or a second-hand pair of wool socks in exchange for the shake. The milkshake vendor prefers to get money in exchange for his product: he can buy other things readily with the cash.

In a very simple market, true, it may be possible to get along without money. The alternative to money is *barter*: the direct exchange of one good for another good, without money passing from hand to hand. In some of the remote parts of the world, barter still is a means of trading. For that matter, swapping (bartering) still survives in many an American neighborhood. An advantage of barter is that buyers need not use cash which they wish to reserve for other purposes.

In general, nevertheless, exchange through barter is complicated and time-consuming. If no money is involved, who can say what the precise value of bartered articles may be? Is a milkshake truly equivalent in value to several tomatoes or fifteen minutes of washing dishes or a pair of old socks? One of the strong advantages of money is that money provides a means for comparing the value of one good with another, to find out if the two goods are equivalent.

Also, barter is difficult because goods may not be readily divisible. Suppose that a trained shepherd dog seems to be worth three sheep and that the owners of the dog and of the sheep wish to trade. But suppose also that the owner of the sheep has only two sheep available to trade. The dog owner cannot cut off two thirds of the dog to swap for two sheep. If these people have money available, however, the sheep owner can pay the dog owner wholly in money, or else partly by his two sheep and partly in cash. Most money is readily divisible into smaller units. Dogs and some other forms of property are not readily divisible.

In addition, barter often requires much time and bother. All sellers with different goods to offer, in different quantities, must go about looking for somebody who has precisely the different material good or service they want, in the desired amount. And that somebody must want precisely what some other swapper has to offer, in precisely the right quantity. One might waste days or months in such a search.

The Pine-Tree Shillings

So people in advanced societies turn from barter to money, the medium of exchange. The Puritan colony of Massachusetts had no proper money of its own until the middle of the seventeenth century, when the government arranged for the minting of its first coins, which bore the emblem of a pine tree: the pine-tree shillings. The following description of how Massachusetts shifted from barter to money is taken from Nathaniel Hawthorne's book *Grandfather's Chair*.

Captain John Hull was the mint-master of Massachusetts, and coined all the money that was made there. This was a new line of business, for in the earlier days of the colony the current coinage consisted of gold and silver money of England, Portugal, and Spain. These coins being scarce, the people were often forced to barter their commodities instead of selling them.

For instance, if a man wanted to buy a coat, he perhaps exchanged a bear-skin for it. If he wished for a barrel of molasses, he might purchase it with a pile of pine boards. The Indians had a sort of money called wampum, which was made of clamshells, and this strange sort of specie was likewise taken in payment of debts by the English settlers.[1] Bank-bills had never been heard of. There was not money enough of any kind, in many parts of the country, to pay the salaries of the ministers, so that they sometimes had to take quintals of fish, bushels of corn, or cords of wood instead of silver or gold.[2]

As the people grew more numerous and their trade one with another increased, the want of current money was still more sensibly felt. To supply the demand the general court passed a law for establishing a coinage of shillings, sixpences, and threepences. Captain John Hull was appointed to manufacture the money, and was to have about one shilling out of every twenty to pay him for the trouble of making them.

Hereupon all the old silver in the colony was handed over to Captain John Hull. The battered silver cans and tankards, I suppose, and silver buckles, and broken spoons, and silver buttons of worn-out coats, and silver hilts of swords that

1. **Specie:** coin, as opposed to paper money.
2. **Quintal:** a measure, of Arab origin, amounting to a hundred pounds, or a hundredweight, or a hundred kilograms.

had figured at court,—all such curious old articles were doubtless thrown into the melting pot together. But by far the greater part of the silver consisted of bullion from the mines of South America, which the English buccaneers—who were little better than pirates—had taken from the Spaniards and brought to Massachusetts.

The magistrates soon began to suspect that the mint-master would have the best of the bargain. They offered him a large sum of money if he would but give up that twentieth shilling which he was continually dropping into his own pocket. But Captain Hull declared himself perfectly satisfied with the shilling. And well he might be, for so diligently did he labor that in a few years his pockets, his money-bags, and his strong box were overflowing with pine-tree shillings.

Discuss

1. Why did the people of Massachusetts find barter a somewhat unsatisfactory way of marketing goods?

2. Would you agree to print dollar bills for the United States at your own expense if you were given a contract with the government guaranteeing you one dollar bill for yourself out of every twenty one-dollar bills you should print? Would making such a contract be a good way for the American government to save money today?

3. From what you know of American history, can you suggest why the Puritan colonists of Massachusetts Bay lacked "hard" money so late as 1652, more than three decades after the first settlers had landed at Plymouth Rock? (Think of the system called mercantilism.)

4. Suppose that all paper money in the United States suddenly were to become almost worthless—as the money of Germany, Italy, and the countries of Eastern Europe became at the end of the Second World War. If you were buying goods in such circumstances, what would you use to pay sellers? If you were selling in such circumstances, what forms of payment might you accept? Can you think of any instances in the history of the United States when something of this sort happened to money?

The Four Functions of Money

Most economists agree that money has four principal purposes or functions, listed in the box on page 201.

The Functions of Money
1. To be a medium of exchange
2. To provide a measure of value
3. To provide a standard for deferred payments
4. To provide a convenient means of storing wealth

These functions need to be explained. We already have discussed money as a medium of exchange. But what do we mean when we say that money provides a measure of value?

Why, this phrase **measure of value** means that by using some standard unit of money—the American dollar, the British pound, or the French franc, for instance—we can express how much one material good or service is worth as compared with some other material good or service. Suppose, for example, that your doctor charges you thirty dollars for a brief consultation at his office. By comparing the doctor's fee with other costs and prices, you can see that a consultation with a physician is worth about as much, in dollars, as a twenty-five-mile ride in a taxi or five pounds of steak or a new hardbound book. Money, in short, enables us to measure the value or cost of some particular good against the values or costs of other goods. Knowing such equivalents, you and I can conduct our economic affairs accordingly.

How about money's function as a standard for deferred payments? This purpose of money makes borrowing and lending possible. A borrower promises to repay what he has borrowed from a lender in terms of money. If a person needs to build a house, ordinarily he borrows money to pay for the construction (supposing he does not have sufficient cash of his own on hand). Now, he *could* borrow cement blocks, boards, roofing, plumbing fixtures, and the like—promising to pay back the lender eventually in similar blocks, boards, nails, fixtures, etc. But the lender would not be pleased by such an arrangement, ordinarily. For one thing, he could not be certain that the material things paid back would be identical in quality to those lent. Nor could the lender be sure that, years later, the value of blocks, boards, and the like would be equal to the value of such things as had been lent. Therefore, promises to pay in the future commonly are expressed in terms of some standard unit of money. For the value of money usually changes less than do the values of various commodities.

As for money's function of enabling people to store their wealth, this has been understood for many centuries. "Money is a guarantee that we may have what we want in the future. Though we need nothing at the moment, it insures the possibility of satisfying a new desire when it arises." So wrote the Greek philosopher Aristotle, about 340 B.C. In other words, many forms of wealth are perishable: they rot or melt away. But money lasts. And if we save money, the gold or silver or bills that we put away "against a rainy day" may serve us well when we grow old or when other forms of wealth have decayed or have been destroyed.

Any sort of money performs these functions—although some forms of money are more satisfactory than other forms. An ideal money would have the qualities listed below.

Qualities That Money Should Possess

Constancy (stability) in value
Intrinsic value (worth something in its own right, aside from being money)
Portability (easily carried about)
Durability (slow to wear out)
Standard and recognizable appearance
Divisibility (available for use in both large and small units)

But most money today lacks some of these qualities—particularly the first two qualities.

Discuss   5. In Maryland and Virginia, during the last quarter of the eighteenth century, tobacco was used as money. One could pay debts and taxes in tobacco. Why did those two colonies (later states) choose tobacco for this purpose? Why didn't they use metal coins?

6. The ancient Spartans are said to have used huge pieces of iron as money. Of the several qualities that money ought to possess, what quality would this iron money lack most conspicuously?

7. In Ethiopia, until very recently, bars of salt were used as money; so were rifle cartridges. What advantages and disadvantages did those two forms of money have?

8. Grain and cattle have been used as money in some societies. How well would either of these commodities fulfill the four functions of money? Explain your answer, showing in what respects these commodities can (or cannot) serve as media of exchange, measures of value, standards for deferred payments, and means of storing wealth.

Metallic Money

Until the nineteenth century (and in some countries, until recent decades), when civilized people said "money," they meant metallic coins—of gold, silver, bronze, copper, and sometimes other metals. (Economists often call metallic money **specie.**) A chief advantage of metal money was (and is) that it has **intrinsic value:** the metal, particularly gold and silver, has value in itself for other purposes than use as money. Gold, for instance, is valuable for filling teeth or as jewelry.

Gold and silver, the precious metals, are fairly stable in value, besides. Until the twentieth century, enough gold and silver were available in many countries to supply the mints, but not so much was available that the price of the precious metals would go down. In short, the precious metals always have been scarce. No one would value money made of baked clay, if one had the choice of some better form of money, because supplies of clay are not very scarce. If demand remains constant but supply does not increase, then price remains stable. So it is with gold and silver, most of the time, in most countries.

Coins are also portable and durable. Well-minted coins are standard and recognizable. A regular coinage is divisible into large and small units. (In the United States, we still have dollar coins, half dollars, quarters, dimes, nickels, and pennies; until recent years, the British had half-crowns, florins, shillings, sixpences, threepenny bits, pennies, halfpennies, and farthings.)

Any person possessing bags of gold or silver coins could be fairly certain that his wealth would not diminish in value. A gold coin that would have bought three cows in the year 1600, say, probably still would have bought three cows in the year 1650—or perhaps four cows, considering improvements in animal breeding. Houses might burn; fields might be devastated by drought or flood; ships might sink; merchandise in a warehouse might be damaged. But gold and silver coins, properly safeguarded, would last their owner's lifetime—and could be passed on to heirs.

Even gold and silver "coin of the realm" was not a perfectly sure form of money, nevertheless. Much as today's paper money often suffers from depreciation in value, so it was possible for metallic coins to become worth a good deal less than they had been previously. This form of inflation occurred, both during the course of the Roman Empire and during medieval times, when rulers deliberately *debased* coins. Gold and silver might be mixed with some proportion of *base metals*— lead, zinc, copper, or iron—to produce coins that looked like the old gold or silver coins but which actually did not contain sufficient weight of "noble metal." By requiring subjects to turn in the old coins in exchange for new coins, emperors or kings might make a large profit in gold or silver. Thus, debasing the coinage was a disguised form of taxation.

When people cannot trust the value of one form of money, they will hide away for themselves the kind of money (perhaps coins many years old) that seems more valuable, and will spend the new and less trustworthy money. This principle is called **Gresham's Law,** after Sir Thomas Gresham, adviser to King Henry VIII and Queen Elizabeth I of England. "Bad money drives out good," Gresham said.

When governments issue "bad" money—that is, coins or paper money worth less than the money that had been in circulation earlier— people tend to hoard the old money, taking it out of circulation. That is not the only mischief done by issuing a kind of money that is not really worth, on the market, the **face value** (the asserted value) of the money. For coining or printing "cheap" money is the chief cause of what economists call *inflation* of prices (a topic we will discuss later). When the level of prices in the market greatly increases because too much money is in circulation, the process is called **inflation.** When prices decrease because money seems sounder and more stable, the process is called **deflation.**

By the latter half of the eighteenth century, about the time when the Physiocrats and Adam Smith were founding the science of economics, the great commercial countries of Western Europe, Britain and the Netherlands especially, had established a sound and honest coinage: that is, their metallic coins were constant in value, trusted in every market. This stability of money contributed greatly to the economic success of Britain and other nations that had grown prosperous during the Commercial Revolution of the sixteenth, seventeenth, and eighteenth centuries.[3]

Discuss

9. Suppose you had some large Spanish silver coins called doubloons, minted in the seventeenth century and made of silver that was nearly pure (that is, without much alloy of some other metal). Would those doubloons have an intrinsic value? What could be done with the silver, besides using it as money? If you wished to sell the coins, would you take them to someone who would melt them down for the value of the silver, or to a dealer in antique coins? Explain your choice.

10. In California during Gold Rush days, sometimes little "pokes" (leather sacks) of gold dust were used as money. Would these be a better form of money than United States gold coins of that period?

11. We have pointed out that gold and silver coins might be a safer way of saving than investing in houses, land, ships, or merchandise, because coins are durable and are more or less stable in value. But can you suggest some reason why, nevertheless, hoarding coins might not be the most profitable form of investment?

---

3. **Commercial Revolution:** an economic development, beginning in the fifteenth century, that involved both a great enlargement of trade throughout much of the world and increased specialization of production in various countries. The Commercial Revolution was made possible by progress in the science of navigation and the improvement of seagoing ships.

(Remember some remarks on this subject in our chapter on saving.)

12. During the first administration of President Franklin Roosevelt, all American citizens were required to turn over to the federal government whatever gold coins they possessed (except for those coins that formed part of systematic coin collections) and to accept paper money in exchange. The price of gold coins has been rising ever since, so that in effect those citizens who turned in their coins lost money by the process. Was this demand on the part of the federal government a form of taxation?

13. If today the federal government were to mint and send into circulation twenty-dollar gold pieces of the same weight and quality as those confiscated by the government in the 1930s, what do you suppose would happen to those new gold pieces? (Here you can apply Gresham's Law.) Would those new gold pieces have the same value on the market as twenty-dollar bills?

Paper Money

Few of us do our buying with coins today—although as late as the administration of President Lyndon Johnson, a good many large silver dollars were in circulation. Most of us rarely have in our purses or pockets any coin larger than a quarter. Nearly everywhere in the world, the money in general circulation has become one form or another of paper money. Notes or bills issued by governments or approved banks have become **legal tender:** that is, any seller or creditor has to accept paper money in payment. It still would be lawful to pay sellers and creditors in bags of pennies, nickels, dimes, quarters, half dollars, or dollars; but few buyers or debtors go to all that bother.

Paper money developed gradually in Western Europe, beginning in the sixteenth century. The earliest forms of paper currency were *promissory notes* and *bills of exchange*. From these privately issued paper documents comes the present worldwide triumph of paper money over coins.

In the beginning, goldsmiths, who acted as bankers in Western Europe, issued notes in which they promised to pay the value of those notes, in gold, on the demand of the persons holding the notes. People owning quantities of gold would deposit their specie (coin) or bullion (gold not coined) with goldsmiths for safekeeping. The receipts of deposit given by goldsmiths to these gold owners were the original forms of paper currency.

These notes from goldsmiths (or sometimes from important merchants engaged in international trade) were more convenient than gold coins and less risky to carry about. This banking business of goldsmiths and merchants was profitable. Bankers discovered that generally they needed to keep on hand only a proportion of the gold that had been deposited. If a London goldsmith should issue notes to the value of a thousand pounds, say, he might need only about two hundred pounds in gold on hand to meet the day-to-day demands of his depositors. It was unlikely that more than twenty percent of the notes a banker issued would have to be exchanged for gold coin or bullion at any given time. Therefore, the banker (originally a goldsmith) could lend out 80 percent of the gold deposited with him—at good interest.

In the nineteenth century, after many small, privately owned banks had sprung up throughout Europe and America, governments began to issue their own notes or bills (paper money)—either through a central banking system chartered by a government or through the government's own treasury. Sometimes these government notes were backed by gold deposits, but sometimes they were backed only by the government's promise to pay coin in exchange for notes.

During emergencies, governments were (and still are) under strong temptation to issue paper money not backed by deposits of precious metals. In times of war, indeed, governments frequently issued vast quantities of paper currency backed by little except the "faith and credit" of the government itself.

The inflation in France during the French Revolution, caused by printing of unlimited **fiat money** (currency backed by nothing but the government's command), showed how wildly prices could rise in a short time when the issuing of paper money was not sensibly controlled. A few years earlier, during the War for Independence in America, both Congress and the state governments had issued masses of paper money not backed by gold deposits and not redeemable in coin. These "Continental" dollar bills soon became worthless. (To establish a sound national monetary system was one of the principal aims of the Constitutional Convention of the United States, in 1787.)

From the painful experience of most European countries during and after the First and Second World Wars, many other examples of the collapse of paper currencies might be given. All these cases of financial collapse on a national or international scale illustrate what happens to the value of money when that particular money has no intrinsic value, is not backed by a substantial reserve of precious metals, or is not controlled in quantity by some other reliable means.

During the American Civil War, both Union and Confederate governments issued many millions of dollars of paper money. Confederate dollars were worthless at the end of the war. Union dollars lost value at the rate of 25 percent per year as long as the war lasted.

For the value of money is measured in terms of the goods for which the unit of money can be exchanged. At the beginning of the Civil War, a United States dollar bill would buy "an honest dollar's worth of groceries." For a dollar in 1861, say, a single person might have bought enough food to last eight days. By 1862, at the end of a year of civil war, a dollar bill might have bought that person a six-day supply of food. By 1863, a dollar might have bought a four-day stock of groceries. By 1864, even though the Union was winning the war, a dollar might have purchased only a two-day supply.

It can be seen readily enough that paper money has its dangers as well as its advantages. To understand how the value of money depends on the supply of goods and on the demand for those goods, look at the table below. (This simplified table does not take into account what economists call "the problem of velocity"—that is, how rapidly money is "turned over," changing hands from one possessor to another. The speed of this turnover of money also affects inflation and deflation.)

Supply of Money in Relation to Supply of Goods		
	Supply of Money	Supply of Goods
Year 1	$10,000	10,000 units
Year 2	$20,000	10,000 units
Year 3	$40,000	15,000 units
Year 4	$10,000	20,000 units

Discuss

14. What was the price in money of a unit of goods in Year 1? In Year 2? In Year 3? In Year 4?

15. In what years was there inflation of the economy?

16. In what year did deflation occur—that is, money disinflation?

17. Economists often say that "inflation is nothing more than too much money chasing too few goods." Explain that statement.

The great advantage of metallic money is the fixed supply of the precious metals—more or less fixed, that is, although the discovery of new sources of gold and silver ore may cheapen the value of gold or silver, as happened with the opening of American mines in the sixteenth century. So the value of gold (and sometimes silver) coin is relatively stable. The great danger of paper money is that a reckless or ruthless government can print as much currency as it wishes.

The economies of the United States, France, and other countries suffered from the printing of far too much paper money near the end of the eighteenth century and the beginning of the nineteenth century. So it is not surprising that many American citizens were suspicious of the use of paper money during the period between the Constitutional Convention of 1787 and the coming of the Civil War. The American agricultural interest especially feared any central bank chartered by the federal government, and opposed the system of paper money and credit created by the federal government and the banks.

The Duel of Randolph and Clay

In April, 1826, Senator Henry Clay and Senator John Randolph were to fight a duel with pistols, on the outskirts of Washington. Clay was a champion of economic expansion; Randolph, a leader of the Southern agricultural interest. By way of preparation for his possible death, John Randolph needed a few gold coins—meaning to give them to friends to make seals that they might wear in memory of him.

What follows was set down by Senator Thomas Hart Benton, one of those friends. The incident suggests the wrath that could be aroused by the debate about hard money versus paper money.

He [Randolph] wanted some gold—that coin not being then in circulation, and only to be obtained by favor or purchase—and sent his faithful man, Johnny, to the United States Branch Bank to get a few pieces, American being the kind he asked for. Johnny returned without the gold, and delivered the excuse that the bank had none. Instantly Mr. Randolph's clear silver-toned voice was heard above its natural pitch, exclaiming, "Their name is legion! and they are liars from the beginning. Johnny, bring me my horse."

Upon Randolph's arriving at the bank, this scene took place:

Mr. Randolph asked for the state of his account, was shown it, and found it to be some four thousand dollars in his favor. He asked for it. The teller took up packages of bills, and civilly asked in what sized notes he would have it. "I want money," said Mr. Randolph, putting emphasis on the word; and at that time it required a bold man to intimate that the United States Bank notes were not money. The teller, beginning to understand him, and willing to make sure, said, inquiringly, "You want silver?" "I want my money!" was the reply. Then the teller, lifting boxes to the counter, said politely: "Have you a cart, Mr. Randolph, to put it in?" "That is my business, sir," said he. By that time the attention of the cashier (Mr. Richard Smith) was attracted to what was going on, who came up, and understanding the question, and its cause, told Mr. Randolph there was a mistake in the answer given to his servant; that they had gold, and he should have what he wanted.

In fact, he had only applied for a few pieces, which he wanted for a special purpose. This brought about a compromise. The pieces of gold were received, the cart and the silver dispensed with; but the account in the bank was closed, and a check taken for the amount on New York.

Senator Randolph, a brilliant orator and a learned man, believed in the gold standard for money and would have kept the federal government altogether out of the banking business. The only real money was gold, he implied in his conversation with the bank teller. Incidentally, neither Randolph nor Clay was wounded in the duel that took place a little later that day.

More than a century and a half since John Randolph demanded gold from the Bank of the United States, the controversy about the gold standard continues in this country. The gold standard still has many supporters. But in 1965, the federal government ceased even to pretend that the United States dollar is backed by gold deposits. Billions of dollars of gold bullion are kept in the vaults of Fort Knox, in Kentucky. Yet if you were to hand a twenty-dollar bill to the Treasurer of the United States and ask for twenty dollars in gold in exchange—why, she would smile politely, taking it that you were joking. Today the United States has a "managed currency" of paper, its quantity determined by federal officials. And not even a rather belligerent United States senator could now get gold pieces from a Washington bank merely by demanding them—not United States gold coins, anyway.

Discuss

18. Why would Senator Randolph have needed a cart to carry away four thousand dollars in silver but no cart to take away the same sum in notes of the Bank of the United States?

19. Why was the bank teller prepared to supply Senator Randolph with four thousand dollars in silver but nothing in gold? Aren't both silver and gold precious metals?

20. If the federal government has buried at Fort Knox the biggest gold reserve in the world, why can't American citizens change their paper money into gold if they wish to? Wouldn't it be better to have the gold in circulation than to keep it buried? Americans are free to buy gold bullion, or the gold coins of other countries. Why shouldn't they be able to exchange paper dollars for gold dollars? See if you can give reasons for the federal government's hoarding of gold. Look up the subject of gold reserves in encyclopedias and other works of reference.

Most Money Is neither Coins nor Notes

No doubt the average citizen thinks that money consists of dollar bills in various denominations, plus "chicken feed"—the small coins in circulation. But remember the formal definition of money: "any article of value which is generally accepted as a medium of exchange."

What media of exchange are there besides bills and coins? Why, bank checking accounts (**demand deposits**); bank savings accounts (**time deposits**); and bank credit cards, which now account for a huge proportion of consumer spending in the United States. Economists call demand deposits a form of money, and any person with a checking account can use them whenever he likes. Time deposits and credit card accounts often are called by economists **near-money.** (When we say "bank savings accounts," we include accounts with credit unions and savings and loan associations. Charge accounts at stores are not readily convertible into cash. This is true also of credit cards with gasoline companies.)

So long as the medium of exchange (money) was cattle, iron bars, tobacco, salt, or something else that could be seen and felt and used for a practical purpose, it was easy for people to understand the nature of money. In the same way, when gold, silver, copper, bronze, and other metals were used as money, it was not very difficult to understand what money was: everybody knew that such metals were scarce. They recognized that a small gold coin, say, might be of value equal to that of a fat cow.

But when paper money began to circulate (beginning with sixteenth-century bills of exchange and promissory notes), a good many people found it hard to understand the relationship between pieces of paper and the goods that such paper money could buy. Bits of paper have next to no intrinsic value. So how can a hundred-dollar bill, say, be of a value equal to that of a new bicycle?

How can it be that a bank creates money when it extends a thousand-dollar loan to a customer—either crediting his account with that sum or giving him the money in bills? It becomes harder still to understand how the form of "near-money" called the credit card is a valuable medium of exchange. When a traveler can pay for lodging and food at a good hotel merely by signing a tiny piece of paper stamped with the impression of a plastic credit card, many people are somewhat puzzled as to how the credit-card slip is equal in value to the hotel's services.

Yet a credit card is a kind of money, or near-money, because that card is a symbol of ability to pay. The card represents money: the hotel manager knows that he can obtain money from a bank or credit-card company when he presents that institution with such little slips of paper, signed by hotel guests. Like paper money, the credit card has next to no value in itself. Instead, it is a medium of exchange. Bank notes and credit cards both are promises to pay.

How much money is there in the United States? The box below (which does not include the near-money of savings accounts and credit cards) gives us an idea of the total. Note that three fourths of American money is in the checking accounts of American bank depositors—most of them people of modest means.

U.S. Money Supply, July 1988
(in billions of dollars)

Currency in circulation	$206.3
Travelers' checks	7.2
Demand deposits in banks	290.6
Other checkable deposits	278.2
Money supply (MI)	$782.3

(Seven hundred eighty-two billion, three hundred million dollars)
Source: Federal Reserve Bank, Cleveland, Ohio.

As the figures above show, most American money isn't buried at Fort Knox; nor is it in the hands of millionaires. It is in demand deposits. The ability to write a check on a bank (confined a century ago to relatively few people) has spread to the large majority of American families. Ordinary citizens who write personal checks and occasionally use credit cards can lay claim to a great part of America's money supply.

The vast bulk of the American money supply is managed by banks, savings and loan associations, and other financial institutions—not by the United States Treasury. Calculating and controlling the money supply is a vastly complicated business.

How on earth can this tremendous apparatus of cash and credit be managed? How is it possible to arrange that enough money circulates to keep the American economy going healthily—but not so much money that inflation of the currency becomes a grave problem?

First of all, the Congress of the United States has a very general supervision over the flow of money. Congress is empowered by the Constitution to "coin money and regulate the value thereof." Under the Constitution, the federal government holds a monopoly of this power of coining (and printing) money. It holds very great power over the national money supply generally. Congress does not usually intervene directly in control of the money supply, nevertheless. Instead, Congress has established, over the years, several different federal agencies to deal with such concerns. Perhaps the most important function of these public and semipublic agencies is to control sensibly the total amount of paper money, and of such other forms of money as demand deposits, that is in circulation at any one time. For *if too little money and credit are available, an economy grows stagnant: commerce and manufacturing slow down. But if too much money and credit are available, serious inflation results, perhaps doing even greater damage to commerce and manufacturing.*

Paper money, in short, is a tricky thing; demand deposits and near-money can be even trickier. So we need to see where our money comes from nowadays and how the money supply is managed.

The Treasury and the Federal Reserve System

The United States Treasury Department (which was established in President Washington's administration, with Alexander Hamilton as the first Secretary of the Treasury) is the source of part of the American money supply. The Bureau of the Mint (making coins) and the Bureau of Engraving and Printing (making notes) are parts of the Treasury Department.

But the greater part of America's money supply is under the control of a central banking system called the **Federal Reserve System.** The six thousand member banks (commercial banks) that belong to the System are not the property of the government. The members of the System's board of governors are appointed by the President and confirmed by the United States Senate. Although the Federal Reserve works with the Department of the Treasury, it is an independent agency.

The chief aim of the Federal Reserve System is to form America's monetary policy. Since 1913, when Congress established the Federal Reserve, the System has issued paper money in the form of Federal Reserve notes. *About 90 percent of the paper money in circulation today consists of these Federal Reserve notes.* The rest are United States Treasury notes.

Acting as a central national bank, the Federal Reserve sometimes attempts to raise or lower interest rates throughout the country. The "Fed" certainly can influence short-run interest rates temporarily, but economists disagree about whether the Federal Reserve System is able to influence interest rates for any great length of time. It is the Federal Reserve's responsibility to see that more money is issued when the country's economy seems to require that, and to discourage the issuing of money when the economy is threatened by inflation.

This Federal Reserve System strongly influences commercial banks (privately owned), which handle people's checking accounts, the biggest source of America's money supply. If the Federal Reserve wants demand deposits increased (an "easy-money" policy), it can encourage the commercial banks to make more loans to their customers. ("Easy money" implies more funds in circulation, through ready granting of applications for loans.)

If the Federal Reserve wishes to have demand deposits decreased (a "tight-money" policy), it can discourage its member banks from making new loans or from renewing some of the loans that already exist. ("Tight money" implies restrictions upon the granting of loans, so that the supply of money made available is reduced, or at least not very greatly increased.)

To express this concept another way, demand deposits at commercial banks consist in considerable part of credits in dollars extended by those banks to their borrowers. *By making more such extensions of credit, or loans, the commercial banks can increase the supply of money in circulation. By making fewer such extensions of credit, or loans, the commercial banks can decrease the amount of money in circulation. The Federal Reserve System can strongly influence the increase or decrease of demand deposits by charging higher or lower rates of interest to the commercial banks that borrow part of their supply of money from the Federal Reserve System.*

Yet the Federal Reserve does not exert complete control over its member banks or over the money supply generally. Suppose that in a time of recession, for instance, the Federal Reserve wishes to adopt an "easy-money" policy to stimulate buying by consumers and so get the economy prosperous again.[4] Therefore, the Federal Reserve wishes its member banks to increase demand deposits. But suppose also that (as often happens) businessmen may be hesitant to borrow money in a time of economic recession; or that commercial bankers may not desire to make many more loans, fearing that some of them might not be repaid. Despite this business reluctance, the federal government's makers of economic decisions believe that the money supply ought to be

---

4. **Recession:** in economics, a period during which the economy recedes, or declines somewhat, causing unemployment and "hard times." A frequent cause of recession is a sharp decline in demand for goods. A recession is not as severe as an economic depression.

increased so as to "fight the recession." In such circumstances, what can be done by the federal government to increase the supply of money in circulation?

Why, in such cases the federal government can intervene in the economy through other agencies than the Federal Reserve System. The United States Treasury, which can issue its own notes and coins when it wishes, then may issue a large quantity of its own notes to supply more money—and thus encourage spending by consumers. Conversely, if the President, the Secretary of the Treasury, and other economic decision makers in Washington think that there is too much money in circulation and that the Federal Reserve's policies are too easy, then the Treasury can refrain from issuing any more notes for some months. Occasionally the Treasury and the governors of the Federal Reserve System do disagree, in this fashion, as to whether the money supply ought to be reduced or increased. If the Federal Reserve Board and the Department of the Treasury disagree very strongly and persist in opposed policies, the President of the United States can settle the dispute by removing either the chairman of the Federal Reserve Board or the Secretary of the Treasury. But disagreement between these two federal agencies rarely goes quite so far as all that.

Most of the time, the Federal Reserve Board sets monetary policy. The Federal Reserve, which is somewhat similar to the governmentally directed central banks of European countries, is able to increase or decrease the amount of money in circulation through the interest it charges its many member banks when the Federal Reserve System lends those banks money. Also, through the Federal Reserve's open-market operations, this central bank system can buy or sell government bonds. Selling bonds in the open market has the effect of reducing the amount of money in circulation. Buying bonds in the open market has the effect of increasing the amount of money in circulation.

In short, the Federal Reserve System functions as a national central bank, control over which is shared by the federal government and by the many commercial banks which belong to the system. It endeavors to control to some degree the total amount of demand deposits (otherwise called *deposit money*) available for lending by commercial banks. By such control, it can influence the interest rates (in the short run) that banks charge to their borrowers; and by influencing those interest rates, it may succeed in encouraging more spending in a time of economic recession—or discouraging more spending during a business boom that may be getting out of hand, with too much money and credit available (and therefore high prices). Also the Federal Reserve, by directly selling or buying the federal government's bonds, may help to prevent the business cycle (alternating periods of boom and recession) from going to extremes.

The Federal Reserve can act either on a national scale or on a regional scale. That is, the "Fed" may decide to increase or decrease the supply of money throughout the whole country. Or, on the other hand, the governors of the Federal Reserve Board may decide that only one of its districts, or only a few of those districts, may require an increase or decrease of money supply; then an appropriate policy is applied only to the district or districts in question.

There are twelve Federal Reserve districts in the United States, and in each district the Federal Reserve Bank is a magnificent building. These grand banks are owned, at least in name, by the system's member banks in each district; but for most purposes they are under the control of the federal government. If you enter one of those twelve splendid banks, with a Federal Reserve note for twenty dollars in your hand, and ask to have it changed into a gold coin—why, you will come off less well than Senator Randolph did. Some of the gold buried at Fort Knox is "backing" for the Federal Reserve notes, but that does not mean you can get your fingers on a little of the gold. If you hand a teller your twenty-dollar bill, he will give you a new twenty-dollar bill in exchange—or some smaller notes totaling twenty dollars, or twenty dollars' worth of small coins: no gold.

In other words, ever since 1933 the United States has not based its money on a gold standard, really, or on any other metal. Nowadays, the United States has a managed paper currency. And the vast monetary resources of the United States are under the elaborate controls of the Federal Reserve System and the Treasury of the United States.

Discuss

21. When the Federal Reserve Board's policies reduce the amount of money in circulation, loans become harder to get. Does the rate of interest on loans then tend to rise or to fall?

22. Do you know the difference between a *tight-money* policy and an *easy-money* policy ? Which policy would increase the money supply? How? Explain clearly.

23. If checks written on a checking account (demand deposits, or demand money) are considered a form of money, then what is the difference between personal checks and Federal Reserve notes or Treasury notes? Do sellers and creditors have to accept checks in payment? If checks are money, why can't everyone write checks to pay for all wants?

24. If agencies of the federal government control the money supply and can print as much paper money as they like, why do citizens have to pay taxes? Why doesn't the federal government print as much money as it needs to pay its bills, and not bother about taxes? Why don't the Federal Reserve System and the Treasury print enough money so that everybody in the United States would be well off?

25. The "welfare" system for poor people in the United States costs much money and often doesn't work well. Someone proposes that we get rid of the welfare system by giving credit cards, a form of near-money, to everybody in need of help. Then the Federal and state governments would not have to raise taxes to pay for the "welfare load." Do you see anything wrong about this proposal? If so, what?

The Use and the Abuse of Money

Metallic money has given way to paper bank notes. Bills and notes have given way to checks. Perhaps checks may give way to credit cards. Yet if a day arrives when everybody in the world possesses a credit card (or a dozen such cards) and uses it for every purchase, still there will be money in circulation.

For money, we need to remember, is any medium of exchange generally accepted. If sellers and buyers generally accept credit cards, and accept them in preference to other media of exchange, then credit cards become the principal money of a society.

It is difficult to imagine any civilization getting on for very long without some form of money. Settled communities of an advanced society have contrived to manage with very little money for some time, as did Massachusetts Bay Colony during the first thirty years of its existence. But barter is cumbersome and time-consuming; it may take a great while to satisfy one's wants by barter. As soon as possible, therefore, people who trade with one another devise a system of money.

If money is lacking, a society has no proper medium of exchange, no reliable measure of value, no standard for deferred payments, and no compact and durable way of storing wealth. These merits of money were discussed earlier in this chapter. Even communist states find it necessary to keep a great deal of money in circulation. Without money as a measure of value, indeed, communist countries (like all other countries) would have no means for calculating productivity, arranging distribution, and keeping track of consumption of goods. Also, many experiments down through the centuries have shown that it is highly difficult to persuade most men and women to work well unless they are paid some money. Some few people will work out of a sense of duty, unpaid; slaves will work under the lash; but most free labor requires a monetary reward.

Every society higher than the most primitive social groups must have money, then. And nearly any individual in a civilized society must have some money—though it still is possible for a thrifty person with simple wants to get along with a very little money, or what seems to the average citizen a very little money. Most individuals in the prosperous technological societies of the twentieth century think that they would like to possess a great deal of money; their wants are limitless.

Yet prophets, poets, and moralists, since the dawn of history, have warned mankind of the illusions and dangers that arise from the appetite for much money. A Greek myth from remote antiquity suggests the folly that results from eagerness for gold.

Midas of the Golden Touch

The richest of all mortals was Midas, king of Phrygia. When he was a baby, ants had carried grains of wheat into his mouth, a sign that Midas was destined to wealth beyond the dreams of avarice. He worshiped especially the god Dionysus, the patron of music, poetry, wine—and disorder.

Into Midas' great rose garden there stumbled, one day, the drunken satyr Silenus, companion of Dionysus. Peasants caught Silenus, bound him with wreaths of flowers, and dragged him before King Midas. Recognizing the follower of Dionysus, Midas treated Silenus with kindness; and after much hospitality, he led Silenus back to the divine Dionysus.

Grateful for this generosity to his companion, Dionysus invited Midas to ask of him one favor. Gods could alter the usual course of nature.

The boon which Midas begged of Dionysus was that he give him the power to turn to gold everything that he might touch. This Dionysus granted.

But gifts from the gods of the Greeks sometimes brought more sorrow than joy. Indeed, everything that Midas touched turned immediately to gold—whether Midas wished it so or not. Things organic became golden metal when Midas' fingers brushed them. The food that Midas raised to his lips was transformed into gold even before he could bite it. No man may dine upon gold.

Dismayed, Midas besought Dionysus to take back his fatal gift. The god instructed the stricken king to bathe in the headwaters of the river Pactolus. There Midas was washed clean of the golden touch, and ever since then gold dust has been mixed with the sand of the river's bed.

Discuss

26. Was some moral lesson intended by this myth or fable of Midas? If you think so, can you explain that moral?

27. Dionysus was the god of intoxication, revolt, excess, and wild living. Why was it natural enough for Midas to turn to Dionysus in his eagerness for greater wealth? Remember that Midas was immensely rich even before he gained his golden touch.

28. Have you heard of any celebrities today who behave rather as Midas did—and meet with his punishment?

Paul of Tarsus on Money

The early Christians, like the Greeks of classical times, perceived that money can be baneful. Paul of Tarsus, who did more than anyone else to spread the teaching of Jesus, wrote to his friend and disciple Timothy, at Ephesus, instructing him that followers of Christ should be content with little in this world:

> For we brought nothing into this world, and it is certain we can carry nothing out.
> And having food and raiment let us be therewith content.
> But they that will be rich fall into temptation and a snare, and into many foolish and hurtful lusts, which drown men in destruction and perdition.
> For the love of money is the root of all evil: which while some coveted after, they have erred from the faith, and pierced themselves through with many sorrows.
>
> —1 Timothy 6:7–10

It should be noted that the apostle writes "the *love* of money." (Often this phrase of his has been misquoted as "money is the root of all evil.") And by "*all* evil" is meant "all manner of evil" or "a multitude of evils." Paul makes it clear elsewhere that there exist other strong evils besides the love of money.

The apostle Paul is saying in these lines that to worship money, as if money were an idol or even a living spirit, is temptation and a snare. Jesus, in his Sermon on the Mount, had declared, "Ye cannot serve God and mammon." (Mammon is "the god of this world"—that is, the spirit of material things and possessions. In the Syriac language, *mammon* means "riches.") In short, the human being who *loves* money must worship a false god. For only God and human beings are deserving of love. To love a bag of gold is a "foolish and hurtful lust," because gold (unlike God and human beings) cannot return one's love.

Money can buy a great many things—perhaps more things than it should. But it cannot buy good character, or honor, or the love of created beings—or the love of God. Having said much in the first part of this chapter about the usefulness of money, it is only fair for us to mention at the end that for some purposes money is quite useless. Gold and silver coins were of no use whatever to Robinson Crusoe on his island: when there is no one to trade with, who needs a medium of exchange?

Similarly, money can buy comfort, but it cannot buy happiness. The love of money may turn a human being into a selfish and lonely miser, far distant from happiness. Out of the love of money, men and women sometimes commit ghastly crimes, so distorting or destroying their own souls. Proverbs chapters 15 and 16 admonish the reader to establish priorities concerning money. We are told in Proverbs 15:16, "Better is little with the fear of the Lord than great treasure and trouble therewith." Proverbs 16:8 is a parallel passage with a similar emphasis; "Better is a little with righteousness than great revenues without right." These Scriptural portions do not discredit wealth; they only warn of the dangers which can be associated with it. Another verse which serves as a model is shaping one's attitude toward money is found in Proverbs 16:16. "How much better is it to get wisdom than gold! and to get understanding rather to be chosen than silver!"

Money in itself is neither good nor evil. Everything depends upon the uses we make of money. Prudent and charitable use of money is praiseworthy. Arrogant and wasteful use of money is despicable. Intelligence, imagination, and moral principles determine our choices of how to employ money. So the science of economics is not "a law unto itself." To make good economic choices—including choices of ways to use money—every person must look beyond demand and supply, and beyond interest tables, to the teachings of religion, philosophy, and imaginative literature. The principal founder of modern economics, Adam Smith, was a professor of moral philosophy. If we would use money well, we need to understand (as Smith did) that above the laws of economics there stand the laws of morality.

Discuss   29. If it were possible to abolish poverty and make everyone rich, would all human beings be kind, honest, and moral in their conduct? Why or why not? Why does the apostle Paul say that rich people, or those who wish to be rich, "fall into temptation and a snare"?

30. In his Sermon on the Mount, Jesus told his followers:

Lay not up for yourselves treasures upon earth, where moth and rust doth corrupt, and where thieves break through and steal:

But lay up for yourselves treasures in heaven, where neither moth nor rust doth corrupt, and where thieves do not break through nor steal:

For where your treasure is, there will your heart be also.

—Matthew 6:19–21

Does this teaching mean that Christians should not save money? If so, why are there many rich Christians today? What would happen to society if everybody laid up treasure only in heaven? (Look up interpretations of the Sermon on the Mount in various dictionaries of the Bible and other works of reference.)

31. Some men and women work very hard, voluntarily, without any pay, for religious, moral, or political purposes. Does this fact mean that society really could get along quite well without money, with every person working as best he might without monetary reward?

Few people have all the money they desire; others have it for a time and then lose it. For them, "riches certainly make themselves wings; they fly away as an eagle toward heaven" (Proverbs 23:56). Some people have more money than is good for them. Were everybody plentifully supplied with money—real money that would purchase limitless goods—probably the human race would ruin itself by eating and drinking and sleeping excessively. Certainly not very much useful work would be accomplished, were everybody rich. So when you find yourself short of money, think on these things.

CHAPTER 10

Government and the Economy

Chapter 10
Government and the Economy

- How Much Should Government Do?
- The Meaning of Macroeconomics
- American Attitudes toward Government in the Economy
- How Governments Can Damage Economic Systems

How Much Should Government Do?

Since very early times, people have lived under some form of civil government—from very simple governments in the beginning to the complex governments of the twentieth century. What we call **government** is the political organization of a society. Governments enforce laws and protect a people against enemies.

The aim or object of all government is to keep the peace. That is, government restrains people from injuring one another. Government may be said to be a gigantic policeman. Within any country, the government prevents (or punishes) crimes of violence, theft, fraud, and other "breaches of the peace." And on the frontiers of a country, the government holds off raiders or invaders. As medieval scholars put it, government has two functions: to administer justice and to defend the realm.

Governments are political organizations, in short, not economic organizations. Until the twentieth century, governments did not often try to produce many goods. How far should governments concern themselves with economic matters? That question is hotly disputed in our time.

The Greek philosopher Plato, four centuries before Christ, said that the political state should not interfere with the economy: economic concerns should be left to merchants and craftsmen. Adam Smith, in the eighteenth century, argued that government should not intervene in the economy more than seems necessary. In America, from colonial times to the present, there has been a strong tendency to keep separate the country's politics and the country's economic system. But in every civilized society, necessarily, the government always has regulated economic matters to some extent.

Even in the United States, the general government increasingly has extended its controls over the economy during the twentieth century. Other major industrial countries have gone farther in their regulation of the economy. In totalist political systems, governments direct every aspect of a nation's economy.

In the box on page 229, we list a number of ways in which governments of one country or another, during the past four centuries, have become involved in economic matters.

The government of the United States never has undertaken some of the activities listed. Yet even in America, the part of the government in the economy has grown so large that most economists speak of the economy's *private sector* and of its *public sector*—meaning by these terms the portion of the economy controlled by private enterprise and that portion controlled by federal or state governments.

Clearly, governments in the twentieth century do more than keep the peace. Yet originally governments became involved in economic concerns through the peace-keeping function of political authorities. For governments, ever since people settled in permanent communities, have been the protectors of markets.

Thieves and robbers must be kept out of markets. Buyers and sellers who cheat must be dealt with by judges. Contracts made in markets must be enforced by governmental officials. Standard weights

Some Forms of Political Involvement in the Economy

- Controlling the supply of money
- Granting patents and copyrights
- Granting monopolies to organizations or individuals
- Taxing imported goods
- Taxing exported goods
- Subsidizing certain agricultural and manufactured goods
- Imposing heavy taxes on certain forms of economic activity
- Regulating wages, prices, and conditions of labor
- Regulating markets, including stock markets
- Allocating use of scarce resources
- Rationing commodities
- Directing labor (who shall work where)
- Operating central banking systems
- Encouraging technological and industrial developments
- Controlling or changing the physical environment
- Carrying on economic projects deemed too big for private resources
- Damaging the economy, or stimulating it, through war
- Encouraging or forbidding forms of foreign trade
- Operating state industry and state agriculture
- "Nationalizing" (confiscating) economic enterprises
- Planning and directing all production and consumption
- Transferring income and property from one social group to another

and measures used in markets must be certified by local or national governments. In these and other ways, markets are made possible by political authorities. Otherwise, buyers and sellers could not come together to exchange goods safely. *Without political protection, even the most simple market economy would collapse.*

Discuss

1. "In order to keep the peace, government holds a monopoly of force." What is meant by that statement? What happens to the public peace when armed gangs or private armies arise within a country?

2. How does a government protect a market by controlling the supply of money?

3. Look at the chart "Some Forms of Political Involvement in the Economy," page 229. List the forms of intervention that never have taken place in the United States.

4. The Constitution of the United States authorizes the federal government to tax goods imported into the country but forbids the government to tax goods exported from the country. How does this distinction in taxes stimulate American economic production?

5. Before the income tax was adopted in the United States, taxes on imported goods were the federal government's major source of revenue. How did these import duties (called *tariffs*) help the government to perform its peace-keeping functions?

Certain episodes in American history demonstrate that there cannot be a safe market and a prosperous economy unless there is a strong government to enforce laws. Here is one such episode.

Gold Rush Days

In January 1848, a workman found raw gold on the California ranch of John Sutter, where California's capital of Sacramento now stands. When President Polk announced the discovery to Congress, people in all walks of life quit whatever they were doing to join in one of the great migrations of history. They made their way to California, expecting to grow rich within a few weeks or months.

Yet few of these men and women were prepared for the dangerous trip, the difficulties of mining gold, or the hardships of life in California. By land and sea they went, all the same. Within a year, some eighty thousand Easterners, the "Forty-Niners," had arrived on the Pacific Coast; their sudden coming turned California into a land without law and order.

Most of the gold-hunters became squatters, disregarding the property rights of the landowners. Great numbers of these newcomers had to live in tents or in the open. Necessities, being very scarce, cost huge sums of money. Because there was little paper money or coin in circulation, gold nuggets and gold dust were used to pay for goods. Here are some Gold Rush prices:

pound of pork	$ 6	one barrel of flour	$400
one pick	$20	one pan	$ 10
one quart of whiskey	$20	one pound of sugar	$ 4
one candle	$ 3	one shirt	$ 40

Even by comparison with the inflated commodity prices of the 1980s, these are extravagant prices; yet 1849 was a time when a skilled workman in the eastern United States might earn as little as two dollars a day. In California, the price of a rowboat for crossing streams rose from fifty dollars to four hundred dollars. Because the miners had no safe means of shipping their gold to New York or Boston, they sold their gold dust and nuggets to commercial dealers in gold. In the East, the price of gold stood at $17.50 an ounce, but the price that dealers paid to the miners in California was as little as $4 an ounce.

Since California was not a state or even an organized territory in those days, there was no civil government beyond the coastal towns. The small force of American soldiers stationed there could not keep order. There existed no system of courts and no way to enforce justice. Murder, robbery, and other crimes usually went unpunished. For more than a year, there was anarchy in the mining regions.

But some degree of order was restored by two influences. First, many of the newcomers understood that if they stood alone as individuals, they would be robbed or killed, and so communities called *mining camps* took form. Life was primitive in the camps, but some protection could be found there. The leaders of these rough communities had knowledge of local government in the East, and the rules they established brought some security.

Second, and more important, the President of the United States sent a representative to California in 1849 to establish an orderly government. In September, a constitutional convention met. After the constitution was adopted, elections were held to choose a governor and the members of a legislature. When that task was done, it became possible for human society, including the market, to function with relative safety. Property was protected, violence and fraud were suppressed by the courts, and debts were collected. The entrepreneur could invest without being in terror of the gunslinger's six-shooter. Natural resources, labor, financial resources, and the resources of ability could be combined, under the shelter of the territorial government, to produce a real prosperity in California.

Discuss

> 6. Note the prices paid for gold in California and in the eastern states in 1849. Compare those prices with the cost of an ounce of gold today. (There is an active market in gold nowadays, and most daily newspapers publish the current price on their financial pages.) If the price has risen since 1849, can you suggest why?
>
> 7. Why did prices rise so rapidly in California when crowds of newcomers moved into that territory? (Apply what you know about the relationships between demand and supply.)
>
> 8. Can you name other countries or regions where law and order have collapsed in recent years? What happens to prices in such countries? Why?

Clearly, there must be close relationships between a country's economy and a country's government. But we still need to ask the question, "How much should the government do to influence the economy?"

The Meaning of Macroeconomics

To seek for answers to the question of how much economic activity the government should undertake, we need to turn to economics on a big scale. Economists have a term to describe large-scale public economic activity. That term is *macroeconomics*.

In our previous chapters, we have been concerned mostly with *micro*economics. We need to distinguish between these two aspects of economics.

The word *micro* is Greek for "small." The word *macro* is Greek for "large." **Microeconomics,** "little economics," has to do chiefly with markets and basic principles of economic science. **Macroeconomics,** "big economics," has to do chiefly with the total wealth of a society, including national economic policies, the economic role of government, and general productivity.

So when we discuss the part of government in a nation's economy, we enter the field of macroeconomics. But there is no great wall between microeconomics and macroeconomics; the two are merely different aspects of a country's economy. Public economic policies can be as well understood in microeconomic terms as in macroeconomic terms. Macroeconomics deals with such abstract concerns as the *gross national product*, the *national income*, and large-scale questions of investment: what economists call "fictitious aggregates."[1]

Microeconomics is the economy as the typical producer or consumer sees it. Macroeconomics is the economy as the national political administrator or national economic planner sees it.

The government of every industrialized country with a productive economy has to be concerned with questions of macroeconomics, but *in a country with a market economy, most economic decisions are decisions in the field of microeconomics. In a country with a command economy, most economic decisions are decisions in the field of macroeconomics. There are many decision makers in a market economy and few decision makers in a command economy.*

This fact does not mean that macroeconomics is unimportant in a market economy such as America's. From the beginnings of the modern study of economics, economic thinkers have recognized that governmental policies have a great deal to do with the success or the failure of any economy. The peacekeeping power of government can make possible a prosperous economy. Yet because government has a monopoly of force, the political authority called government has power to injure an economy as well as to help it.

Adam Smith, in his book *The Wealth of Nations,* had a good deal to say about macroeconomics—even though the term *macroeconomics* had not been invented in his day. Smith emphasized that the Mercantilist system of European states diminished the wealth of nations through elaborate controls upon production and distribution and through its monopolies and restraints upon trade.

But Adam Smith also recognized that the state (or government) must be strong enough to maintain law and order—and to protect and

---

1. **Gross national product (GNP):** the sum of all goods, including services, produced in a country during one year. This estimate of the value of total production includes the services of government.

encourage markets. He wrote that the powers and resources of government may well be employed when economic projects are too large for any individual or private company to undertake. The building of harbors, canals, and highways, Smith said, falls within the proper scope of government. Smith saw the need for paying the cost of such large projects through general taxes.

Yet Smith reasoned that the government should not interfere greatly in a nation's economy, that a nation's wealth will grow when individuals are left free to do their own work in their own way. In a society that is economically free, Smith argued, people who work for their own advantage actually work for the whole country's advantage: for the more wealth is produced by individuals for themselves, the more prosperous a nation becomes.

At the time the American colonies won their independence, most public leaders tended to agree with Adam Smith that although governmental policies can affect the economy for good or ill, still the management of any economy ought to be chiefly in the hands of individuals and companies. "That government is best which governs least," said Thomas Jefferson.

Jefferson and his friends were suspicious of national banking systems, governmental debts, governmental encouragement of industry, and other macroeconomic policies favored by their political opponents of the Federalist party in the early years of the United States. Yet even Jefferson, when President, became involved in "big economics" on the part of government. When Jefferson purchased from France the huge territory of Louisiana, he engaged in macroeconomic policy. That is, he bought Louisiana because he believed that possession of all that land would increase the prosperity of American agriculture and commerce.

Thus, macroeconomic policy always has been important in America, even though most economic decisions in the United States are microeconomic choices, which are made by individuals and corporations, not by governmental officials. Basically, in America the political authority has lent a helping hand to the economic system. In certain ways, the political authority (federal and state governments) has regulated that economic system. Yet the United States never has had a command economy, or directed economy, like that of socialist countries. The Constitution of the United States and decisions of federal and state courts have restrained federal and state governments from various forms of intervention in the economy that occur in many other countries.

Today the American economy remains primarily a market economy, or private-sector economy. Freedom of choice among producers and consumers, competition in price and quality, the profit motive, and private property still dominate economic institutions in the United States. The part in the economy played by the general government has increased greatly since the adoption of the federal Constitution, but the economic principles of Adam Smith have not been pushed aside in America by the economic concepts of Karl Marx and other radical thinkers. In terms of producing goods, including services, the private sector remains much bigger than the public sector.

Discuss

9. Adam Smith wrote that by "an invisible hand" the selfishness of producers working with their own advantage in mind is converted into the general benefit of a whole country. Can you explain what Smith meant?

10. Can you think of macroeconomic decisions that have affected your own family?

Even though the American economy is run largely by the private sector, it will not do for us to forget about macroeconomic policy. Almost daily, in every newspaper, we see long accounts of the economic measures of the President of the United States—as if the President were personally responsible for everybody's relative prosperity or relative poverty. Governmental spending is a major source, in one way or another, of the incomes of half the people in the country. Governmental borrowing is the major cause of inflation of the dollar. Political decisions about relations with other countries may change the course of the whole American economy—particularly when the nation goes to war. Federal and state laws may greatly encourage some forms of production but virtually wipe out other forms of production.

So the remaining chapters of this book will have much to say about the public economic measures that economists classify as macroeconomics. There is more to macroeconomics than governmental policies, but the major economic decisions by governments are part of macroeconomics.

Discuss

11. Here is a question to test your knowledge of history and geography. At present, of the following list of countries, what ones have market economies (for the most part), and what ones have command economies (for the most part)? The Irish Republic, Taiwan (Nationalist China), the Soviet Union, Switzerland, West Germany, East Germany, Cambodia, Canada, the Republic of South Africa, Poland, Japan.

12. From your knowledge of recent history, can you suggest how the military policies of the United States since 1941 have affected the economy of the United States?

13. Why is it that most countries with fairly free governments seem to have fairly prosperous economies?

14. If a woman decides to buy a house costing a hundred thousand dollars, is she making a microeconomic decision or a macroeconomic decision? Explain what you mean.

15. If the legislature of California decides to increase the retail sales tax by one half of one percent, is that a macroeconomic decision or a microeconomic decision? Why?

16. If the President of the United States invests his personal savings in a building-and-loan association, is that a macroeconomic or a microeconomic decision? If the President, in a television address, urges American citizens to buy American-made automobiles, is he trying to influence microeconomics or macroeconomics?

American Attitudes toward Government in the Economy

If American adults were asked today the question, "How much should the government do economically?" it seems probable that the majority of them might answer, "Not more than it is doing already." People who had studied economic science might reply, "Not too much macroeconomics, please."

About 1932, when Franklin Roosevelt was elected President, apparently a good many Americans thought that the federal government should do far more about the economy than it had done in the past. The election of 1932 was held in the depths of the Great Depression, when millions of Americans were unemployed, bank deposits were in danger, and many businesses were bankrupt.

During the half century since the administration of Franklin Roosevelt, federal, state, and local governments have influenced the economy far more than in any earlier period of American history. An index to this development of governmental economic activity is the number of public employees. In 1930, when the United States had a population of some 123 million, there were approximately 3,223,000 employees of federal, state, and local governments. By 1986, when America's population reached roughly 239 million, there were nearly 17 million public employees. Of those, 9.8 million worked for local governments; 4.1 million for state governments; and 3.0 million for the federal government. (These figures do not include military personnel.)

In short, during a period of fifty-six years, the general population had not doubled, but the total of public employees had increased fivefold. (The total number of employed persons in the United States, by the summer of 1986, was more than 117 million: the private sector of the American economy employs today more than six times as many persons as does the public sector.)

Most of the growth in the number of public employees has resulted from the increased economic activities of government. Social Security, unemployment insurance, and large-scale welfare benefits to the poor have been merely three of the more elaborate and costly public measures intended to improve economic conditions in the United States. All such benefits have to be paid for—either through higher taxes or through inflation of the dollar (that is, through higher prices). The majority of Americans now seem resentful of either way of paying the heavy bills. Commerce and industry complain that they are over-regulated and overtaxed by agencies of government.

Even so, American government interferes with the country's

economy less than does the government of any other great nation. Here are some of the things that the governments of many other large countries do, but the government of the United States does *not* do.

The American political authority does not—

- produce many goods in government-owned plants

- take most of anyone's income in federal income tax

- impose very heavy inheritance taxes

- "nationalize" (confiscate) industries

- tell citizens where and at what they must work

- take farmland away from some people and sell or give it to others

- dictate what goods must be produced, or how much of such goods

- set wages and salaries (except for minimum wages)

In these and other ways, the United States has a freer market economy than do other major nations. (Some small countries, notably Switzerland, have less governmental control of the economy.) Most Americans, including most leaders of labor unions, are opposed to **socialism**—that is, to *government ownership and control of the means of production.*

Indeed, the majority of Americans apparently think about governmental control of the economy much as the British statesman Edmund Burke thought about it. In 1795, Burke published his pamphlet *Thoughts on Scarcity.* Here are some sentences from what he wrote:

> To provide for us in our necessities is not in the power of government.
> It would be a vain presumption in statesmen to think they can do it.

The people maintain them, and not they the people. It is in the power of government to prevent much evil; it can do very little positive good in this, or perhaps in anything else.

Burke went on to declare that the state (government) ought to confine its activity to "everything that is *truly and properly public,* to the public peace, to the public safety, to the public order, to the public prosperity." He argued that the political state should interfere with the economy no more than was genuinely necessary.

That was the attitude of the large majority of Americans, too, at the time Burke wrote. And to the present day, the majority of Americans seem uneasy when the central government assumes more power, including economic power. Almost nobody is in favor of higher taxes and more governmental regulation, generally speaking.

Yet when it is proposed to reduce governmental expenditures and regulations of the economy, various groups of citizens object to reducing particular kinds of benefits from government. Elderly people may be alarmed when it is suggested that the Social Security program might be reduced—because elderly people receive Social Security benefits. Young taxpayers, on the other hand, might like to reduce their heavy Social Security taxes by reducing Social Security benefits. Yet some of those young people might object strongly if the federal government were to reduce its educational benefits, which generally help the young. Elderly citizens might be more willing to see federal grants for college study reduced. In short, Americans often do not agree on what particular economic benefits the government should confer, or on what economic activities the government should undertake. Yet, in general, most Americans seem to favor a free market economy, without excessive governmental regulation.

Tobacco growers usually favor federal subsidies for tobacco crops, but they may oppose federal subsidies for milk production. Dairy farmers may accept federal money and controls readily, but they may say that tobacco subsidies harm the nation's health. Yet both these groups of producers may declare themselves in favor of a market economy, as against a command economy. *A free-market economist would say that both tobacco subsidies and milk subsidies by the federal government are costly economic mistakes.*

Why do most Americans apparently approve of a competitive market economy, when many other countries have turned to socialism or some other sort of command economy? There are two chief reasons for this preference. First, America's market economy has been highly productive, supplying great quantities of goods. Second, Americans pride themselves on being a free people, and they see some connection between economic freedom and other forms of freedom. These two reasons deserve some discussion.

First, productivity. "The proof of the pudding is in the eating," an old proverb runs. That is, we learn about the goodness or badness of a thing by our experience of it—how it tastes. The United States has a more productive economy, with more material goods and services for everybody, than has any other major country in today's world. The American free market economy is not the only reason for this productivity, but it is one of the more important reasons. And every generation of Americans, since the Republic was established, have found themselves better off economically than were their parents' generation. In other words, the American economy has tended to satisfy most people's expectations of economic improvement. So men and women in the United States tend to say to themselves, "If the American economy of the free market and freedom of choice works so well for us, why think of exchanging it for some other sort of economy that may not work at all? Why kill the goose that lays the golden eggs?

Second, freedom. The American people have been accustomed to a higher degree of personal freedom than any other great nation has known (with the possible exception of the British until recent years). They cherish their economic freedoms as they cherish their religious, intellectual, and political freedoms. They always have enjoyed the freedom to buy and sell as they like, the freedom to work where and at what occupation they choose, the freedom to set up their own businesses if they have the ability, the freedom to get ahead economically if they work hard, the freedom to grow affluent or even rich if they know how to do that. When, during emergencies, the national government has fixed prices and wages, rationed foodstuffs, and in other ways imposed temporarily some aspects of a command economy—why, the American public has disliked such controls and has gotten rid of them as soon as possible. And a good many American citizens suspect that if they should lose their economic freedom of choice, soon they might lose also some of their civil and political liberties.

Everybody has to eat, obtain shelter and clothing, and, in general, make a living. So if a central political power controls the way people make their living and what they buy and sell—why, that political power can compel most people to do whatever the central political authority desires them to do. In a totalitarian country, those men and women who do not obey the central authority are deprived of their livelihood. Many Americans are aware that if some central political authority can direct labor, capital, and management as it chooses, that authority can direct citizens' private lives. *Therefore, the American attachment to a market economy is connected with Americans' belief in freedom generally.*

During the twentieth century, the tendency of most nations has been toward command economies—and loss of political freedom. Probably a free and productive economy can endure in America only if a great many Americans come to understand clearly how their economy works and the relationships between a free economy and political liberties.

Discuss   17. What did Edmund Burke mean when he wrote that it isn't in the power of government "to provide for us in our necessities"? Why can't a government provide all citizens with the food, clothing, and shelter they need?

18. What are the most essential things that a national government does? Who provides the material goods and services, or the money to pay for these essential activities? If the budget of the United States government had to be reduced by 50 percent, what federal activities could be eliminated, in your opinion?

> 19. Try to list ten benefits that your family receives from federal, state, and local governments. How many of these are economic functions of government?
>
> 20. The inhabitants of some small states in the Arabian peninsula have higher incomes, on the average, than do average American citizens. Is that because such Arab states have better economic and political systems than does the United States? [2]

How Governments Can Damage Economic Systems

Without a reasonably strong government, there can be no prosperous economy. By prudent public policies, a government may encourage and stimulate an economy.

But governmental policies may also injure or even stifle an economic system. Adam Smith pointed out convincingly how the Mercantilist system of the seventeenth and eighteenth centuries, intended to increase a country's strength, actually had worked to discourage sound economic growth. In ancient times, state policies sometimes ruined economic development—especially during the later Roman Empire, when imperial taxation and political corruption became major causes of economic and social decay.

Today, in the countries controlled by communist regimes or other totalist governments, political domination of national economies tends to discourage economic growth. Even in the United States and in the other Western democracies, the tremendous cost of "welfare states"

---

2. In 1987, per capita income in the United States was about $13,450. But per capita income in the tiny, desolate, and almost treeless Arab state of Qatar, on the Persian Gulf, was approximately $27,000; while that in little Kuwait, near the head of the Persian Gulf, was about $23,000; and the figures in the vast desert kingdom of Saudi Arabia, and in the United Arab Emirates, also exceeded per capita income in the United States. It is true that income was more equally distributed in the United States than in these Arab countries; but also it is true that the Arab states supplied their inhabitants with various public services that are not furnished free of charge in America. Per square mile, the richest country in the world, during the 1980s, was the Republic of Nauru, a coral island of only eight square miles, in the western Pacific Ocean. Eight thousand people live there, and during the 1980s their per capita income exceeded $20,000. Their wealth came from the exporting of phosphate deposits—which may soon be exhausted.

makes it uncertain whether the economy of the West will continue to grow.

Here is a short list of some of the ways in which governments, over the centuries, have done harm to economic systems.

1. **Excessive taxation.** When taxes on commerce, real property, and (in recent times) personal and corporate incomes become too heavy, the following succession of unhappy events often occurs:

    a. Individuals and firms cannot save enough money out of current income to provide for replacing their capital goods (which necessarily wear out gradually) or for new capital investments intended to increase production.

    b. When there is little or no new investment in capital goods, and worn-out capital goods are not replaced, production of material goods and services diminishes.

    c. When the supply of goods diminishes, prices go up and people's wants are not adequately satisfied.

    d. Then, perhaps, (in Roman times or in our age) the government, to satisfy public demands, tries to provide for people's wants by furnishing food and other goods to the poor at low prices or free. To do this, taxes must be raised. When taxes are increased, there is still less saving of capital. The economy continues to spiral downward, perhaps toward national bankruptcy.

2. **Inflation, or debasement of the currency.** When a government does not properly control the supply of money, prices rise rapidly, investment is discouraged, the rate of interest increases until borrowing becomes very costly, and most people suffer economically. This process, generally called inflation, will be discussed more fully in Chapter 13.

    From ancient times, governments have been tempted to debase the coinage or (in the modern age) to print paper money without adequate backing or (in the twentieth century) to "create" money through a central banking system. Such measures temporarily give a government sufficient money to spend, but within a short time such inflationary policies do immense damage to an economy. And sooner or later those policies do mischief to the government itself. Deliberate inflation by governmental policy sometimes occurs when governments dare not increase taxes.

3. **Excessive public expenditure**—on wars of conquest, on magnificent public works (as in ancient Athens), on impractical political and economic schemes, on huge **bureaucracies** (systems of public employees). When much of a nation's productivity is consumed by such grand designs, the means of production tend to lack capital. Then consumers must get along with fewer goods—even, sometimes, to the point of starvation. In order to pay for such expenditures, commonly governments resort either to excessive taxation or to inflation of the medium of exchange.

4. **Excessive regulation and direction of the economy.** A government can kill an economy—or at least make it very sick—by seeming kindness. A host of inspectors, tax collectors, and governmental regulators can greatly discourage entrepreneurs (or management), capital investment, and the whole process of economic production. In a command economy, central decision-making for the whole economy can result in gigantic blunders, causing suffering by consumers worse than any consequences of recessions and depressions in a market economy.

5. **Political plundering of the economy.** Bad governments—controlled by malevolent dictators, selfish or fanatical factions, or simply by politicians more interested in their own advantage than in the public good—frequently use their political power to rob the economy. This plundering may be done by demanding bribe money from producers, by putting the government's friends and supporters into well-paid posts

in business and industry, by demanding a share for the government in every economic enterprise, or through the simple scheme of using police and troops to confiscate the property of individuals or classes unpopular with the government.

Many instances of such plundering occur in the "emergent nations" of twentieth-century Africa or the unstable political systems of certain Latin American states. The grim practical result of such misgovernment is that people with property tend to invest their capital abroad—in Switzerland or the United States, perhaps—or to convert it into gold that they conceal underground. This means that productivity is low and poverty is taken for granted in such a land.

Several other ways might be described in which incompetent or unscrupulous governments damage economic structures and diminish the wealth of nations. Government may be a protector of the economy, but also government may foolishly lay waste its own economic foundation. *It is not only totalist governments that sometimes try to ignore or defy the laws of economics.*

Discuss

21. Suppose that the government of some American state should impose a tax of fifty percent upon all profits by business corporations. What would tend to happen to businesses in that state? If such a tax were in effect for five years, by the end of the fifth year would the state government have plenty of money to meet public needs?

22. Suppose some African government decrees that no citizen will be permitted to inherit real or personal property. The property held by any man or woman at the time of death will pass to the state, to be used for public purposes. Does this provision seem fair? Why or why not? Does it seem economically sound—that is, would it have good economic consequences or unfortunate consequences? Explain your answer.

23. Suppose that there should be introduced in Congress a bill intended to improve conditions in hospitals. This piece of legislation provides that all increases of hospital charges must be approved by a federal board; that all hospitals must submit complete written reports, weekly, in quadruplicate, to a Wash-

ington office; that all hospital personnel must report weekly for medical examinations; that federal inspectors are authorized to close any hospital, on one week's notice, that they find unsatisfactory; that physicians and surgeons working in hospitals may be arrested and brought to trial if any three patients enter serious complaints against them. Would such regulations tend to improve hospital services in the United States?

Despite many ruinous economic mistakes made by twentieth-century governments, in nearly every country the majority of the population tend to look to the central political authority for economic help in time of emergency—or perhaps for economic help in ordinary circumstances. It needs to be remembered that (except in communist or socialist states) the government does not itself produce food, clothing, and shelter. Nor can any government make a nation prosperous merely by printing plenty of paper money or borrowing huge sums through a central bank. Economic production is something quite different from force. If we want milk delivered daily to our door, we do not telephone the police station; we telephone the local dairy. It seems unwise to expect government to perform economic functions for which sound and free government never was designed.

CHAPTER 11

Successes and Difficulties
in the Market Economy

AMERICA
The World's Breadbasket

PEOPLE'S CHOICE AWARD
FRIDAY
SATURDAY
SUNDAY
MONDAY
TUESDAY
WEDNESDAY

THE FAIR

Chapter 11
Successes and Difficulties in the Market Economy

- What the Market Economy Has Achieved
- Opportunity Costs and Comparative Prices
- Criticisms of the Market Economy
- Recessions, Depressions, and Unemployment
- Is a Market Economy Unjust?
- The Economics and Politics of Envy

What the Market Economy Has Achieved

No economic system ever has satisfied everybody. Yet for centuries the economy of a civilization has continued to function with little change and little or no increase of prosperity—and, nevertheless, with little protest against the economic system. So it was, most of the time, in ancient Egypt, or during the Roman domination of the cultures of three continents, or during the Middle Ages of Europe.

Today, however, there occurs frequent and widespread complaint about the faults of the market economy. Modern Western civilization doubtless has many defects; every civilization in every age has suffered from defects, caused by human nature, though not the same defects. But it is somewhat odd that a good many people should complain about the *economy* of modern civilization.

For *production of goods is far greater in present-day countries with market economies than production ever has been in any civilization of the past or in any country with a command economy today.* In the economically developed countries of our century—especially those with competition and private enterprise—the great majority of people obtain adequate food, shelter, clothing, and medical services.

It was otherwise in nearly all cultures of the past. Even in the more prosperous periods of earlier civilizations, most people were not really well fed or clothed or lodged or otherwise provided for economically—not by present American standards of comfort and health.

Take a case in England during the thirteenth century, nearly seven hundred years ago. That was a time of high achievements in architecture, sculpture, and philosophy. In that thirteenth century, some people lived in splendor (though not, by our standards, in comfort): nobles, bishops and abbots, and some merchants. But the average man and woman lived in what we would consider poverty.

In the year 1293, there died an English farmer named Reginald Labbe. A copy of his last will and testament still exists. Labbe's farm was small, yet probably Labbe was better off than most of his neighbors. He did not own the land he cultivated, but leased it. (In England, until very recently, farmers were not ordinarily landowners, but rented their land.)

At Labbe's death, his goods were found to be worth thirty-three shillings and eight pence. That sum, in British money today, would be only three dollars and fifty cents, but English coins were worth much more in purchasing power during the thirteenth century than they are today. Here is a list of the goods Labbe possessed when he died:

- one cow and one calf
- two sheep and three lambs
- three hens
- a bushel and a half of wheat
- a seam of barley (a seam is a sack of eight and a half bushels)
- a seam and a half of fodder for cattle
- a seam of mixed grain
- clothes, consisting of a hood, a tunic, and a tabard (a kind of coat)
- a bolster (pillow)
- a rug (blanket)
- two sheets
- a tripod or trivet (for cooking food)

He had no ready money. There was no furniture in Labbe's cottage, and apparently he owned no tools. (Probably the tools he used were owned by his landlord.)

One penny was paid for digging Labbe's grave, twopence for tolling the church bell at his funeral, sixpence for making his will, and eightpence for "proving" the will (court fees). Refreshments for the mourners (including the pallbearers) cost eight shillings and sixpence. (The mourners were provided with bread, cheese, and beer.) The clerk who drew up this account for the executors of the will was paid threepence. Altogether, the expenses for the will and the funeral used up a third of Labbe's estate.

If we compare Labbe's goods with the numerous goods left by nearly any small farmer in America today, we get some idea of the great difference between the poverty of most people in previous periods of history and the prosperity of most people in a developed economy today.

This success of today's market economy has several causes—some of them political, some of them bound up with a nation's history, some of them economic. Here we have space only to list some of the economic causes.

Why the Market Economy Is Productive

1. It permits and encourages entrepreneurs to commence or expand industry and commerce.
2. It is based on competition, which lowers prices and improves quality.
3. It makes possible private saving and the acquiring of private property.
4. It offers personal rewards for hard and intelligent work.
5. It functions without deadening control by a central political bureaucracy.
6. It encourages inventions and the development of new technology.

The United States, Japan, West Germany, Canada, Switzerland, Taiwan, The Netherlands, Singapore, and Belgium are some conspicuous examples of developed countries with successful market economies. Other prosperous countries have **"mixed" economies,** partly based on the market but partly directed by political authority: Britain, Sweden, and Italy, in one degree or another, are examples of "mixed" economies.

In our time, no country whose economy is thoroughly directed by central political authority is nearly so prosperous as countries possessing market economies (nor so prosperous as countries having mixed economies in which the market element remains fairly strong, such as Sweden).

Economic success is not the only standard by which a civilization may be judged. Some countries or regions that are economically poor nevertheless may be pleasant places to live, with a healthy culture. But so far as economic productivity goes, *nations with market economies clearly achieve more than do nations with other economic systems.*

Discuss   1. From your knowledge of the history of the twentieth century, can you suggest reasons why the following countries, which formerly had market economies, now have command economies? Poland, Hungary, East Germany, Algeria, Cuba.

2. Would you prefer to live in a quiet, old-fashioned town situated in a handsome countryside, but where your income would be relatively low; or in a bustling, ugly city with a high crime rate, but where your income would be relatively high? Give your reasons.

Perhaps the best way to judge a country's economic prosperity is by the relationship of prices to wages. If people have to work very hard to buy necessary things and harder still to buy some desirable goods that are not necessities—why, such people are poor. A country where such unhappy relationships between prices and wages prevail either is economically inefficient, or else the rulers of such a country keep the fruits of production in the hands of the central government.

Note the chart "What's the Difference?" (page 254). It compares the prices of certain goods in five large cities of different countries. According to the chart, if we measure prices in terms of the minutes of work time required for earning enough wages to buy what one wants, the market economy of the United States generally offers the lowest prices. In America, this chart shows, a weekly basket of groceries costs a good deal less in terms of work than would a comparable basket in Russia, England, France, or West Germany. The Moscow basket, indeed, costs nearly four times as much as the Washington basket.

Of the countries mentioned on the chart, the United States and West Germany have predominantly market economies. Britain, and to a lesser extent France, are mixed economies in which the political state directs the economy to some degree; in Britain, some of the means of production are owned by the state. The Soviet Union has a huge command economy.

Of the five cities, Washington is the capital of the most "capital- istic" nation. In this city, the chart shows, most items have lower prices in terms of work time than do comparable items in any of the other four cities. (It should be understood that this chart measures prices in terms of the number of minutes, hours, or days required to earn enough wages to buy the desired goods listed on the chart—not in dollars, pounds, francs, marks, or rubles. This is because some governments claim for their unit of currency a value that it does not really possess in international exchange.)

Discuss   3. Some goods appear to be cheaper in Moscow than in Washington. Explain why in the Soviet Union these things are relatively cheap, if measured in work time.

4. Do you notice any items on the list that seem remarkably costly in Washington, as compared with other cities? If so, how may we account for these high prices?

5. The Soviet Union has so much petroleum within its boundaries that the Soviet empire does not need to import oil. Yet in Moscow the price of gasoline is nearly ten times the price in Washington. What possible explanations exist for this startling difference?

What's the Difference?

Commodity	Washington	Moscow	Munich	Paris	London
Food and Beverages					
Unit of measurement: 1 kilogram/2.2 pounds unless otherwise noted					
White bread, unwrapped	6	17	25	20	11
Corn flakes	21	NA	45	54	24
Rice, polished, white	6	49	10	30	16
Chicken, fresh or frozen	18	189	17	31	20
Hamburger meat, beef	30	72	60	75	38
Steak, sirloin	83	195	93	109	123
Sausages, frankfurters	30	145	74	75	70
Cod, frozen	76	33	77	124	80
Tuna	36	183	40	129	50
Potatoes	9	11	5	9	3
Carrots	10	11	5	5	9
Beans, packaged or frozen	9	84	17	29	17
Oranges	10	(112)	9	15	12
Apples, eating	18	28	16	16	14
Ice cream, vanilla, qt.	13	107	17	21	11
Milk, fresh, qt.	4	20	6	8	6
Eggs, 10, cheapest	5	50	9	17	10
Cheese, fresh, Gouda-type	81	167	53	59	45
Sugar, white, granulated	6	52	8	11	8
Butter	40	195	37	63	38
Tea, 100 g	12	42	19	20	6
Orange juice, qt.	7	151	7	18	9
Cola, qt.	7	58	7	21	5
Transportation					
Car, medium (months)	9	84	12	15	15
Gasoline, regular, 10 1/2.5 gal.	17	167	47	66	64
Bicycle, men's, cheapest (hours)	17	49	17	29	23
Taxi fare, 3 km/2 mi.	25	34	29	20	31
Bus fare, 3 km/2 mi.	7	3	7	5	9
Clothing					
Jeans (hours)	4	56	7	10	5
T-shirt, cotton, white	28	184	70	55	56
Panty hose, one pair	16	279	16	17	14
Men's shoes, black, office (hours)	6	37	11	8	6
Men's office suit, 2-piece, dacron (hours)	18	118	33	34	16
Household Items and Services					
Refrigerator, small, 120-liter (hours)	44	102	31	30	30
Washing machine, automatic cycle (hours)	46	177	49	61	52
Television, color, 61 cm (hours)	30	669	54	106	75
Rent, monthly, 50 sq. m, unfurnished, subsidized apartment (hours)	55	11	24	15	26
Telephone, monthly rent	20	139	126	287	95
Miscellaneous					
Toothpaste, 75 g	6	22	12	16	7
Aspirin, 100, cheapest	7	33	75	44	9
Deodorant, spray can, 200 ml	18	139	11	39	17
Baby-sitter, per hour, excluding fare	44	279	47	37	43
Haircut, men's, dry, no extras	62	34	75	92	61
Suburban movie, best seat	40	28	42	48	52

NA denotes a product not generally available. Parentheses denote a known price for a product not found at the time of the survey.

Opportunity Costs and Comparative Prices

This chart "What's the Difference?" suggests another aspect of the prices we pay for goods, and the way those prices tend to differ in market economies and command economies.

We discussed opportunity cost in connection with our analysis of the market in chapter 5. There we pointed out that when we buy one thing, usually we have to refrain from buying something else that we might like. Or if we choose one gainful occupation, usually we have to forego, or renounce, some other gainful occupation that we might follow. Economists call the second-choice good, which is given up for the sake of the first-choice good, the *alternative foregone.* This choice of alternatives involves costs: the costs of abandoning one opportunity for the sake of a different opportunity.

This concept of opportunity cost may be applied to the work time price of goods listed in the chart "What's the Difference?" In order to acquire some of the goods listed, buyers must make choices: they must sacrifice, or give up, other goods that they want. Economists have a formal phrase that defines this opportunity cost: "cost as a renunciation of alternative utilities." The opportunity to acquire one thing, that is, compels us to renounce (give up or postpone) the opportunity to acquire some different thing which would have utility (usefulness) for us.

If we apply this concept to the chart, we find that opportunity costs in Moscow generally are high, if compared with opportunity costs in Washington. Even when work time prices are about the same in those two cities, the real cost of goods generally is higher in Moscow, and often much higher. For real cost, remember, is accounting cost (money price) plus opportunity cost.

Suppose, for instance, that Ivan Rostov, in Moscow, wishes to acquire a new refrigerator. It would cost him 102 hours of his work time to pay the price fixed by state authorities. (In Russia, during 1986, the average hourly take-home pay was $1.59, expressed in dollars, so the refrigerator would cost him, in rubles, the equivalent of $162.18.) Russian wages considered, that would be a large purchase. To get the refrigerator, Ivan might have to postpone his intended purchase of a new suit, which would cost him 118 hours of work time (or about 187.62). The opportunity cost of the refrigerator would be rather high for Ivan.

Now suppose that Harry Thomson, in Washington, wants a new refrigerator and a new suit. The refrigerator would cost him 44 hours of his work time; the suit, 25 hours. (American take-home pay averaging $6.77 per hour in 1986, the price of the refrigerator would be about $297.88; of the suit, $121.86, approximately.)

The Moscow refrigerator would cost, in cash, somewhat less than the Washington refrigerator; the Moscow suit would cost a trifle more than the Washington suit—if we think only in terms of money prices. But in terms of how much work the buyer would have to exchange for the desired goods, the prices of both would be far higher in Moscow.

And, balancing American wages against Russian wages, opportunity costs would be far higher for Ivan than for Harry, in these and other cases. That is, Ivan would have to renounce opportunities to obtain various other goods in order to make his purchase of refrigerator or suit, while Harry would not find it necessary, probably, to give up so many other things in order to find the money for refrigerator and suit.

Harry would be paying only thirty minutes of his work time for a kilo of ground beef, for instance, while Ivan would have to pay seventy-two minutes of his work time for the same quantity of meat; Ivan would also have to pay more than Harry for sugar, butter, cheese, eggs, apples, tea, and most other staples of diet—not to mention a luxury such as color television.

Thus, in terms of money price, for some goods Ivan would be paying about the same sum as Harry. But in terms of work price, Ivan would be paying far more than would Harry for practically everything except fuel gas, electricity, fish, bus fare, and haircuts.

And in terms of opportunity cost, Ivan would enjoy far fewer options than would Harry. To gain one good, Ivan would have to resign himself to postponing some other want. Harry presumably would be compelled to renounce, temporarily, only such a relatively costly want as a new car, requiring months of work time—and, with loans readily available for new cars in Washington, even that cost might occasion Harry no painful postponement.

Should Ivan want a television set, he would have to devote all his earnings over a period of four months (supposing a forty-hour work week) to that one purchase. That would be a very high opportunity cost, relatively or absolutely, requiring much abstinence from alternative wants such as hearty meals. It would take Ivan more than nine times as long as it would Harry to buy a small car: another high opportunity cost.

Discuss

6. Do these comparisons of five cities seem fair to you? Why or why not? Can you name some items on the chart that reflect Washington tastes more than the tastes of the other cities? If possible, relate your answer to the concept of opportunity costs.

7. Do industrial and commercial firms have to take opportunity costs into account? Explain your answer.

In terms of opportunity costs, it appears, the market economy—in Washington particularly, but in other countries also—distinctly offers more freedom of choice than do existing forms of the command economy. For whether or not the money price is about the same in various countries, the real cost (including the opportunity cost) today usually is lower in countries with a market economy. That is because market economies today produce more abundant goods and services than do command economies.

Is the market economy just? Why, *perfect justice never has been attained in any society*. But the market economy ordinarily provides just economic rewards for intelligent work. The same cannot be said, in most instances, of the commmand economy. In a market economy, the typical citizen is far more free to choose; he has larger opportunities than does the citizen in a command economy.

Criticisms of the Market Economy

This apparent success of market economies, as contrasted with command and mixed economies, does not signify that there are no economic difficulties in the United States, Canada, Western Europe, and other countries and regions with competitive economic systems. Nor does this success persuade everybody living in a market economy country to rest content with what he has. On the contrary, there runs on in free market lands an almost endless debate about the health of the economy. (Such frank discussion ordinarily is discouraged in countries with command economies.) In today's world, market economies often are criticized severely on three grounds.

The first of these criticisms is a complaint about **business fluctuations**. This term means that periods of high prosperity seem to be followed by periods of decreased economic activity and considerable unemployment. *Recessions* and *depressions*, periods of "slump," put out of work many who were employed during a preceding period of full production. Such downward fluctuations of the economy cause public suffering and discontent. Is this fluctuation an inevitable fault of a market economy?

The second of these grounds for criticism of the market economy is inflation of money and prices—that is, "too much money chasing too few goods." During inflationary periods, prices rise more rapidly than does purchasing power. People's savings, as a result, lose much of their value. By the late 1970s, inflation of prices became the chief economic problem of the United States and of many other countries. Was it the greed of industrialists and merchants that caused the inflation?

The third principal charge against a market economy has been that a competitive economic system is hard and greedy and unjust. Sometimes there is bound up with this argument a belief that a competitive economy produces an ugly and dreary society.

In these charges there is some substance—and also some exaggeration. First of all, it needs to be pointed out that *recessions and depressions occur in command economies as well as in market econo-mies, though the people who run command economies try to conceal economic fluctuations.* As for inflation, that too occurs in both command and market economies; the subject of inflation will be discussed systematically in Chapter 13. The modern industrial system indeed has its hard and ugly aspects—in command economies no less than in market economies. In short, it is not the market economy alone that suffers from certain grave faults.

Discuss

8. From what you know of history, can you suggest any era more productive economically than the twentieth century?

9. During the 1960s and early 1970s, hundreds of thousands of young people—sometimes called "flower children" or "hippies"—tried to withdraw from the market economy and from ordinary employment, hoping to lead a simpler life, to "drop out" of the usual processes of production and consumption. How did they expect to provide for their essential economic needs? Can you suggest practical alternatives to holding a regular job in industry or business?

To assess charges against the market economy, we need to take up the large topic of business fluctuations. Ever since the Great Depression that commenced in 1929, people have been arguing about the causes of sudden changes in the economy's health—the changes that we call *business cycles* or business fluctuations.

Recessions, Depressions, and Unemployment

To understand business cycles, we need to remember something about the laws of supply and demand. In any market economy, frequent changes in supply occur, and also frequent changes in demand. Small adjustments go on all the time in any market economy, tending to balance out supply with demand.

This means that in one month, say, the business of a particular firm or industry may be especially good. In some other month, the same firm's or industry's business may be remarkably poor. Every entrepreneur or manager, expecting such fluctuations to happen from time to time, tries to prepare for them.[1]

As an example, take the management of a department store. During several weeks before Christmas, demand for goods increases sharply, because people are buying presents. Every store manager, months earlier, orders more goods from his suppliers, anticipating this Christmas-season demand. And during the month of December, he hires a good many temporary clerks and warehouse personnel, because he will need more labor during the "rush season." Such preparations are part of the department store's normal business cycle.

About the middle of summer, on the other hand, demand falls off at most shops and merchandising centers. People are away from home on vacation, or do not go shopping because of the heat. Therefore, store managers try to reduce their supply of goods by holding sales at reduced prices—perhaps "sidewalk sales" outdoors. They may lay off some of their clerks during the hottest weeks, there being few customers for the clerks to serve. This too is part of the normal and anticipated cycle of business for department stores. There is nothing strange or unjust about it.

So it goes, most years, with every industry, commercial undertaking, or other form of economic enterprise. Taking such fluctuations pretty much for granted, manufacturers, farmers, and service-industry people plan their annual operations accordingly. In agriculture, for instance, employment tends to be seasonal: that is, farmers employ more help in summer than in winter, because of the cycle of nature. Even in a totalist economy, there is no way to abolish such business fluctuations.

Yet sometimes bigger fluctuations occur in the market, affecting a great many firms and industries: changes on a national or an international scale, perhaps. Sometimes demand grows great; supply

---

1. **Fluctuations:** irregular changes, like water rising and falling; as a term of economics, the rising and falling of demand or supply; or the fluctuations of business tendencies.

does not respond promptly to demand; so prices rise. Then people invest more capital in production, because good returns can be made by producing more goods. The demand for labor increases as a result, and so everyone who wishes to work can find employment. Such a period is called a *boom*.

But after a short business boom or a prolonged one, something quite different may come. Supply outruns demand and prices fall, causing producers to reduce their output and lay off some employees. Consumers have less money to spend, and nationally or internationally, business falls off. Such a period is called a **recession.**

When a recession comes, one of two events may follow. If recovery from a recession goes well, business will get rid of excess supply. Prices may be stabilized, and production may increase once more. Demand may then increase, and business may return to normal conditions—perhaps moving on toward another boom.

But the other event, far less pleasant, may happen. The recession may grow worse. More and more people may fall out of work. Demand then may continue to shrink. This continued decline in business may become a *depression,* a widespread and serious blow to the economy. If that occurs, many people will be unemployed for a long time, and business may be able to recover only slowly.

There is no general agreement about what causes any particular depression. The cause sometimes may be ill-guided monetary policies on the part of government or of the central banking system. Or sometimes the cause may be excessive speculation on the stock market and excessive buying on credit—that is, trying to satisfy too many wants all at once. Or a widespread depression may result from the slackening of demand because of the ending of a war or the diminishing of some other huge source of demand. Other causes of depressions might be listed. Sometimes these causes combine and coincide to bring about a major depression.

These business fluctuations—booms, recessions, depressions, business recoveries—economists call the *business cycle.* Of course, there are frequent ups and downs in the huge markets of industrial

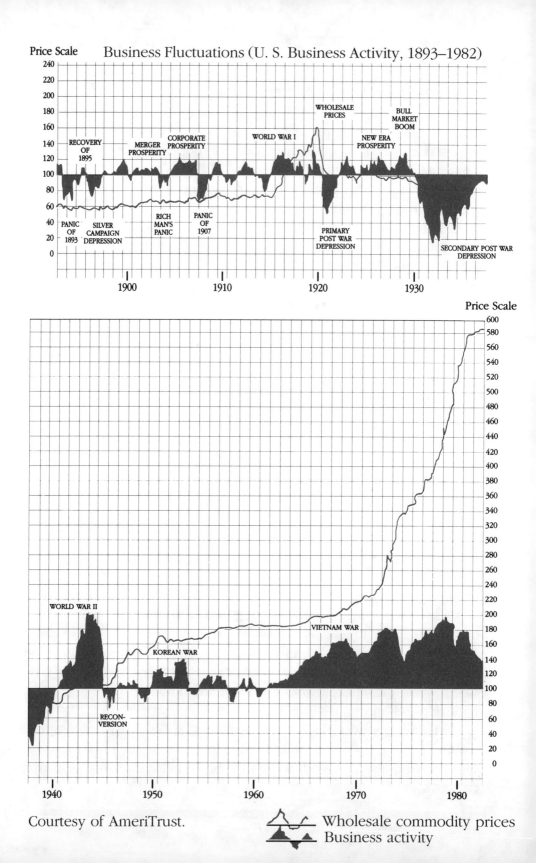

Business Fluctuations (U. S. Business Activity, 1893–1982)

Price Scale

240
220
200
180
160
140
120
100
80
60
40
20
0

RECOVERY OF 1895

MERGER PROSPERITY

CORPORATE PROSPERITY

WORLD WAR I

WHOLESALE PRICES

NEW ERA PROSPERITY

BULL MARKET BOOM

PANIC OF 1893

SILVER CAMPAIGN DEPRESSION

RICH MAN'S PANIC

PANIC OF 1907

PRIMARY POST WAR DEPRESSION

SECONDARY POST WAR DEPRESSION

1900   1910   1920   1930

Price Scale

600
580
560
540
520
500
480
460
440
420
400
380
360
340
320
300
280
260
240
220
200
180
160
140
120
100
80
60
40
20
0

WORLD WAR II

KOREAN WAR

VIETNAM WAR

RECON-VERSION

1940   1950   1960   1970   1980

Courtesy of AmeriTrust.

Wholesale commodity prices
Business activity

countries, but it would be a mistake to think of these fluctuations as a series of inevitable big booms followed by inevitable big slumps. Rather, these changes are necessary (if somewhat painful) adjustments in the working of the market. And to some extent the unfortunate changes can be foreseen and averted.

The more we learn about business fluctuations, the better we are able to prevent them from becoming extreme. Experts in macroeconomics may note important alterations in the national or the international economy as soon as those changes begin. Then steps may be taken to modify the dangerous trend. National governments may adopt fiscal measures calculated to increase or decrease spending. Central banking systems (or, in the United States, the Federal Reserve System) may increase or decrease the volume of their loans, so as to encourage or discourage the increase of business nationally. Businesses, labor unions, and consumers' organizations also can work to avoid extravagant booms or sudden recessions. But experts in macroeconomics, being human, now and again make mistakes. They do not possess perfect knowledge of all economic trends and possibilities, and they cannot safely be expected to foresee all large economic changes and then take steps to modify dangerous trends.

One of the principal economic problems with business cycles is to discourage "forced draft" increase of incomes and business activity, for too sudden economic growth tends to result in a temporary boom and then in a recession.[2] In recent decades, an increase in per capita incomes at the rate of 5 or 6 percent annually has been a sign of a boom that must end in a severe recession. Public measures can be taken to discourage such rapid increase of incomes, but often measures of restraint are unpopular, because many people relish the apparent increase of their personal prosperity and are unaware that recessions, with reduction of personal incomes, result from booms.

In the preceding paragraphs, we have been discussing fluctua-

---

2. **Forced draft:** increased heat or pressure by a strong draft of air, as air may be forced into a furnace to raise the temperature sharply; as a term of economics, pressures and plans to increase economic activity swiftly.

tions in developed market economies. Simple subsistence economies rarely suffer from recessions or depressions on any large scale, but they do suffer from droughts, floods, plagues, and famines, which bring bigger economic fluctuations than do the relatively mild business cycles of an industrial economy. Developed countries have means for keeping to a minimum the evil consequences of natural disasters, but the economic reserves of simple agricultural economies often are insufficient to contend with such disasters. Perhaps business fluctuations are part of the price that technological societies must pay for their escape from the common poverty of subsistence societies.

The United States economy has known several eras of expanding prosperity and several periods of recession or depression. (See page 262.) Four big depressions have occurred—beginning in 1815, 1837, 1873, and 1929. Recessions, less severe, came in 1847, 1857, 1883, and 1907. After the beginning of the Second World War, there came a fairly long period of national prosperity, extending from the middle 'Forties until 1974, although slight recessions were felt in 1949, 1955, 1958, 1961, and 1970. From 1974 to 1980, the American economy was in trouble, with accelerating inflation of prices and no real increase in production of goods. (Inflation began to diminish in 1981.) A recession occurred in 1980–81, followed by a gradual recovery.

Depressions and recessions are times of reduced employment, reduced production, reduced consumption. In the developed countries, most people continue to be employed during recessions or depressions, although some of them for a reduced number of hours per week. People who are totally unemployed usually obtain some form of unemployment compensation or public assistance in every major industrial country. Some firms and investors, and even banks, fall bankrupt. Many people have to postpone satisfaction of their more costly wants for months or even for years.

Yet recessions and depressions in developed countries are not times of starvation and despair. Many economists argue that some such falling off of business is necessary from time to time, because depressions and recessions "weed out" inefficient producers, stimulate competition, use up accumulated stocks of goods, and reduce prices. *If everybody were always prosperous, year in and year out, there would exist small incentive to efficiency or thrift, and then presumably there would arrive, in the long run, a collapse of the economic structure bigger than any depression has been.*

Certainly, depressions and recessions are not arranged by "somebody up there." Business people and politicians dread the approach of a recession, which must cause them loss of income and perhaps loss of office.

Inflation of the currency is bound up with many booms and depressions, but the complex subject of inflation is discussed later, in chapter 13. Here we can say that price inflation certainly is a grave failing of the market economy, as it is of the command economy. But the causes of such inflation ordinarily are political, rather than economic. It is not a free-market economy, based upon competition, which is the primary source of inflationary dangers.

Discuss   10. All industrialized countries today have systems of unemployment compensation. If the unemployment compensation should be nearly as much money as a worker would have earned when employed for wages, can you see any economic problem in such generosity?

11. Consult the chart "Business Fluctuations," on page 262. What relationship do you notice between wars and the amount of business activity? What might cause this connection?

12. What happened to prices during the Great Depression, 1929–40?

13. What happened to prices in the years 1946–75?

14. If a man or a woman loses a regular job during an economic recession, does the unemployed person have any alternative to sitting at home and living on unemployment compensation? What else might such a newly unemployed person do?

Is a Market Economy Unjust?

Some critics of a market economy will concede that a competitive economic system may be efficiently productive. They may recognize that business fluctuations and inflationary dangers occur also in mixed economies and command economies. But the basic trouble with a market economy, these critics go on to remark, is this: such an economy is dominated by selfishness and greed. "Production for profit, not for use," is the purpose of a market economy, these critics insist. And often they argue that a market economy results in a dreary and ugly society.

Certainly much selfishness and greed may be found in countries with market economies. But those vices exist in equal strength in countries with mixed economies and with command economies.

Avarice and gluttony are two of the Seven Deadly Sins that medieval preachers denounced. These two terrible faults—wanting too much and consuming too much—have to be dealt with in every society, in every age, in every sort of economy. These human failings seem strongest today in totalist states where religion is forbidden or sneered at and where state propaganda declares that life is simply for production and consumption.

Nevertheless, the American economy and other free-market economies strongly encourage everybody to "put money in thy purse; and yet again, put money in thy purse"—to borrow a phrase from William Shakespeare. Alexis de Tocqueville, the young Frenchman who was the shrewdest foreign observer of American character, perceived this hard truth a century and a half ago. As he wrote in his *Democracy in America*—

> A native of the United States clings to this world's goods as if he were certain never to die; and he is so hasty in grasping at all within his reach that one would suppose he was constantly afraid of not living long enough to enjoy them. He clutches everything, he holds nothing fast, but soon loosens his grasp to pursue fresh gratifications.

In the industrially developed nations of our time, a great many people think that they will be happy if only they obtain plenty of goods and services. Christians know that this is not true, however. The Bible teaches that happiness comes from being in God's will.

Competition in the market tends to lead people toward desire for whatever can be bought and sold. "Getting and spending, we lay waste our powers," as the poet William Wordsworth put it. Prophets and poets tell us that human life is for more than getting and spending.

Yet if the appetite for goods is too strong sometimes in free-market economies, it is stronger still within socialist countries. And when economic competition is replaced by political competition, the penalty for failure is something worse than bankruptcy. In totalist states, those who fail in political competition face imprisonment or death. So it has been in the Soviet Union, Communist China, Vietnam, Cambodia, Ethiopia, Cuba, and the "captive nations" of Eastern Europe.[3]

Does the market economy produce for profit rather than for use—the socialist charge against capitalism and economic competition?

Certainly, all producers and sellers in any market hope to gain something personally. The farmer hopes to be paid decently for his crop; the factory worker seeks a good wage for his labor; the professional man aspires to a good living; the entrepreneur hopes for a tolerable return upon his investment; the merchant tries to sell his goods for more than he paid for them.

There is nothing dishonest about such hopes. It is not necessarily greedy to try to better oneself economically. The famous profit motive is not evil, unless it is carried to excess. The desire to gain something, in essence, is merely the desire to survive. Without that powerful natural desire, none of us would be alive on this earth.

Who would produce for loss? In a market economy, the very people who produce for profit are the people who produce for use.

No farmer means to grow crops that nobody wants. No factory operative fancies that he could get paid for turning out useless objects. No captain of industry manufactures odd trinkets for which no demand

---

3. The **captive nations** dominated by the Soviet Union ever since World War II are Poland, Czechoslovakia, Rumania, Bulgaria, Hungary, East Germany, Lithuania, Latvia, and Estonia. Yugoslavia and Albania have had Communist governments since the Second World War but do not obey Russian commands. Some other countries are dominated by the USSR but are not usually listed among the captive nations—in some cases because they were not conquered by Russian troops, in other cases because resistance to Russian power continues within their frontiers. These latter states with Russian garrisons or "military advisors" include Cuba, Ethiopia, Mozambique, Angola, Afghanistan, and Nicaragua. The Chinese claim that Mongolia is held captive by Soviet Russia.

exists. No doctor or lawyer fritters away his office hours without helping patients or clients. No shopkeeper deliberately stocks goods that customers would reject. The more useful a thing is, the more likely it is to make a decent profit for the person who manufactures it or sells it.

In a market economy especially, all production is intended for somebody's use. Indeed, it may be a fault of the market that economic competition has small regard for the beautiful or the ornamental. Things that have no commercial or practical application are not much in demand in the marketplace of modern times.

In a free market, then, "production for use" and "production for profit" really amount to the same impulse and process. The competitive economy may turn out some silly things—but only if there is a consumer demand for those particular silly things. In a command economy, consumer preferences tend to be ignored. Shoddy goods often are produced in a command economy—but through bureaucratic stupidity. (More of this in the next chapter.) At least as many useless objects are turned out in a command economy as in a market economy.

Discuss

15. If every producer took no thought for his own advantage, but produced simply for the use of other people, do you think production would increase or decrease? Do you know of any social experiments in America or elsewhere at various times in history which were attempts to abolish "production for profit"?

16. If all of us did nothing but pursue our own private advantage in economic life and other fields, what probably would happen to society? Suggest in detail, if you can, some of the consequences.

17. Marxists teach **dialectical materialism**—the doctrine that the physical world about us is the only form of existence, and that all of humanity's objects in life are material purposes. Tocqueville wrote that materialism never can triumph totally in the United States, so long as Americans remain attached to religious belief. Can you suggest ways in which Americans' religious convictions tend to encourage American political and economic freedom?

The Economics and Politics of Envy

Earlier we mentioned that avarice and gluttony cause trouble in the market economy—as in all other economies. A third vice threatening the market economy in recent years is another of the "Deadly Sins"— envy. For an example of how envy damages a market economy, we turn to the mild and recent difficulties of the kingdom of The Netherlands.

One of the more prosperous countries of Europe is The Netherlands, often called Holland. Ever since the Middle Ages, the Dutch people have been successful at commerce, banking, transportation, and agriculture. They are called thrifty and cautious. Until the Second World War, The Netherlands held large territories overseas in the East and West Indies.

Per capita income in The Netherlands is double per capita income in Britain, though less than that of Switzerland.[4] The Dutch economy is a market economy, basically; yet there are features of governmental direction and intervention. The Netherlands government takes about 70 percent of the national income through heavy taxation and social security payments.

For after World War II, the Social Democratic party of Holland, together with other political groups, established an elaborate "welfare state" in the country. This has cost a great deal of money—and trouble for the economy.

By 1982, the financial condition of The Netherlands had become alarming. About 11 percent of the working people were unemployed, and the deficit in the government's budget stood at 11 percent of the national income. "Social benefits" to the unemployed, the disabled, the elderly, students, and other groups of "underprivileged" had become so lavish that the government did not know what way to turn for the

---

4. The figure called **per capita income** (that is, income per head of population) is calculated by taking the total income of a nation (or a state or some other unit) and dividing that amount by the total number of people in that nation (or other unit). Thus, if a country had one million inhabitants and a national income of one billion dollars, the per capita income would be one thousand dollars.

necessary money. Governmental direction of many forms of economic, social, and educational activity had been extended so far that the country seemed struggling through a forest of paper work. The price of wages had gone sky-high by any previous standard or even by comparison with the current wage levels of most of the rest of Europe. Governmental control of rents and governmental intervention in housing had brought about a painful scarcity of housing. To the surprise of many Dutch people, a large black market in money had commenced to flourish—because the state demand for equality, and its costs, had stopped the functioning of the regular markets.

Presently, all parties came to agree that in seeking "social justice"—that is, economic equality—the architects of the Dutch welfare state had gone much too far. Governmental expenditures must be reduced, as the first reform. Otherwise, the economy might be wrecked. Indeed, it had come to appear that Dutch society itself might fall apart unless the welfare state should be restrained.

Netherlands industry had begun to find it difficult to secure the necessary capital for development or retooling: taxation was taking so much of the gross national product that it had become hard, very hard, for the Dutch to save and invest.

Still more discouraging, incentives to work had diminished. For a Dutch statute of the welfare state prescribed that no unemployed person would receive unemployment compensation less than the amount earned by a person working at the minimum wage. In other words, for many forms of labor a person would be paid as much while not working as he would have been if he had been employed. This policy offered no encouragement to seek employment—except for those persons liking work for its own sake.

In the name of equality, the government had taxed the wealthier citizens and subsidized the poorer citizens until a person in the highest income bracket in Holland could keep only four times as much income as a person earning the minimum wage. And the typical person in the highest income bracket had to work 50 percent longer every week than did a worker earning only the minimum wage. No longer could any entrepreneur hope to earn a fortune for himself—or even to obtain a very superior style of living. It had become difficult to fall into real poverty in The Netherlands, but it had become still more difficult to grow, or remain, really prosperous.

A leading Dutch public man, Andries van Agt, prime minister of The Netherlands for a time, memorably called the mentality and the economic condition created in Holland by this welfare state "a society of envy."

By 1983, The Netherlands government was attempting to reverse or modify many of the policies that had brought about the society of envy. But it is not easy to undo the power of envy, once that vice has been heavily subsidized by public funds.

A society of envy, and related complex economic difficulties, came to pass by the 1980s in other nations that had built up elaborate "welfare states": Britain, the Scandinavian countries, to some extent Italy, France, and lesser states. It began to appear that the market economy and the welfare state were uncomfortable as partners. Perhaps a society of envy would have to endure a command economy.

What did Andries van Agt mean by his phrase "a society of envy"? He referred to the belief that "one man is as good as another, or maybe a little better." (That witticism comes from Mark Twain, not from Van Agt.) A society of envy is a culture in which envious people make public policy. The envious try to pull down to their own level the hard-working, the ingenious, the imaginative, the learned, the strong, the successful, even the handsome.

Dictionaries define envy as "discontent or ill will at another's good fortune because one wishes it had been his; dislike for a person who has what one wants."

In politics and economics, envious politicians and envious voters try to level off incomes: to impose such heavy income taxes that there can be no wealthy men and women. One of the troubles with these policies of envy is that if such measures are adopted, ability and hard work are not rewarded. Economically considered, a policy of social envy tends to reduce production. Incentives to intelligent work, and motives to ordinary integrity, have been found necessary in every society of the past.

In the market economy, it is not assumed that "one man is as good as another, or maybe a little better." The vast majority of economists are well aware, as was Adam Smith, that men and women are not as much alike as peas in a pod. Some people are stronger than most, some cleverer, some more beautiful, some swifter, some wiser, some harder working, some thriftier, some more imaginative, some braver, some more artistic, some more systematic. And also, some people are deficient in most of these qualities. The market rewards those qualities which result in successful production and distribution. The market refuses to reward those habits or failings that do not produce material goods or services.

Similarly, the political system established in the United States by the federal Constitution of 1787 is not founded upon envy. The constitutional republican pattern of life that has developed in America opens many opportunities for people who hope to rise. But also, both Consititution and custom in America tend to restrain envious people from pulling other people down.

A widespread envious state of mind may be a greater menace to a healthy economy than is the power of the totalist states. Even the most vigorous economy may be enfeebled by excessive taxation, inflationary financial policies, discouragement of saving, fussy overregulation of economic concerns, hostility toward entrepreneurs, and creation of a huge, centralized political bureaucracy, much of which produces little in the way of services and less in the way of material goods. *Envious politicians sometimes are able to obtain a considerable degree of economic equality, but it is the equality of equal poverty, produced by the doctrine of equal misery.*

Even the masters of the Soviet Union have discovered that equality of rewards brings low production of goods. Karl Marx demanded complete equality of condition, but such equality has been achieved only at brief moments in the history of nations—through violence. And then it has been an equality in suffering.

A society of envy, in short, is a self-destroying society that must dissolve. For the bond that unites human beings is friendship, not hatred. And the prospering economy is one in which producers and consumers, buyers and sellers—or most of them—often think of how they can benefit one another, not of how they can pull down one another.

Discuss

18. From what you know of history, can you suggest how necessary hard work was for the Dutch people in previous centuries? (Consider Holland's geography.)

19. During the seventeenth century, there were more rich people in The Netherlands than in any other country. Today, although there are still rich Dutch citizens, it is almost impossible to build a fortune by cleverness or hard work. Can you suggest where all the riches have gone?

20. Holland has much rich soil (a good deal reclaimed from the ocean), great ports, and capital accumulated over several centuries. Switzerland has little arable land and not much by way of natural resources (aside from water power). In the nineteenth century, the per capita income was relatively high in Holland, while per capita income in Switzerland was low. Yet nowadays the per capita income of the Swiss exceeds that of the Dutch. Can you give some probable reasons for this change?

21. Does the emotion called envy ever do any good in society? (In its more favorable sense, envy sometimes is called the desire to *emulate*.) What does the Bible say about envy?

A market economy encourages people to hope and work for more goods. But because not everybody is equally successful in earning more goods, envy arises. And that envy tends to injure the market economy—perhaps to ruin it. So the worst trouble of the market economy may be its very emphasis on material success.

The command economy experiences difficulties of a different character—to which we turn now.

CHAPTER 12

Promise and Performance
in the Command Economy

Chapter 12
Promise and Performance in the Command Economy

- •What the Command Economy Tries to Achieve
- •Touring a Command Economy
- •Permanently Depressed Economies
- •Commands Often Have Unpleasant Results
- •Permanent Perplexities of a Command Economy

What the Command Economy Tries to Achieve

In a command economy, the production, distribution, and consumption of goods are planned and directed by a central political authority. In command economies with the kind of government called communist (or, in some cases, with governments that call themselves merely socialist), all the major means of production belong to the political state.

In non-communist command economies (such as that of Germany under Hitler, or that of Argentina under Perón during the period of the Second World War), most of the means of production may remain in private ownership, but the government strictly directs production, distribution, and (in part) consumption.

Today there exist some examples in Africa, Asia, and Latin America of command (or "directed") economies under the control of governments that are **nationalist,** not communist. These nationalist regimes declare that they have taken command of the economy in order to strengthen the nation, especially in military power.

Also there are democratic nations that have in their economic systems some command features, and yet their economic systems are not wholly socialist. Britain and Sweden are examples of these "mixed" economies, in which the private sector remains large and the operation of markets has not been abolished.

In this chapter's discussion of the command economy, we will limit ourselves to examples of the fully developed command economies of the countries belonging to what is called the **communist bloc.** In those lands, the market economy is forbidden by law. The Soviet Union (the USSR) and the People's Republic of China (mainland China) are much the most powerful and the most populous of these totalist countries with command economies.

Beginning with the Bolshevik Revolution in Russia, in 1917–18, more and more of the world's population has come under the domination of totalist governments that have established command economies. The box below suggests how thoroughly the communists have crushed the market economy, along with the old social and political order, of the countries where a communist revolution has succeeded.

Radical Economic Measures of Communist States

Confiscation of nearly all private property
Abolition of economic competition
Monopoly of production and distribution by the communist state
Control of consumption by rationing and quotas
Abolition (or else absorption) of labor unions
Nationalization of the banking system
Fixing of all wages and salaries
Total planning of the economy by the state

Also, in country after country, these totalist regimes have swept away constitutional governments, democratic political processes, and civil liberties. They have persecuted religious belief and destroyed voluntary organizations of all kinds. But here we are concerned with the economic policies of totalist governments rather than with the political features of totalist systems.

What have Communist parties hoped to accomplish by thus destroying market economies (along with peasant economies and other economic forms)? What is the purpose of the Communists' command economy?

The declared economic aim of the Communists is to create an economic system in which everybody shares equally. In the words of Karl Marx, **communism** is a future system of production, distribution, and consumption in which every person works "according to his ability" and every person receives goods "according to his need." The Communists, or Marxists, maintain that "capitalism" (the market economy) must be totally destroyed to make way for their revolutionary new system of "scientific economics."

So the professed aim of Marxist economics is complete equality of condition. In theory, this means that everyone under communism would live the same sort of life. There would be no rich, no middle class, no poor. Indeed, there would be no city and no countryside: Marx thought that when communism had triumphed, people would live in little straggling communes (communist villages) scattered across the face of the land.

"In order to establish equality, we must first establish inequality," Marx wrote in his famous book *Das Kapital,* of which the first volume was published in 1867. He meant that to achieve communism, first there must come violent political revolution, and next "the dictatorship of the proletariat," in which a nation would be ruled sternly by soviets (committees) of workers. All property would be confiscated by this dictatorship of the proletariat, and the old ruling and propertied classes would be wiped out.

Eventually, Marx believed, the dictatorship of the proletariat would come to an end. Then, true communism would be established throughout the world, all opposition having been destroyed. Marx was not wholly clear about what this universal communism would be like. He assumed that there would be sufficient goods for everybody, equally shared, and that work would be light and enjoyable. In a condition of communism, Marx mentioned, every man would perform nearly all tasks for himself and his household, without much need of buying and selling anything. When communism arrives, Marx continued, every man "will fish in the morning, hunt in the afternoon, breed cattle in the evening, and criticize at dinner just as he pleases." This is the Marxist ideal of *utopia,* or the perfect society.[1]

The reality in the communist countries of our day is very different from Marx's dream. Vladimir Lenin, the first Communist dictator of the USSR, commenced a program of heavy industrialization of the Soviet Union. "Communism is socialism plus electricity," Lenin said. Contrary to Marx's prediction, the dictatorship of the proletariat that commenced in 1918 has not withered away, along with the centralized state. Instead, a ruthless secret police and a huge army keep the dictatorship in power in the Soviet Union right to the present day.

Even though the Communist dictatorships of today bear little resemblance to Marx's utopia, in portions of Asia, Africa, and Latin America, Communist organizations continue to seize power and to establish command economies. *More people in our time live under command economies than under market economies.*

Let us see how a command economy actually works. "The proof of the pudding is in the eating," an old proverb instructs us. Theory is one thing; practice may be different. Does a command economy actually provide plenty and equality for everybody in a society?

Discuss
1. Can you name ten countries in which Communist parties control the government today?
2. Do you think you would be contented in a society with complete economic equality, where everybody would live just as everybody else lives? Why or why not?
3. Can you name some countries in which socialist parties are powerful today, but which are not communist states?

1. **Utopia:** an ideal place or state, with perfect laws. The word is derived from Greek words meaning "nowhere."

4. Marxists argue that everything important in human history has been caused by economic motives. They believe that economic concerns matter more than anything else in life. Can you suggest some other point of view?

Touring a Command Economy

It is possible to travel within a few hours from a city that has a market economy to a city that has a command economy—indeed, within a few minutes. It is easiest to do this in Berlin, once the capital of all Germany, but since the Second World War a city divided into halves. The western half of Berlin is part of the Federal Republic of Germany, often called West Germany. The eastern half of Berlin is the capital of the German Democratic Republic (East Germany).

West Berlin, under the democratic government of the Federal Republic, enjoys a vigorous market economy. It is a bustling and prosperous city, full of well-dressed people, many of them cheerful and smiling. Good restaurants and cafes are numerous; so are fashionable shops and department stores. West Berlin has been thoroughly restored and rebuilt since Russian troops virtually destroyed Berlin near the end of the Second World War.

A high, grim wall separates West Berlin from East Berlin—a wall built by the Communist East Germans and their Russian masters to prevent East Germans, and others, from escaping into West Berlin. One can pass through this wall only at heavily guarded gates. Anyone who tries to climb over the wall may be shot by East German sentries.

Although it is difficult for East Berliners to visit West Berlin, tourists usually are permitted to cross from the western part of the city to the eastern—returning to West Berlin in the same day. The contrast between the two halves of the city startles nearly anyone.

For East Berlin is an ugly and grim place. The chief avenues are lined with hideous gray public-housing projects. Shabbiness pervades everything. The inhabitants are poorly dressed and often sour and hostile in manner. Few decent shops exist; in those, few goods are displayed. Eating-houses are rather dismal places, most of them, with grudging service. Consumer goods are rationed. One receives an impression of unending poverty. Everywhere are police of one sort or another.

West Berlin has a market economy. East Berlin has a command economy.

Now, the difference of economic systems is not the only reason why East Berlin is poor and disagreeable, while West Berlin is affluent and lively. For one thing, East Germany (though nominally independent) is dominated by a foreign power, the Soviet Union. The government of the Democratic German Republic, despite the name of the country, is a Communist dictatorship subservient to the Soviet Union. East Berlin is run from Moscow, so to speak. East Germany is kept poor by trade agreements with Russia which are thoroughly unfavorable to the East Germans.

The economy of East Berlin does no more than supply a bare subsistence to most of the inhabitants of that city. Some of the reasons for this poverty are economic, some political. True, there is more equality of economic condition in East Berlin than in West Berlin. But it is equality in misery. Everyone, except for a few high officials who are eminent members of the Communist party, is as poor as everyone else.

Startling contrasts between market economies and command economies are not confined to Europe. Take an Asiatic example. The island of Taiwan (or Formosa) is the most densely populated country in the world. It has few natural resources except stone. Yet since the Second World War, Taiwan has become a major exporter of food in the Orient, outselling Hawaiian pineapple even in the United States. Even more surprising, little Taiwan is second only to Japan, among Asiatic countries, in shipbuilding and other heavy industries.

Taiwan is governed by the Republic of China—that is, the anti-

Communist leaders of the Kuomintang party. Taiwan enjoys a market economy. The island is highly prosperous, and there are next to no unemployed people.

Only the Formosa Strait, a hundred miles of water, separates Taiwan from mainland China. It is now possible for some foreign tourists to visit, on the mainland, the cities of Foochow, Amoy, and Swatow, opposite Taiwan. Mainland China is governed by the People's Republic of China, the Communist regime. Foochow, Amoy, and Swatow, like the rest of mainland China, are part of a command economy.

The cities of mainland China are poverty-stricken in comparison to the four large cities of Taiwan—so near in space, so distant in economic development. On the mainland, nearly everyone dresses in uniform; individual enterprise is scowled upon; most people appear to have just enough to eat. Taiwan, meanwhile, continues to grow in industry and agriculture, and many inhabitants of the island can afford luxuries.

Or consider an African example. Tanzania and Kenya are neighboring countries of East Africa, both ruled by Britain for a considerable time, now independent "emergent nations." In climate and resources they are similar. The economy of both is chiefly agricultural. Each country is governed by a single political party. These two large countries are nearly equal in population and have about the same rate of literacy.

If one flies from Nairobi (the capital of Kenya) to Dar-es-Salaam (the capital of Tanzania), a distance of less than four hundred miles, one finds that Nairobi is a far better place to live than is Dar-es-Salaam. The contrast is even greater when one visits the villages and rural regions of both countries.

The population of Tanzania is far poorer than it was before independence from Britain. The government of Tanzania manages the whole of the economy, and manages it badly. The only portion of the population which seems to thrive is the massive bureaucracy. Indeed, the only way for young Tanzanians to get ahead is to be permitted to join the bureaucracy.[2]

Kenya, however, is relatively prosperous by African standards, and relatively well governed. Property is secure; laws are enforced with some efficiency. This is one region of Africa that attracts investors. Many African refugees from tyranny or anarchy have taken up residence in relatively stable Kenya.

Kenya has a market economy and friendly relationships with Britain, Western Europe, and the United States. Tanzania has a command economy and a close relationship with Russia.

It is not simply the differences in economic structure that distinguish West Berlin from East Berlin, Taiwan from Red China, or Kenya from Tanzania. In part, the advantages of a market economy account for the vigorous societies of West Berlin, Taiwan, and Kenya; while the disadvantages of a command economy account in part for the listless and depressed societies of East Berlin, mainland China, and Tanzania.

Recent statistics show that economic productivity per capita is much higher in these three market economies than in these three command economies. What matters still more than economic productivity is the survival of human hope and human freedom. Hope and freedom have better prospects in these three societies with market economies than in their command counterparts.

Discuss

5. Every year since the Berlin Wall was built, many people have tried to get over or under the Wall, at the risk of being shot by guards or of being caught and imprisoned. All these people have been endeavoring to cross from East Berlin to West Berlin. Why do no people try to escape from West Berlin to East Berlin?

6. If Taiwan has few natural resources, how have the island's people become major exporters of both industrial and agricultural goods? What other factors of production seem important in Taiwan?

---

2. **Bureaucracy:** government by groups of officials; concentration of power in administrative bureaus.

7. Although Kenya is fairly prosperous by African standards, it is a poor country by European or American standards. Indeed, with the exception of the Republic of South Africa, all African populations are poor by Western standards. Can you suggest reasons for the prevalence of poverty in the African continent?

If the proof of the pudding is in the eating, command economies seem incompetent at cookery. True, there have been some examples of success by command economies. Hitler's elaborate system of controls over the German economy and his measures to stimulate production— including production by prisoners in Nazi concentration camps—did obtain results that helped him in his military adventures. And it seems probable that Russia's huge prison camps in Soviet Asia are run at a profit to the Soviet government. But such economic cookery also produces disagreeable puddings.

Permanently Depressed Economies

It is charged against market economies that sometimes depressions occur because of the business cycle. It certainly is true that in market economies prosperity diminishes from time to time. But it does not follow that command economies are stable.

Great mistakes frequently are made by the bureaucracies that direct command economies. The planners may greatly underestimate the amount needed of some good, and then there is underproduction, with shortages and disorders in consumption. Or the state planners may overestimate the potential demand for a good, and then, on a grand scale, overproduction occurs, with unpleasant consequences very similar to disruptions of market economies. Command economies, too, experience their recessions and their depressions, often more severe than those of the market—though the governments of totalist states endeavor to conceal the evidence of such economic disorders.

But a worse fault of most command economies is that they tend to be inefficient and stagnant, changing too little, rather than too much.

Thus, many command economies are in a kind of permanent state of depression, producing little, distributing that little incompetently, and compelling consumers to wait in ration lines for hours, days, or even weeks.

Solzhenitsyn the Accountant

For a practical illustration of these failings in the command economy of the Soviet Union, we turn to an episode from the life of Aleksandr Solzhenitsyn, the most famous Russian man of letters of recent years. In 1945, when Joseph Stalin was dictator of the USSR, Solzhenitsyn was sent to a prison camp on vague charges of being a political dissident. In 1953, he was released from prison but was kept in the status of "exile," forbidden to return to European Russia for several more years.

In the vast desert region called Kazakhstan, Solzhenitsyn managed to obtain a job as accountant at the Kok-Terek District Consumer Cooperative— a district center for the distribution of goods of all sorts. He was hired because it was time for the annual inventory and price reduction (what we would call a clearance sale), on April 1.

When Solzhenitsyn arrived (with the title of Planning Officer) at the cooperative's offices, he found fifteen people already working on the inventories. The whole local distribution system was a marvel of incompetence. Much theft by salespeople occurred.

General stores in villages served by the cooperative sent in their inventories of goods on their shelves. Here is one of those inventories:

1.	Bicycle nails	1/2 kilo
2.	Shoo	5
3.	Ash-pan	2
4.	Glashes	10
5.	Fencil case, child's	1
6.	Glope	1
7.	Match	50 boxes
8.	"Bat" lamp	2
9.	Tooth past	8
10.	Gingerbread	34 kilo
11.	Vodka	156 half-liters

(The misspellings of "shoe," "galoshes," "pencil," "globe," and "paste" occur in the Russian of the original.)

This was the entire stock of one general store—which suggests the genuine scarcity of nearly all manufactured goods in the Soviet empire. The gingerbread, Solzhenitsyn speculates, probably was left over from before World War II.

Until the cooperative's district office completed its repricing, no store in the district was permitted to sell anything to anybody. The indolent and incompetent staff were a week behind schedule. To catch up, the chairman of the cooperative ordered all employees to sleep only four hours a night, working at their desks from seven in the morning until two the next morning.

Only Solzhenitsyn was courageous or foolhardy enough to disobey this outrageous order from the director; he continued to leave the office at 5 P.M., directly defying his superior. That director told the other employees that he would have police take Solzhenitsyn a hundred kilometers into the desert and leave him there as punishment. And he might have done so, under Stalin. Happily for Solzhenitsyn, that writer found a post in a local school and so departed from the cooperative.[3]

This is a small incident, mildly amusing. But it serves to suggest keenly the inadequacy of distribution by the central agencies of a command economy. The consumer scarcely is consulted by the petty bureaucrats who make their living by this inefficient system. And the poor consumer has no escape from this frustrating system: the state and its agencies hold a monopoly of distribution, competition being forbidden. This episode suggests also the virtual helplessness of working people when a state bureaucrat or manager decides to bully them under a command economy. It is not merely the minister of transportation or the minister of economic planning who gives those commands: it is a matter of commands from a long series of officials, all the way down to petty village functionaries.

No doubt there are a number of reasons for the incompetence in distribution within the USSR that Solzhenitsyn describes. One of the

---

3. See Aleksandr Solzhenitsyn, *The Gulag Archipelago, 1918–1956*, V–VII, New York, Harper & Row, 1976.

more important causes of this difficulty seems to be the lack of incentives offered under the communist form of the command economy. The central state or some agency of the state owns the distribution centers, the stores, and the goods offered in them. Salaries and wages ordinarily are fixed by central authority. Therefore, the "capitalistic" profit motive does not operate, because managers and employees have nothing personal to gain through greater efficiency or better treatment of customers. After all, customers have nowhere else to go. And as for selling more goods—why, practically all consumer goods are scarce always in such an economy, and are rationed. A store cannot sell what it does not have in stock.

The assumption of the Russian Bolsheviks on seizing power in 1918 was that when capitalism and the old political regime had been overthrown, people would work together for the sake of the whole community, not seeking much personal reward. *For Marxists, like some other radical groups, maintain that men and women are naturally good when not corrupted by private property and religion.*

This dream of the early Marxist revolutionaries has not been fulfilled. Cases of large-scale theft and corruption arise frequently in the Soviet Union today, and heavy sentences are imposed upon offenders.

The leaders of the Soviet Union have found it necessary, after all, to introduce special monetary incentives into factories to increase production. In communist China, a severe problem for years after the Chinese communist revolution was the difficulty of finding competent people to manage factories. For the manager of a Chinese factory has greater responsibility and strain than anybody else in the factory, but until recent years he was paid no better than any other worker. So no competent person sought the manager's post. As Edmund Burke said in the eighteenth century, "Ordinary integrity requires the ordinary rewards of integrity."

Discuss   8. Economic planners in totalist countries declare that the more they centralize production and distribution, the lower the cost of goods will be, because of mass production, standardizing of

products, and accurate estimating of demand. Do you think this
argument is sound? Why or why not? Is standardizing of goods
always an advantage to consumers?

9. At the Kok-Terek District Consumer Cooperative, Solzhenitsyn found that there was no calculating machine; to do his work
efficiently, he had to borrow a half-forgotten calculator from the
District Statistics Administration. Presumably, no office in the
United States with more than fifteen employees, and a need for
keeping accounts, would lack a calculating machine. Can you
suggest reasons why, in a communist system with a command
economy, accurate accounting may have been thought unnecessary?

A Marxist regime has been established in Russia since 1917. Total
economic planning on a grand scale, including ruthless speedy industrialization, commenced with the Soviet Union's first "Five-Year Plan,"
adopted in 1928. The Russian peoples had an elaborate political and
social structure for centuries before the Bolshevik Revolution. So it
seems fair to judge the performance of a thoroughgoing command
economy by how such an economy has functioned in the Soviet Union.

A short time after Yuri V. Andropov became dictator of the Soviet
Union, an experienced writer for the *New York Times* spent a month in
the Soviet empire, assessing its economy. He found Russia's economic
structure enfeebled, though in no immediate danger of collapse. Here
are some of the failings this investigator described:

- A lack of incentives for both working people and managers.
- A shortage of skilled workers, technicians, and managers.
- Virtual exhaustion of many natural resources in European
  Russia, with coal, petroleum, timber, iron ore, and other
  minerals all used up by the command economy.
- An economic structure rigid, overcautious, secretive, bureau-
  cratic, obstructive.
- Difficulty in deciding how to allocate scarce resources.

These, the *New York Times* journalist suggested, were the fruits
of communist ideology, "summed up in the Marxist-Leninist doctrines
calling for state ownership of the means of production, the abolition of

private property, a dearth of competition, and the so-called dictatorship of the proletariat, as administered by bureaucrats."

Soviet agriculture is inefficient: although the Soviet Union has ten times as many agricultural laborers as there are in the United States, Soviet farm output is only three fourths as large as American agricultural production.

Industrial growth has slowed down in the USSR, and industrial plants are decaying. A Soviet economist told the American journalist that a barrier to efficient production "is the inability of the government-run enterprises to fail. Without a profit-and-loss system, the sheriff never comes. Monopoly, the overwhelming pattern of industrial organization in the Soviet Union, obviates failure, but not inefficiency." Also, it is very difficult for a manager to dismiss an incompetent worker; so workers' productivity is low in factories.

Soviet economic planning is confused and hesitant. Planning difficulties "extend to the entire control-and-response system of economic enterprises, in the absence of a flexible market-price mechanism to guide decisions." In other words, the Soviet State Planning Committee seems unable to solve grave questions of supply and demand. Nearly all goods are in short supply.

The Soviet Central Bank denies that currency inflation troubles the USSR. But as the *New York Times* puts it, "In fact, however, the economy appears to suffer from disguised inflation, which takes the form of endless shortages and queues of people waiting to buy goods, no matter how shoddy the goods may seem.

"Suppressed inflation and shortages appear to be the hallmark of this centrally planned economy. . . . The fruits of such an economy are inefficiency, low productivity, low morale, grumpiness and surliness in the provision of services."

The chief engineer of a Siberian coal mine told the writer from the *Times,* "Do you know what I think is the fundamental thing wrong with this country? The absence of competition."[4]

So competition and personal incentives, prominent features of

4. See Leonard Silk, "Russian Economy Gives Andropov Huge Problems," *New York Times*, Sunday, June 12, 1983, pp. 1, 10.

any market economy, begin once more to be recognized, even in the Soviet Union, as essential to a thriving economy. After more than seven decades of trying to achieve prosperity through a command economy, the Communist leaders of Russia grope for some way to approach the success of the market economies of the West. The economic story is the same in other communist dominations.

In the People's Republic of China, especially, efforts are being made to reward hard work, provide economic incentives to efficiency, and encourage investment of private capital by foreign firms—all this in a huge country still nominally Marxist. After a recent tour of China, an American man of business remarked, "What is occurring is the early phase of what may well become a broad-scaled transition from a centrally planned economy to a free market capitalist system within a Communist-controlled nation." This tactic of momentarily releasing the stranglehold on the economy has been used before. The key point to remember is that historically it has always been *temporary*.

Such Communist-ruled states as Bulgaria and Poland, unlike China, have not yet modified "pure Marxism" in their economic programs; so they sink deeper into poverty. When Communist parties established themselves in power in Bulgaria and Poland, they declared that the Marxist principle of "production for use, not for profit" would result in abundant consumer goods and permanent peace. It is interesting to contrast the present industrial reality in those two countries with this initial promise.

During the 1980s, Bulgaria's largest export was weapons, sold to "Third World" countries. United States officials had evidence that these purchases of Bulgarian arms were financed in part by production and sale of narcotics by the importing countries.

Also during the 1980s, Poland's most profitable nationalized industry was the distilling of vodka. The state-operated alcohol monopoly, called Polmos, made a profit of some $3.8 billion dollars in 1983, while the second most successful Polish state-owned industry, oil refining, was far less profitable. It was estimated that a third of the typical

Polish family's yearly budget for food and drink was spent on alcohol. In 1984, the Polish underground free labor union, Solidarity, collaborated with the Catholic church in an appeal to Poles to drink less. "There was a great revival in the struggle against alcoholism when Solidarity was created," said the priest in charge of the sobriety program in the archdiocese of Warsaw. "People became aware that because of alcohol the nation is unable to decide about itself. Alcohol always reappears when people want to escape from reality into a world of illusions."

Marxist economic promises are one thing; Marxist economic performances are something quite different, it appears.

Discuss

10. The Soviet dictator Yuri Andropov addressed workers in a Moscow machine-tool factory in 1983. He lamented that, throughout the Soviet Union, wages had been rising more rapidly than productivity. "The main road for us is to increase production," he said. "Everything we do and produce must be done and produced, to the highest degree possible, at minimum cost, high quality, quickly, and durably." The rate of industrial growth in the Soviet Union had fallen every year since 1977; agricultural production was still worse off. In November 1981, Andropov's predecessor as head of the Soviet system, Leonid Brezhnev, had declared, "The food problem is, economically and politically, the central problem."

In view of these admissions by the masters of the Soviet Union, and of the failings of the Soviet economy described by Leonard Silk (the *New York Times* journalist), why don't the Russians and other peoples of the Soviet empire radically change their economic system? Can you suggest obstacles to such a change?

11. If in Poland one third of the price of a week's basket of groceries goes for vodka, the typical Polish household is sustaining (as in the Soviet Union) a very high opportunity cost in order to obtain distilled drink. In other words, often the purchaser of vodka must abstain from buying the good he would like next best to vodka. Yet alcoholism is a terrible social problem in Poland: a survey of public opinion made by the weekly Communist newspaper *Polityka* in 1984 showed that "Poles feel more endangered by the threat of alcoholism than by another world war." Three out of every four murders, rapes, and assaults in Poland are committed by drunken persons. This being so, why do many Poles continue to drink excessively? And why doesn't the government of Poland take action to diminish alcoholism? Can you suggest reasons?

Commands Often Have Unpleasant Results

Few people in the United States or in other democratic countries admire the command economies of the totalist states. Still fewer folk living in countries with market economies would find any good to say about a command economy if they had personal experience of life under such an inhumane system.

Nevertheless, some features of a command economy exist in such democratic, industrialized countries of the West as Britain, Sweden, Italy, and France. Socialist and Social-Democratic parties in those countries advocate a "directed economy" or "planned economy" which, they argue, would guarantee prosperity for the working classes. Even in the United States, now and then certain public measures based on the "command" theory of economics have been tried—with consequences that the people who planned such policies never intended.

Take one example of such attempts to improve economic conditions by governmental commands in a democratic society: the control of rents. We discussed rent controls near the end of chapter 4; now we take a more detailed look at them.

During periods of war or inflation, prices of all goods rise rapidly. Among these prices is the price of renting houses or apartments, agricultural land, and commercial buildings; tenants (renters) complain loudly that rent increases are a heavy burden on them, while people who own their residences, farms, or business premises do not suffer from the increase of rents.

Tenants bring pressure upon governments, therefore, to control rents: that is, to fix rents at what they were before war or inflation began—or at least to fix rents at some level less than the new "market" cost of rent. In democratic societies, tenants have votes, and governments tend to pay serious attention to tenants' political influence. So ever since the First World War (1914–1918), from time to time various governments have established systems of rent control.

Once established, rent controls are difficult to remove—even when the emergency justifying the controls has passed. In the United States, most rent controls were abolished after World War II, but the controls lingered in New York City for many years and have not yet been entirely removed there. In recent years of inflation, rent controls have been imposed in Santa Monica, California, and a few other towns. In Britain and some countries of Western Europe, systems of rent control that began in World War I or World War II are still partially in effect, though modified in recent years.

At first, rent controls may seem only fair to the majority of citizens. If government instructs landlords that they may not charge more rent, life seems easier for tenants, who, like most other citizens, have to "tighten their purse strings" in times of inflation or war.

But rent controls do not make life easier for landlords. As all other prices rise, the owners of rental property have to meet heavy costs. They must pay more for repairs and improvements to their buildings. They must find the money for higher taxes. Their own living costs are going up rapidly. Is it just for a society to discriminate against one class of citizens—landlords?

Before long, tenants usually find that rent controls have unpleasant consequences for them, too. Hard-pressed property owners make only minimal repairs and improvements to their rental properties, because they cannot afford to do more. If they pay for a building's utilities, perhaps they try to reduce the heat. Possibly roofs begin to leak and are not fixed properly. Apartment houses and dwellings fall into decay; some become uninhabitable, and the tenants move out, if they can find any other place to live.

If rent controls last a considerable time, investors cease to put their money into construction of new housing. Because interest rates tend to rise during war or inflation, landlords and builders find it very costly to borrow money for new construction. If rents are held low by governmental command, landlords cannot get enough out of their rents to pay for the maintenance of their buildings—let alone get a tolerable income out of rentals. So new building almost ceases. That means serious trouble for tenants, or people who would like to be tenants, young couples especially. Sooner or later, a serious housing shortage results from fixing rents at a level below the level of other prices.

People have to live somewhere. If existing housing is in short supply and few new buildings are being constructed, what becomes of men and women who do not own houses or apartments? Why, pressure grows to have a governmental agency provide housing for people who are homeless or in danger of becoming homeless.

So governments begin to construct massive housing projects. Public housing, which costs a great deal of money, must either raise taxes for everyone or else cause the government to borrow great sums. Such borrowing may increase the rate of inflation, to everybody's harm. And public housing projects commonly are less agreeable places to live for many tenants.

Entering the housing business compels a government to adopt another feature of a command economy, the direction of housing construction and living patterns—when originally the advocates of rent control may not have intended that a new costly responsibility would be imposed upon government.

And often the governmental agency in charge of public housing construction finds that no matter how many projects it builds, older housing falls into decay and is abandoned more rapidly than public housing can be erected, because landlords cannot afford, under rent controls, to maintain and repair their properties. Sometimes property owners simply stop paying their taxes and let their buildings go to ruin. In some American cities during recent years, less scrupulous landlords have hired arsonists to burn their buildings down so that they may collect insurance and thus get something out of their bad investment in rentals.

Rent controls, in short, commonly tend to create slums, where rates of crime are high. Older quarters of cities may fall into sad decay under rent controls. New public housing projects may be ugly, monotonous, unpopular, and unsafe. A policy of "rent ceilings," intended to help folk with low incomes, frequently has the opposite effect: in the long run, such a policy may leave renters worse off than they were before.

In Britain, as a result of rent controls imposed during World Wars I and II, hundreds of thousands of houses fell into ruin. The government attempted to replace them by huge "housing schemes," often so ugly that the socialist leader Aneurin Bevan compared them to "goods-waggons on a railway siding." Rates of violence and crime generally rose higher in the new housing schemes than they had been in the old low-rent districts of British towns.

Another bad effect of rent controls is that such policies tend to favor one class or group of people at other people's expense, for most rent-control acts apply only to existing housing and exempt new buildings. Thus, tenants who are established in older buildings (and cannot be evicted so long as they pay their low rent) may be charged only half as much rent as the tenants of more recently built apartments or houses. These conditions discriminate against people whose lodgings are not included under rent controls.

In New York City, major landlords often have found it profitable to demolish big, handsome apartment buildings—even on fashionable Fifth Avenue—and to erect new apartments or offices on the same site. Why? Because they could get only low rents from the older buildings, under rent control, but they can obtain high rents from new buildings exempt from controls. This situation causes waste and disruption of urban living, and it forces the tenants of the older buildings to pay much higher rent in new buildings, or else to move to less desirable housing.

Rent control is a fairly simple example of how the intrusion of a "command" economic policy into a market economy may work mischief—especially to the very people the policy was intended to benefit. Control of rents, like governmental control of other prices, generally results in scarcity. It has been said that the most effective way to destroy a city, aside from bombing, is to impose rent controls.

Discuss

12. Suppose that Enrique and Maria Fernandez, a married couple with four children, living in Santa Monica in a frame house built about 1900, have been paying a monthly rent of $350 for the past several years. Because of inflation, the old woman who owns the house tells them that she must increase their rent, beginning next January, to $425. But before January comes round, the city government of Santa Monica imposes rent controls, fixing the house's rent at $375. At first this action pleases the Fernandez family.

But Mrs. Andrews, who owns the house, has only the rent money and Social Security payments for her support. The house needs a new coat of paint and improvements to the plumbing. Previously, Mrs. Andrews has paid for modest repairs when her tenants asked for them.

When Enrique Fernandez asks his landlady to have the house painted and the plumbing improved, she replies, "I'm sorry, but painters charge so much, and plumbers too, that I just don't know how I could find the money for those things. Even if I had raised your rent, it would have been difficult. I have my own bills to meet. If you want the work done, I'm afraid you'll have to pay for it yourself."

Mrs. Andrews, a widow, has a total monthly income (counting the rent) of $950. Mr. Fernandez, an automobile mechanic, has a monthly income of about $1,700. Mrs. Andrews does own her residence, but she has to pay heavy property taxes on it. Mr. Fernandez has five dependents.

Does rent control benefit the Fernandez family? Should Mrs. Andrews sell the house where the Fernandez family lives? If so, could she get a good price for it, under rent controls? Should Enrique Fernandez buy the house from her? Suppose Mrs. Andrews would sell for as little as thirty-eight thousand dollars, and that interest on home mortgages stands at 10 percent. The Fernandez family would have to find thirty-eight thousand dollars to pay Mrs. Andrews. Would Enrique and Maria Fernandez be better off by buying the house or by continuing to rent? Is rent control fair to Mrs. Andrews, a capitalist in a modest way? (Many or most American landlords are people of modest means.)

13. Suppose that a state legislature, trying to fight inflation, should pass an act commanding all sellers of meat to "roll back" their prices of beef, pork, and mutton to the price levels of 1970, when the cost of meat was much less. Would this measure help poor people to have a high-protein diet? Would supermarkets and

butcher shops supply their customers with meat at 1970 prices? Might a black market in meat develop? Explain.

14. If a Marxist government should come to power in some Latin American country, nationalize all housing, and let tenants live rent-free, would that be a benefit to most people?

Permanent Perplexities of a Command Economy

If a command economy suffers from all the failings described in this chapter, why do any people tolerate such mismanagement of their economic affairs? Because in the beginning—ordinarily after a political revolution of the kind the Nazis worked in Germany or the Bolsheviks in Russia—the masters of the state promise that central direction of the economy will produce prosperity and economic equality. By the time events have proved these promises false, it has become difficult or impossible to return to an earlier political and economic system. A grim, entrenched bureaucracy, commonly supported by a secret police and a powerful army, runs the economy chiefly for the benefit of a political elite, usually members of some fanatic party.

Yet it is conceivable that a command economy might be directed by sincere and well-intentioned leaders who believe that a society would benefit from wise central economic planning. Even given good intentions, nevertheless, command economies ordinarily blunder, producing less than do market economies. This observation has been conspicuously true in the new African states that achieved independence after the Second World War.

At best, the tendency of command economies has been to overestimate or underestimate the needs and resources of a country. One reason for this deficiency has been the command economy's lack of the "signals of the market" discussed in chapter 5.

In a healthy market economy, these signals by consumers give producers and distributors a fairly clear notion of the demand for goods.

Lacking such signals, the political administrators controlling a command economy make their decisions without sufficient information, arbitrarily. From this "deciding in the dark," waste and scarcity result. *So it comes about that while market economies may suffer occasionally from depressions, command economies plod along in a perpetual state of depression.*

Yet the command economy has one advantage (so far as efficiency is concerned) over the market economy. In totalist states, that one advantage is force. Totalist governments can apply ferocious penalties to those accused of failing to produce.

In Soviet Russia (especially under Stalin) and in communist China (especially under Mao), annually thousands of working people were denounced and sentenced as *saboteurs*, and sent to compulsory labor in prison camps.[5] In such concentration camps, hundreds of thousands of men and women literally were worked to death; on a smaller scale, Hitler's Nazis committed similar atrocities in German labor camps during World War II. (The forced labor of prisoners starving in those camps considerably helped the Nazi war effort.) Although there has been some diminishing of cruelty in Russia and China during recent years, it remains true that "slave labor" is an important factor in the economies of those great countries. The government of communist Vietnam is believed to have transported to Asiatic Russia thousands of Vietnamese citizens, prisoners of war or political opponents, to labor under compulsion for the USSR. There is also evidence that Angola has shipped thousands of children off to work in East Germany.

This ghastly record is a principal reason why the big American labor unions have opposed, for many years, the political regimes and command economies of the totalist powers. Although union leaders in the United States may advocate various modifications of the market economy, few of them favor large-scale economic direction by the federal government.

---

5. **Saboteur:** a workman who damages machinery or otherwise interrupts industrial production. The term was used first in nineteenth century France to describe rebellious workmen who thrust their wooden shoes (*sabots*) into the machinery.

The incentive offered by the market economy is the carrot. The incentive offered by the command economy is the stick.

CHAPTER 13

The World's Distressed Economy

Chapter 13
The World's Distressed Economy

- •Worldwide Economic Perplexities
- •Pollution, Waste, and Ugliness
- •Dread Inflation
- •Political Causes of Inflation
- •Inflation and Allied Difficulties in a Command Economy
- •Secondary Causes of Inflation
- •Remedies for Inflation

Worldwide Economic Perplexities

Often it is said that we now have a world economy, rather than separate national economies. This is because decisions in the great centers of exchange soon affect even remote undeveloped countries and regions, the political measures of the major powers promptly have worldwide economic consequences, and investments by multinational corporations create a huge financial network involving every continent.

This integration of national economies into a worldwide system took place throughout the twentieth century. In 1928, the collapse of the financial empire of Ivar Kruger, the Swedish "match king" (head of an international trust producing matches) was a cause of the Great Depression that afflicted Europe, America, and much of the rest of the world from 1929 to 1932. Civil war in the Congo (now called Zaire) during the 1960s brought about a shortage of copper in America and Europe—and intervention by the United Nations. Drastic increases in the price of crude oil (the Arab Oil Embargo) in 1973–74 gravely menaced industrial production and transportation in the major industrial countries; so did the revolution in Iran in 1979.

Scores of similar examples of economic interdependence today might be offered. Complex international exchange of raw materials and manufactured products, international banking on a tremendous scale, and international trade agreements of a permanent character (of which the European Common Market is the best example) have joined the nations in a common economy.

This network of international economic arrangements has much increased the prosperity of many countries, but it has also brought about large economic difficulties which are shared in some degree by every nation. "No country in the world is independent, except perhaps the U.S.," says Fernand Braudel, the French historian. "Not France, not the Soviet Union. Even Japan is a fragile economy." Braudel declares that the whole world is in the midst of a social, political, and economic crisis.[1]

In this chapter, we discuss two of the economic aspects of this prolonged worldwide crisis: first, the complex problem of environmental pollution, wasted resources, and urban blight; second, the urgent problem of inflation. These troubles are common to market economies, mixed economies, and command economies. A vast deal of intelligence, imagination, and character will be required to diminish them.

Discuss
1. Can you offer other examples of how recent economic and political events have affected virtually the whole world?
2. How might the United States (although only the United States) contrive to be independent economically, should another world war or some other catastrophe cut off exchange with other countries?

Pollution, Waste, and Ugliness

The several industrial revolutions since the eighteenth century have provided the human race with more goods than were dreamed of in earlier ages. Whether those goods have provided the human race

1. See Lawrence Minard, "A Chat with Fernand Braudel," *Forbes,* June 21, 1982, pp. 132–134.

with a corresponding degree of happiness—why, that question may be debated.

Massive industrial development has brought pollution to the environment and dreary conditions of life to whole regions. When Adam Smith published *The Wealth of Nations*, his town of Kirkcaldy was a picturesque and pleasant place to live, with good architecture. In the twentieth century—particularly since state-directed industry was established at Kirkcaldy in recent years—the town has become ugly and cheerless.

Throughout the economically developed countries, with few exceptions (Switzerland being one of those few exceptions), industrial technology and industrial patterns of life have brought such changes for the worse. These unhappy alterations of the natural environment and of urban life occur in market economies, mixed economies, fascist economies, communist economies: for the "smokestack industries" belch smoke wherever they are, regardless of who owns and manages them. And modern scientific technology has developed tools of production more harmful than the old smokestack industries, efficient though the new technologies may be in economic terms. The grim problem of trying to dispose of the radioactive wastes from nuclear power plants is a case in point.

In an attempt to satisfy demand in the Age of the Consumer, modern industrial production has been using up forests, fossil fuels, mineral deposits, and other natural resources at an alarming rate. In many regions of the world, the soil itself has been depleted by excessive cultivation, excessive use of nitrate fertilizers, or bad agricultural practices; some of the best soil in the United States has disappeared before urban sprawl or has been covered by great highways. Even the layer of ozone (a form of the gas oxygen) that occurs in the earth's stratosphere is said to be threatened by certain gases now industrially produced. (The ozonosphere, or ozone layer, absorbs ultraviolet radiation from the sun that would severely damage living organisms on the earth's surface.) Some fears of the depletion of the earth's resources may be exaggerated, a topic that will be discussed in the last chapter of this book; but certainly the waste of natural resources in our time has become a problem that cannot be ignored.

Often the social consequences of industrial development are as serious as pollution or waste of resources. Concentration of industrial production has caused gigantic urban sprawl—with bored and discontented urban populations. The automobile and the building of superhighways have changed the long-established pattern of life in many countries, have increased pollution of the atmosphere, and have given us the permanent irritation of traffic snarls.

Much of this damage has been done thoughtlessly by the private economic sector; yet governments and governmentally controlled organizations can do more damage. Here is an American example. About the end of the 1960s and the beginning of the 1970s, environmental scientists discovered that Lake Michigan, one of the biggest reservoirs of fresh water in the world, was suffering gravely from pollution by substances poured into the lake from ports along its shores; fish were dying, and the whole great body of water was in danger of becoming a "dead sea."

Upon more investigation, it was found that the major polluter of Lake Michigan was not some industrial firm at Chicago, Gary, or Muskegon, but instead the Great Lakes Naval Training Station, on the southern shore. The state governments of Illinois and Indiana could not control pollution by the Naval Training Station, since it was in the jurisdiction of the U.S. Navy. Only an executive order by President Nixon, as commander in chief of military and naval forces, sufficed to stop this pouring of wastes into the lake. After this, the condition of Lake Michigan improved sharply.

One might expect controls upon environmental pollution, use of natural resources, and urban living conditions to be more effective in socialist countries, where there frequently is talk about "conserving the people's resources" and about the wickedness of "capitalist exploitation" of the environment. But the reality in command economies is quite the contrary.

An American writer, traveling in the Soviet Union some years ago, came to Lake Baikal, a huge expanse that used to contain the purest water in the world. Having settled in a hotel, he went down to dinner in a salon overlooking the great lake. On the long menu were listed many fish—some of them varieties that this traveler never had tasted or even heard of. These species were found in Lake Baikal. The American ordered a fish dish. But the waiter shook his head: "Not available." The traveler ordered a different fish: also not available. The American ran through the whole menu of fish dishes: none available. "Why?" the traveler inquired.

The Russian waiter bent close to the traveler's ear. "All dead. The lake is poisoned."

That was too true. A huge Soviet pulp-and-paper mill at the lake's northern end had been pouring into Lake Baikal industrial wastes that destroy aquatic life. The protests of Russian environmentalists had been unavailing. Perhaps newsprint for propaganda publications was regarded as more useful than fish and clean water.

Under Marxist governments in Eastern Europe, industrial pollution has spread widely. In Rumania, large districts, industrially polluted, have been fenced off and closed to the public. In Czechoslovakia, the great Danube River is too filthy now for swimming. Even public authorities declare that Bratislava, capital of the region of Slovakia, has the worst environment and the most pollution in Europe. Next door to the beautiful old estate of the novelist Leo Tolstoi in Russia, a vast chemical plant has been built, poisoning the forests of oak and pine. Grand medieval Russian churches are converted into factories.

Some countries with market economies or mixed economies are as reckless as the totalists of natural resources and seemingly as incapable of maintaining a decent environment. For many years, Venice, Italy—often called the loveliest of cities—was sinking into the Adriatic Sea, its underground water table reduced by the diversion of water to industrial uses on the mainland. Although the sinking has been stopped, Venice remains dangerously exposed to the storms of the Adriatic Sea, and its marvelous sculptures are being destroyed by industrial fumes from the mainland industrial sprawl of Mestre. The glittering cities of Venezuela and Colombia are ringed about by hideous slums, the result of industrial growth and agricultural decay.

Twentieth-century damage to the environment, abuse of natural resources, and ugly patterns of living appear, in considerable part, to result from hasty and ill-planned industrialization. Since this book is not about ecology, natural resources, or urban sociology, we lack space to discuss thoroughly here the possible remedies for these sorry conditions. It is quite possible, if intelligent action is taken, to resist and reverse these dangerous trends; yet such action is costly, involving long-range economic calculations.

Speaking only in terms of the world economy, it must be said that if people today do not act to reduce pollution, conserve resources, and restore tolerable patterns of living, our descendants will be impoverished. The world belongs not merely to the living, but also to the men and women who are to follow us in time: to those human beings yet unborn. The generation living today, in the Age of the Consumer, have no right to consume everything available to them at the moment.

The short-run costs of pollution prevention, conservation, and urban restoration are high. Yet the long-run costs to humanity of neglecting those economic responsibilities would be far higher. Steps already are being taken, especially in the United States, to preserve mankind's natural and cultural inheritance. An economy that fails to provide for future generations is like a farmer who consumes his own seed-corn intended for next year's planting. Such economic problems must be faced boldly in the future.

Discuss   3. The United States now has a federal Environmental Protection Agency; most American states have similar agencies or commissions, and so do the countries of Western Europe. These have been established in quite recent years. Why was little public attention paid to environmental problems until recently?

Dread Inflation

An ogre is stalking across the world. He devours the prosperity of every land. The chief men of great states surrender to him whatever he demands. This giant is especially ferocious when he encounters the aged and the poor. Unless some bold men and women resist him forcefully, he will smash every economy.

The name of the ogre is *Inflation*.

In the latter half of the twentieth century, nearly every country has suffered badly from inflation. The economic damage done by inflationary policies has been obvious in countries with market economies or mixed economies. In command economies, attempts are made to pretend that inflation cannot occur, because of controls on prices. Yet, in truth, the economic mischief worked by inflation has been more ruinous in communist states than in the Western democracies. The consequences of inflation have been less severe in the United States than in any other major country; still, during the 1970s it began to appear that inflation might stifle the growth of American production and perhaps have unpleasant political consequences.

We gave some account of inflation in Chapter 9, discussing money; also in Chapters 11 and 12. Now we turn to a closer description of the economic disease called inflation. *For in both market economies and command economies—and mixed economies, too—during recent years, the most persistent trouble has been inflation.*

When economists employ this word *inflation*, they mean a very rapid increase of prices, so that goods become far more expensive than most consumers ever had expected them to be. To put matters another way, during inflationary times the dollar, or the franc, or the pound, or the yen, or the mark, or the peso—for all currencies have been afflicted by inflation in our time—will buy less and less in the way of goods. If inflation proceeds far enough, these units of money may come to buy only a small fraction of the amount of goods they would have purchased before inflation began. *Prices go higher and higher as money becomes worth less and less.*

But how can money become worth less and less? Isn't a dollar, say, always worth a dollar?

No, it isn't. That is, the dollar of 1988 was not worth nearly so much as the dollar of 1938. Fifty years earlier, the dollar would have bought much more in the way of most goods.

For the value of the dollar, or of any other national unit of money, is not stable, or constant—not nearly so constant as it was in the days when most countries used gold as the basis of their money. (Even the value of gold has fluctuated considerably over the centuries; for that matter, the price of gold may vary widely within a single year.) *A dollar, or any other monetary unit, is worth only what goods it will purchase in the market.*

Once upon a time, in the 1940s (indeed, for years later than that), a dollar would purchase twenty good-sized candy bars. In the 1980s, a dollar would purchase, at best, four candy bars (somewhat smaller than the bars of the 1940s). The dollar, in short, was not worth nearly so much in the 1980s as it had been forty or fifty years earlier: the dollar has suffered from inflation, especially since the middle 1960s.

This American inflation became most severe during the 1970s. Trying to restrain or diminish this inflation became the chief economic problem of the American national government during the 1980s.

But the United States has suffered less from inflation than have most countries. Some of the worst inflation has occurred in command economies. Consider, for instance, the currency of Yugoslavia, a country ruled by its Communist party since the Second World War. During 1981 and 1982, inflation grew so rapidly in Yugoslavia's economy that the *dinar* (Yugoslavia's unit of currency) had to be devalued twice within eighteen months.[2] The first devaluation amounted to 30 percent of the claimed value of the dinar; the second devaluation, to 18 percent. In other words, the Marxist government of

2. The term ***devaluation*** is formally defined as "a reduction in the exchange value of a country's monetary unit in terms of gold, silver, or foreign monetary units." In other words, governments devalue their monetary unit, or currency, when they find that they cannot sell their goods abroad because the country's inflated prices are too high. That is, as price inflation moves higher in Poland or Yugoslavia, and as the zloty or the dinar loses value in relation to sound currencies like the German mark, the American

Yugoslavia found it necessary to declare that their own money was worth little more than half of what they had previously claimed it was worth in international exchange. Yugoslav inflation of the dinar during this period was about ten times as great as American inflation of the dollar's purchasing power. Or, to put it another way, Yugoslav prices expressed in dinars (on the black market, anyway) went up ten times more than American prices expressed in dollars, during the same period.

Since then, inflation of the dinar has continued. During 1983, Yugoslav currency suffered a devaluation of 83 percent: that is, in international exchange, the Yugoslav government was compelled to acknowledge that the dinar had lost 83 percent of its value in a single year. Inflation of the *dinar* continued throughout 1984. During 1985, the country suffered from 90 percent inflation; during 1986, inflation reached 130 percent. And during 1987, Yugoslavia's money lost its value by 170 percent (official figures of the Yugoslav government)!

By autumn 1984, a million Yugoslavs were unemployed, and a million more had gone abroad to find employment. The pay of many workers was drastically reduced by government policy. The labor unions—even under a totalist regime—were protesting angrily. The vice-governor of Yugoslavia's National Bank declared publicly that there had occurred "a drastic tightening of Yugoslav belts." He warned that economic suffering had reached "the point where political problems arise."

Yet Yugoslavia is not an extreme example: inflation was greater in some other Marxist and Third World countries and in some market economies. (Yugoslavia is the only Communist-governed country that supplies more or less accurate statistics about inflation, and Yugoslavia's command economy is not total—that is, small elements of the private

dollar, or the Swiss franc—why, people in other countries cease to buy overpriced Polish or Yugoslav goods; instead, consumers buy from other countries or from domestic sellers in their own country.

So in order to save its export trade, the nation-state suffering from inflation—Yugoslavia, Poland, or some other country—must admit that the dinar or the zloty no longer is what it used to be, in terms of international exchange. The government in question devalues its monetary unit: that is, the government now will give more zloties or dinars in exchange for marks, dollars, or francs. Then, after devaluation, the country suffering from inflation can sell its products again, because now they are cheap in terms of foreign currencies.

sector survive, and, in theory at least, some independence of decisions is left to workers' syndicates and to the several "people's republics" that make up Yugoslavia.)

So inflation is a worldwide difficulty, and a very grave one. What causes this economic disease to spring up everywhere?

The basic cause of inflation is this: a large increase in the supply of money at a time when the supply of goods is not increasing much, or is diminishing. Money becomes relatively plentiful, but goods remain scarce or grow scarcer. Therefore, the dollar, or franc, or mark, or pound, or zloty, or dinar, will buy fewer goods during an inflationary period than that unit of money would have purchased before the money supply was increased. *Too much money is chasing too few goods.*

Commonly, in inflationary times, too much money has been put into circulation by central governments for political reasons—even though severe inflation may lead to a government's downfall. Political instability often causes economic inflation; and economic inflation, in turn, often contributes to political instability.

To understand the relationship between political strategy and inflation, consider the following episode. The Republic of Costaguana is imaginary, but the lesson this example teaches is true.

The Miscalculations of His Excellency Enrique Padron

With the support of the urban unemployed in his country's chief towns, and especially through the raising of bodies of armed peasants to intimidate his political opponents, Enrique Padron has made himself dictator (with the title of president) of the Republic of Costaguana.

Once in office, President Padron determines to build himself a splendid new presidential palace—and simultaneously to double the monthly government payment to unemployed persons in Ciudad Costaguana, the country's capital, where more than 40 percent of the male inhabitants lack permanent employment. The dictator believes that the latter measure, at least, will make him still more popular and secure him in power.

"But, your excellency, where are we to find the money for all this?" inquires the minister of finance.

"Borrow it, my friend," the dictator replies, with a wink that is not altogether pleasant.

"From what source, your excellency? We have difficulties with the International Monetary Fund, and the American and Swiss banks have declined to advance more credits to us, because we have been unable to pay the past three installments on our existing loans."

"It is quite simple, my friend: direct the National Central Bank of Costaguana to issue new bank notes to a value of ten billion *populares* [the familiar name for the Costaguanan unit of money]. That done, our government will accept a loan, secured by government bonds, from the National Central Bank. The amount of this loan will be ten billion *populares*. We shall spend it all quite promptly."

The minister of finance obeys. The money supply of Costaguana is increased abruptly by ten billion *populares*. The National Central Bank sells the government's bonds (at a heavy discount) to such investors, domestic and foreign, as the bank can attract. A new presidential palace is erected; and certain contractors, the dictator's brother among them, do very well out of that job. The cash incomes of persons on unemployment relief are doubled. For a short time, everybody seems to have plenty of *populares* to spend.

But the price of nearly all goods in Costaguana has commenced to rise. For although the Central Bank has been able to print more notes, this does not mean that the peasants of Costaguana have been able to produce more foodstuffs, or that the fishermen of Puerto Costaguana have been able to net more fish.

Unemployed people who used to buy a loaf of bread for half a *popular* now discover that such a loaf costs four *populares;* for though there are more *populares* in circulation, there are not more loaves of bread in circulation. In foreign exchange, the value of the bank note called the *popular* has fallen very sharply, because the central banks and the finance ministries of other countries now distrust the reckless spending of Costaguana. This fall of the *popular* abroad means that imported goods cost a great deal more in Ciudad Costaguana than they did before the printing of those ten billion *populares* in new bank notes.

Printing of the money has increased the demand for goods; but it has not increased the supply of goods. When demand increases, but supply remains constant, prices always rise. They rise swiftly and tremendously, indeed, in Costaguana.

Costaguana's inflation brings on a severe economic recession of the sort that economists call *stagflation*—that is, rising prices combined with a stagnant business condition and high unemployment.

The dictator attempts to cure the recession by yet more spending on a grand scale. As before, his government finances these new public expenditures by having the Central Bank issue more paper money, unsecured by anything but the government's word.

This measure produces "**double-digit inflation**"—that is, prices rise more than 10 percent within a few weeks. By the end of the year, it is **triple-digit inflation:** prices are 217 percent higher than they were at the same time in the previous year.

Many Costaguana businesses fall into bankruptcy. People with small incomes are hardest hit, for their little money will buy next to nothing now. The savings of people with bank deposits are greatly reduced. In the backlands, small landowners and farm laborers refuse to pay taxes, because the prices of food and other necessities have increased outrageously.

The dictator doubles the number of secret police—one way of relieving unemployment. Nevertheless, the proportion of unemployed in the capital continues to grow. Army colonels and navy captains begin to mutter that the dictator is incompetent. A National Central Bank of Costaguana note for a thousand *populares* falls in international exchange to a value of three cents in United States currency.

Now the dictator regrets his rashness in issuing billions of *populares* with no real value behind notes or bonds. He perceives at last that mere "printing press money" does not represent genuine wealth. But he does not know how to undo the inflation he has caused. Army and navy mutiny, overthrowing the dictator, who flees to Cuba.

The new government, a military junta, repudiates all the debts of the dictator's regime. All people who bought the bonds of the previous regime suffer a total loss of their investment. The junta abolishes the note called the *popular,* replacing it with a new monetary unit called the *orden.* The National Central Bank is directed to call in all *populares* within thirty days, exchanging them for *ordenes* at the ratio of 1 *orden* = 1,000 *populares.* By the junta's decree, the value of the *orden* is fixed at one tenth of one Swiss franc. The country's economy begins to improve—but only slightly and slowly.

Though there exists no actual Republic of Costaguana, events similar to those related above have occurred in many countries during the twentieth century. The actual process of inflation and its results usually are somewhat more complex than this imaginary episode in Costaguana. Political instability often causes economic inflation; and economic inflation, in turn, often contributes to political instability.

Discuss

4. If the dictator's giving more money to unemployed Costaguanans doubled their incomes overnight, why in the long run were those unemployed worse off than before? Or were they worse off? Can you explain?

5. Why did the price of bread in Ciudad Costaguana rise swiftly by 800 percent? Did this increase result from a plot by the bakers? If the government had decreed that no loaf of bread should be sold for more than half a *popular,* what might have happened?

6. If you had been a Chilean dealer in agricultural implements, shipping tools and plows to Puerto Costaguana and other ports, would you have accepted a contract with a Costaguanan rural cooperative to send them twenty plows, at the previous month's price, to be paid in *populares*—after the dictator and the National Central Bank had issued ten billion new *populares?* Why or why not?

7. Other than by inflating the currency, by what means might the dictator have raised funds to the equivalent of ten billion *populares?* Why didn't he choose other means?

8. If you had ten thousand dollars in currency and suspected that swift inflation of prices was about to occur, how might you invest your money to "hedge" against inflation?

9. Even during the height of American inflation during the late 1970s, many foreign investors converted their money into dollars and deposited it in American banks. Why did they do so?

Political Causes of Inflation

The major factor in the inflation of prices and the devaluation of money is governmental policy.

Every year, governments are tempted to spend more money than they obtain through taxation. One reason for this situation is the unstable political condition of the world nowadays and the danger of war that results from such instability, prompting governments to spend

gigantic sums upon armaments. Another reason for excessive governmental expenditure (especially in democratic societies) is the demand
by interest groups for ever-increasing "welfare" benefits at public
expense.[3]

If governments do not or cannot obtain enough money through
taxation, they must borrow the rest of the money they spend. Therefore,
governments adopt **deficit budgets:** That is, they go into debt to obtain
the funds they require.[4]

*When a government runs up deficits in its annual budgets, a
country is in danger of inflation of prices of goods.* If the deficit is only
temporary and the government's credit is very sound, such financing will
not result in higher prices. But if the deficit grows year after year and
the government's level of spending amounts to a large part of a nation's
gross national product, the time comes when most prices begin to rise
swiftly upward. (The **gross national product** is a year's total output
of goods and services.)

How does this happen? Why, only the government can "create
money"—that is, authorize the printing of more currency. *If a
government needs more money than it is obtaining from taxation, that
government must either borrow the additional funds or else simply print
more currency without any sound backing for that currency.* Simply to

---

3. **Interest groups** are blocs of people, often organized, who seek to advance or defend their
common interests—which may be economic, political, cultural, or religious. Commonly these interest
groups are represented by lobbies (political agencies) at Washington and at state capitals, in the United
States. There is the "concrete lobby" (representing firms that build highways and other public projects);
there exists the "welfare lobby" (representing the numerous people who desire more of such benefits from
the federal government as aid to households with low income or fatherless dependent children,
unemployment benefits, medical benefits under Medicare and Medicaid, public housing, etc.); also the
"education lobby" (representing the interest group, including teachers' unions, that desires more federal
grants for schooling). Among the many interest groups are industries advocating high tariffs (to reduce
foreign competition with their products); organizations of black citizens; associations of milk producers,
tobacco planters, sugar-cane growers, and cotton farmers (all of which obtain federal subsidies); leagues
for tax reduction; opponents of abortion; citizens wishing to make prayer in public schools lawful; citizens
of Mexican origin; and scores of others. All these interest groups seek legislation or grants favorable to
their especial interests.

4. A **deficit** is the amount by which a sum falls short of the total needed. When a firm or a government
has an excess of outgo over income, in terms of money, that firm or government is "running a deficit." A
deficit may be remedied, temporarily at least, either by borrowing or by reducing expenditures. In the case
of governments, a third remedy is to increase taxes.

print more money results in immediate ruinous inflation; only ignorant and irresponsible governments resort to such a measure, or else governments that are desperate for more funds to fight a war, like the Union and Confederate governments, described in chapter 9. If the supply of goods remains the same, but ten times as much paper money is put into circulation as was circulating before, prices must rise to ten times their former level, and the result is galloping inflation.

But the governments of the major countries today do not simply print more currency: they know that would ruin the economy. Instead, governments borrow the money they require (in addition to taxes). Yet excessive borrowing also causes inflation, though less directly and without effect upon a nation's economy so immediately disastrous.

Ordinarily, a government borrows money chiefly through its central banking system (in the United States, the Federal Reserve System, described in chapter 9). The central bank of a country is supposed to be more or less independent of the government; in practice, however, governments in power can exercise strong pressure upon central banks to cooperate with the government's financial policy. By inducing the central bank to lend the government vast sums of money (and ordinarily issuing government bonds that are given to the central bank as security for such loans), a government in effect authorizes the central banking system to create much more money.

For on the basis of the government bonds (the government's promise to repay such loans), the central bank proceeds to put a corresponding amount of money into circulation. To find this money to lend to the government, the central bank issues many more bank notes (paper money). The central bank authorizes its member banks, or commercial banks, to extend more credit to customers: more loans are made by banks to firms and individuals. When plenty of money and credit become available, demand for goods increases.

But if supply has not increased meanwhile (and ordinarily it hasn't), prices rise swiftly because of the increased demand for goods, firms and individuals now having more money to spend. And presently there occurs, as a result, the swift and startling skyrocketing of prices that we call inflation.

Now, if government should simply borrow money from its citizens without increasing the money supply, demand for private goods would decrease (there being less private money then available to spend on goods), and so inflation would be avoided. But in recent decades nearly all governments, needing much money both for "welfare" expenditures and to meet military costs, have done something different from this. They have *created* more money by forms of borrowing from central banks that have put much more money and credit into circulation, so vastly increasing demand.

Although prices have risen painfully in the United States, inflation has been less harmful in America than in other major countries, partly because of the reluctance of the Federal Reserve Bank's governors to create so much more money that severe inflation would result. But members of Congress now and again complain that the Federal Reserve is too conservative in its monetary policies. And if the national political administration at Washington thinks that the Federal Reserve is not creating enough money, the President can authorize the federal Treasury to issue its own notes, or can appoint a new chairman of the Federal Reserve Board. Therefore, much of the time the Federal Reserve tends to yield, creating more money in response to the government's borrowing.

In short, government deficits and national debts do not *necessarily* bring about inflation: it all depends upon the size of the deficit and the debt and the methods of borrowing that a government employs. In practice, however, deficit and debt have become major causes of inflation. In the beginning, deliberate inflation of the currency seems to many political leaders the easiest way out of their financial difficulties.

David Hume, the Scottish philosopher who was Adam Smith's closest friend, two centuries ago saw the danger in deficit financing. He expressed the point as follows:

It is very tempting to a minister [chief executive] to employ such an expedient as enables him to make a great figure during his administration, without overburdening the people with taxes, or exciting any immediate clamors against himself. The practice therefore of contracting debt will almost immediately be abused in every government. It would scarcely be more imprudent to give a prodigal son a credit in every banker's shop in London, than empower a statesman to draw bills, in this manner, upon posterity.

Discuss   10. What does Hume mean by his phrase "draw bills upon posterity"?

11. National governments have power to levy taxes of various kinds. Why then do nearly all governments meet deficits by borrowing, instead of raising more money through taxes?

During the administration of President Lyndon Johnson, the federal government of the United States borrowed immense sums to pay for two huge costs: the war in Vietnam, and the "social service" projects of Johnson's "Great Society" plan. (Medicare and Medicaid were among those projects; so was a vastly expanded program of public housing.) The combined cost of these undertakings raised the annual deficit and the national debt to levels almost no one had thought possible a few years earlier. There resulted a very sharp inflation of prices. Because of the tremendous increase of the national debt, and continued deficit financing, that inflation still troubles the American economy—although in recent years the rate of inflation has been considerably reduced.

The following table shows the increase of national debt since 1930 and how much that debt amounted to per capita (for each inhabitant of the United States). In 1930, the national debt stood at 16.1 billion dollars. By 1982, it exceeded one trillion dollars.

Public Debt of the United States

Fiscal year	Gross debt (billions)	Per capita
1930	$ 16.1	$ 132
1940	43.0	325
1950	256.1	1,668
1960	284.1	1,572
1965	313.8	1,613
1970	370.1	1,807
1975	533.2	2,497
1977	698.8	3,216
1979	826.5	3,737
1980	907.7	3,970
1981	997.9	4,329
1982	1,142.0	4,909
1983	1,377.2	5,920
1984	1,572.3	6,688
1985	1,823.1	7,686
1986	2,130.0	8,892
1987	2,355.3	9,725
1988	2,581.6	over 10,000*

*estimated

Interest paid on this national debt, in 1987, came to more than two thousand dollars per American household. The national debt is increased every year by deficit financing—that is, borrowing more money to make up the difference between government revenue from taxation and total government expenditures.

To understand how large the federal deficit has become, we can compare the deficit with the gross national product (GNP)—that is, the country's total annual output of goods and service during one year. The following chart makes this comparison.

In this chart, "The Real Cause of Deficits," the second column shows what percentage of the GNP the federal government takes in taxes. The third column shows what percentage of the GNP is spent by the federal government annually. The fourth column shows what percentage of the GNP the deficit amounts to. Note that in recent years the federal government's budget outlays have taken nearly one fourth of the gross national product—that is, a quarter of the nation's total productivity is taken by Congress for public spending. Part of this wealth is collected through taxation; the rest of it through borrowing (deficit financing).

	Receipts (% of GNP)	Budget Outlays* (% of GNP)	Deficit (% of GNP)
	The Real Cause of Deficits		
1970	19.5	19.8	.3
1971	17.7	19.9	2.2
1972	18.0	20.0	2.0
1973	18.0	19.2	1.2
1974	18.6	19.0	.4
1975	18.3	21.8	3.5
1976	17.6	21.9	4.3
1977	18.4	21.2	2.8
1978	18.4	21.1	2.7
1979	18.9	20.6	1.7
1980	19.4	22.1	2.7
1981	20.1	22.7	2.6
1982	19.7	23.8	4.1
1983	18.1	24.3	6.2
1984	18.1	23.1	5.0
1985	18.6	24.0	5.4
1986	18.3	23.6	5.3
1987	19.4	22.8	3.4
1988	19.3	22.4	3.1*
*estimates			

If the debt and the deficit have been growing so tremendously in recent years, why is there not greater inflation of the American dollar?

The answer seems to be that American productivity—the gross national product—also has been growing in recent years, in part because income taxes have been reduced and more private funds are available for investment in the factors of production. More money is in circulation because of the government's borrowing; but also more goods and services are available because of greater productivity. If the supply of goods increases more rapidly than the supply of money, inflation will diminish; inflation may even cease.

Nevertheless, the national debt and, even more, the annual federal deficit remain menaces to American prosperity. Under certain circumstances, "galloping" inflation of the dollar could start up again; some economists predict that it will.

Discuss

12. Can you suggest why the public debt increased so rapidly between 1930 and 1940? What political and economic events account for that increase?

13. Why was there a huge increase of the debt between 1940 and 1950?

14. The chart "The Real Cause of Deficits" shows that for eighteen years the federal government spent much more money than it received from taxation. What probably would happen to a firm or a household that carried on deficit financing for so long a period? Can the same thing happen to a government?

When a government borrows money excessively, it can work other economic harm besides direct inflation of prices. The more capital a government borrows, the less capital remains for the private sector. Thus, it becomes difficult for many businesses to obtain the capital required for continued operation and growth. As government borrowing continues, the rate of interest rises, because money to lend becomes scarcer. Many producers cannot afford to pay the higher interest; these firms cease to expand, and some may collapse. Thus, as government deficits grow, production of some goods ceases to increase. If governmental borrowing and the increased rate of interest persist for a long time, economic production may diminish—causing a reduction in the supply of goods. When supply shrinks, prices go up: more inflation.

There exists yet another objection to using budgetary deficits as a regular policy of government. Such practices are not merely inflationary for a few years: also they place a burden of debt on future generations of citizens, as David Hume said.

Until recent years, a good many economists believed that it might be possible to end a recession or a depression by resorting to deliberate inflation through public deficit borrowing—so stimulating demand for goods. But during the 1970s and 1980s, it was found that inflation instead may result in what is called **stagflation.** This is a term to describe a condition in which demand is stagnant (neither increases nor decreases), but prices continue to rise rapidly. High interest rates, fears for the future of the economy, and other factors may discourage firms and households from purchasing goods, so that demand is not increased; but meanwhile prices continue to rise because more money is being put into circulation.

Inflation terribly injures people who have no way of keeping up with the increase of prices and wages: the elderly and retired who live on fixed incomes; people with their savings invested in insurance policies, pensions, and savings accounts (all of which lose value during progressive inflation, or at least do not soon produce returns proportionate to the increase of prices); people, such as teachers and farmers, whose incomes tend to rise more slowly than do wages and salaries in many other occupations; and the poor, whose little incomes may remain constant in a time of swiftly rising prices.

Also, inflation discourages many forms of saving. Why buy bonds, say, that would pay interest at the rate of 6 percent per year—when the rate of inflation may be 18 percent? Thus people tend to shy away from long-term, stable investments. With that sort of saving, one's capital might dwindle rapidly. Why not spend one's income right now, to the full, before prices move yet higher? So demand increases, without an increase in supply: more inflation. *A society in which saving is not rewarded eventually sinks into poverty.*

And inflation encourages governments to spend public funds

extravagantly for purposes temporarily popular. "After all," many voters may think, "we're not going to have to pay the principal on all the money the government borrows for a long, long time." If the government pumps out plenty of money—why, that makes it possible for debtors to pay off their private debts more easily, even though inflation greatly hurts the creditors who advanced money to the debtors. For a while, an inflationary era may look like a time of general prosperity. Many citizens, like their government, spend far more than they are prepared to repay, in such times. But in the long run, a day of reckoning comes.

If inflation produces all those evils, why do not governments of great countries do more to prevent inflation? And why do not citizens protest more successfully against continuing inflation?

As for twentieth-century governments, political leaders are under constant pressure to find more money for domestic programs or military expenditures. To obtain that money by increasing taxes might make them unpopular. Also, heavier taxes can depress, rather than stimulate, a nation's economy. The easiest way—though the most unsound way— for a government to obtain more funds is to borrow by one means or another. Borrowing puts more money into circulation, but it does not increase the supply of goods. From the World Bank or from great American and European banks, such countries as Brazil, Nigeria, Yugoslavia, Poland, Argentina, Mexico, Peru, Chile, and Zaire—differing greatly in their economic systems and their politics—have borrowed many billions of dollars or other currencies. By the summer of 1988, all of these countries suffered badly from inflation; and all of them had great difficulty in paying interest on their loans, let alone repaying any principal. Should some of these countries simply repudiate their debts, there might occur a financial crash greater than that which brought on, in 1929, the Great Depression. Deficit financing and inflation can lead to worldwide economic disaster. Eminent politicians may know this— but they trust that the day of reckoning will not come until they have left office, or perhaps until they have ceased to live.

As for the general public—why, many citizens expect to have

their cake and eat it, too. People tend to want more goods than they are willing to work for. Every group in a society desires all the advantages it can obtain. Therefore, governments feel compelled to follow short-term policies of pleasing the public (or much of the public), even though the long-run results of inflationary policies may be disastrous for nearly everybody. Once powerful political pressure groups have fallen into the habit of demanding larger grants and subsidies from the government every year, politicians find it most difficult to reduce public expenditures. Too many citizens, in every country, seem to think that the central government has limitless financial resources which ought to be used to benefit whatever group asserts a claim for public assistance. Some people even will say, "Well, why doesn't the government just print more money so there will be enough for all good projects?" Many of these people really are ignorant of the fundamental principles of economics. They do not know that money is a symbol representing somebody's labor; that goods are scarce; that a limitless supply of money, uncontrolled inflation, would result in sky-high prices; and that uncontrolled inflation ends in a country's economic collapse and general poverty. Such people do not understand that the political state itself is not the source of wealth, or that the funds which government spends must come from the economic structure of the country. Thus it is that a good many citizens, not understanding the problem of inflation, demand public expenditures that in the long run will be harmful to those citizens themselves.

It is the policies of governments, not the ways of buyers and sellers in a competitive market, that produce the inflation which distresses the world's economy today.

Discuss   15. President Franklin Roosevelt once told the American public not to fear the growth of the national debt, for "We owe it to ourselves." Would it be possible to get rid of inflation simply by canceling the national debt? Would anyone lose by that cancellation, if Americans merely owe the debt to themselves? Would a reduction of the debt make the dollar worth more or less? Why?

16. Can you name some groups of people or economic interests that seem to profit by continuing inflation?

17. Suppose that Mr. Thomas Sikorski bought a house in 1960, paying for it by a thirty-year mortgage at 5 percent interest. Suppose that in 1980, the interest rates on such mortgages should have risen locally to 18 percent. Would this increase of the interest rate have anything to do with the general inflation of money and prices that had occurred during the intervening twenty years? If so, what and how? So far as his mortgaged house went, would Sikorski be better off because of inflation, or worse off?

18. Suppose that our friend Thomas Sikorski, in 1950, had taken out a thirty-year "endowment" insurance policy, on which he had to pay a substantial premium every year. He would become sixty-five years old in 1980, and he originally had expected to retire in modest comfort at that age, combining his Social Security retirement benefits with the annual sum the insurance company would pay him on this endowment policy. (That sum would be $175 monthly.) With respect to his insurance policy, did Sikorski gain or lose as a result of general inflation? Explain.

19. Suppose that you were a major stockholder in a firm manufacturing school buses—one form of automobile for which there has been increasing demand, in America and abroad, over the past quarter of a century. Even at the height of inflation, your firm had no difficulty in selling its product. As the price of goods (including labor) went up generally, your firm merely raised its own prices proportionally. Nevertheless, your company as a corporation, and you personally, protest vigorously against governmental policies that accelerate general inflation. Why should you object, if your firm still can sell its product? Can you think of ways in which continuing inflation might adversely affect both your firm's return on investment and your own pocketbook?

Inflation and Allied Difficulties in a Command Economy

The ogre Inflation has been savage enough, during recent years, in market economies and mixed economies. Let us see how he behaves in command economies. Consider one Marxist state, Poland—seen through the eyes of one Polish household.

During the years 1980 and 1981, a strong movement of protest against the Communist government arose in Poland. An important cause of this protest was the inflation of prices. A popular demand for more freedom and a tolerable economy took form through a national independent labor union, called *Solidarity*. But in December 1981, the central government declared martial law and crushed the labor union by force.

Among the members of Solidarity was Dr. Rett Ludwikowski, professor of political science at the ancient Jagiellonian University, in Krakow. When the Communist regime crushed Solidarity, Dr. Ludwikowski was harassed by the secret police; at the university, he was ordered to teach the alleged benefits of martial law. Refusing to do that, Ludwikowski contrived to escape to the United States, together with his wife and children. In America, he obtained political asylum, and he is now a professor of law at a major university. Dr. Ludwikowski's account of Poland's economic condition, as told to American journalists, suggests the shortcomings of the typical command economy and how inflation torments Communist-ruled countries.

In the beautiful old city of Krakow, the Ludwikowskis were better off economically than the great majority of Poles. Russian troops had occupied Poland at the end of the Second World War, establishing a Polish Communist government there. But the Communists had not been able to break the influence of the Catholic church, to which nine out of ten Poles still belong. And although a centralized socialist economy had been forced upon the Polish people, still Poles stubbornly resisted Soviet domination. More than the other "captive nations" of Eastern Europe, the Poles clung to some control over their own national economy.

Even so, the Polish economy was mismanaged. Incompetence and corruption among the bureaucracy at its upper levels were notorious. A great deal of money was in circulation, but the prices of most goods were very high, and many goods were available for purchase only rarely. These are the usual results of galloping inflation.

By 1980, the Polish economy seemed near collapse. Food was scarce, although before Communist rule Poland had been one of Europe's major agricultural producers. Industrial production, which the government had tried to enlarge, was inefficient and had difficulty competing in international markets. The government depended on more loans from the West to make up for its immense budgetary deficits. The depressed state of the economy, indeed, was a principal reason for the rise of the Solidarity union. One Communist regime after another had failed to make the Polish command economy function successfully. Prices whizzed steadily upward.

In this depressed society, the Ludwikowskis held respected and tolerably secure positions—Dr. Ludwikowski as a senior professor, his wife as a lawyer for the municipal government. Although their household income was considerably larger than that of most Poles, in 1980 and 1981 they found that actually their combined salaries would purchase little.

The Polish monetary unit is the *zloty.* In 1981, the official value of the zloty (as declared by the Polish central bank) was thirty to sixty zloties to the American dollar. (If one brought dollars into Poland, wishing to exchange them for zloties, banks would pay thirty zloties per dollar. If one were leaving Poland and wished to buy dollars to take abroad, the Polish banks would charge sixty zloties to the dollar. In a market economy, banks are unable to manipulate the exchange of currency on this scale.) Yet in international exchange, by 1980 and 1981, the zloty was worth next to nothing.

Even in other Communist-ruled countries of Eastern Europe—East Germany, Czechoslovakia, Hungary, Rumania, Bulgaria, Yugoslavia—banks, hotels, and shops refused to accept any zloties in payment. For the Polish economy was falling apart, and nobody trusted the financial promises of the Polish government, which was kept from fiscal ruin only through huge loans obtained from the West. The ogre Inflation was abroad in the land.

In the Polish black market, it took four hundred fifty zloties to buy one American dollar. Only in the black market, within Poland, could zloties be exchanged for foreign money.

The average wage in Poland was six thousand zloties per month. In terms of the black-market value of the zloty, that was little more than thirteen dollars monthly. To put it another way, any Pole who had been permitted to spend his monthly income on foreign goods would have found (supposing him to have earned an average income) that his month's labor would have gained him merely thirteen dollars' worth of American goods. Even in terms of Polish goods, prices, and currency, the typical Polish worker earned only about eighty-two dollars per month.

Nearly all goods are sold in state-owned stores at prices fixed by the Polish government. In some state shops, during 1980 and 1981, prices of certain goods still seemed reasonable: food, shoes, baby clothes, soap, and gasoline were not excessively costly—if one could find them.

The trouble was that, at the officially fixed prices, these goods seldom were available, and then only in scanty quantities. Such goods were rationed—that is, they were sold only when customers presented official coupons entitling them to make such purchases. Soap, for instance, was rationed at one bar every two months for each person. Shoes, meat, sugar, imported fruits, butter, margarine, coffee, rice, eggs, tinned fish, and most articles of clothing were some of the articles strictly rationed.

To succeed in buying such items at the official prices—even if a consumer had ration coupons and the money—one had to wait in line a long period. Sometimes, indeed, it was necessary for the intending purchaser to return to that long line the next day, or even for several days. Frequently, people hired elderly or unemployed persons to stand in line as their representatives. One might have to wait in line all night to obtain gasoline. Deep resentments at such treatment were another influence behind the growth of the Solidarity union.

The Polish state also maintained another type of store: the "dollar shop," selling chiefly to tourists from the West, where all sorts of goods were available—at extravagant prices payable only in American dollars. A very few private shops selling costly goods were permitted to exist in Poland.

But if one urgently wanted scarce goods, one turned to the black market. Under cover, almost anything might be bought there. "Under-the-counter" goods cost plenty of money. Ordinarily boots might cost forty thousand zloties on the black market—half of that price to be paid in American dollars.

In the black market, ski jackets cost between eighteen thousand and thirty thousand zloties; tennis shoes, about eight thousand zloties. Automobiles, foreign books, medicines, and much else might be gotten in the black market—for a price. Sometimes the dealers would demand their entire payment in American dollars. Their dealers, too, had to pay very high prices to their underground sources of supply. In the case of goods smuggled into Poland, dollar payment ordinarily was demanded.

In wartime, rationing sometimes occurs in market economies, and most people accept it without much complaint. But in command economies, rationing and ration queues (lines) may continue during years of peace; and many people bitterly resent such controls. Especially they resent being treated like sheep.

Marguerite Ludwikowska, Dr. Ludwikowski's wife, stood in a long line early in 1982, hoping to buy candy for the Ludwikowski children. Waiting beside her was a trembling eighty-year-old man. They stood in line together for more than two hours. When the old man reached the counter, he was told that he could not have any sweets, that candy could be bought only with coupons for children.

"So I cannot get any candy?" the old man asked, a tremor in his voice. He repeated his question, as if in disbelief. Then, humiliated, he stumbled out of the shop.

"I wished to offer him our children's coupons," Marguerite Ludwikowska said after arriving in America, "but another woman restrained me, remarking that it might hurt his feelings." A man standing in line with them said, "I'd kill the ones who brought about this state of things. We worked so hard for so many years, and we're not able to sell candy to an old man. I hate them; I'd kill them all."

The angry man was referring to the Communist officials governing Poland. It was their blunders, he declared, that had ruined the Polish economy. Thousands of little incidents like that at the candy counter roused Poles to their massive protests against the Communist government in 1980.

Dr. Ludwikowski, in that year, heard that twenty-five bicycles were to be sold at a state store. He hired someone to stand in line for him. Ludwikowski was Number Twenty-Five on the list of customers.

When the shop opened and the first twenty-five names were called out, a woman who was twenty-sixth demanded to see the list. On being given it, she stuffed the list in her mouth and ate it. Then it could not be proved who was entitled to buy a bicycle, and all the cycles were shipped to a different store.

"Yet no one was angry with the woman," Dr. Ludwikowski said later. "We all understood what it feels like to lose one's chance. But can you imagine eating the list?"

By 1980, in short, nearly all goods were painfully scarce in the command economy of Poland. It was clear that communist economic theory and practice had brought poverty, not prosperity, to the Polish people. Why?

Because of miscalculations on a huge scale by the central planners, it appears. These mistakes were caused in part by an attempt to follow Marxist theories in agricultural and industrial policy rather than trying to form practical and realistic policies for the country.

Take agricultural economics. Marxism teaches that the land should belong to "the nation"—that is, be the property of the centralized state. Obeying this theory, in the 1970s the Communist government tried to wipe out peasant agriculture and establish "collective farms" and rural cooperatives. Not only was there bitter resistance to this scheme, but presently the government discovered that the agricultural yield of the collective farms and cooperatives was much lower than the yield from farms and small holdings in private hands. Also, the collectives and cooperatives were costly to administer. Agricultural production in Poland had sunk dangerously.

The government then abandoned its policy of collectivization, but great damage had been done. In order to keep the price of food reasonable in the towns, the government fixed low the prices paid to peasants. Therefore, the peasants had small incentive to produce food for others: they grew only what they needed for themselves, or little more. The government encouraged young people to leave the farms for jobs in industry—the shipyards, the steel mills, the mines. This left only the elderly and feeble to work the land. Agriculture was denied capital for machinery and improvements, because the government wished to concentrate upon industrial development. So, remarked Rett Ludwikowski, "Poland, which was once able to feed half of Europe, became a starving country."

Take industrial economics. "Early in the 1970s, it was decided by the government to accomplish great industrial developments in Poland," Ludwikowski said. "This grandiose plan failed because of low production. Although the Polish government borrowed billions of dollars from Western banks, this was not enough capital for the great plan. Also, an economic recession occurred in the West, reducing the market for Polish industrial products. And inflation in the West, on which the Polish planners had counted, did not go so high as the Polish government had expected. But Polish inflation went on wildly.

"Then the government realized that its jump in development was too swift, and it moved to slow down the rate of industrial growth," Professor Ludwikowski pointed out. "Millions of dollars' worth of equipment was left with nobody to utilize it. There were enormous losses.

"Nevertheless, the government then tried to shorten the periods required for completing industrial projects. Everything was uncoordinated." Perhaps the worst confusion occurred at Katowice, where a tremendous steel-making complex was constructed. Wages paid there were twice or thrice wages in factories elsewhere in Poland; so workers at Katowice consumed more. All goods began to disappear from the shelves of stores. Polish production having been geared for export, consumer goods were not available to refill those shelves. With prices rising swiftly and no gold to back the zloty, the Polish government simply printed more paper money. Thus the zloty would buy less and less, at Katowice or elsewhere: galloping inflation.

"We have central planning in which prices are set by planners who have no information," Ludwikowski concluded. "They try to cover their great mistakes by slogans and pretenses of reform."

This first-hand account of Polish economic sufferings is confirmed by many other recent reports. Similar conditions, or worse, prevail in other totalist lands with command economies. Whatever may be said in favor of the command economy, it is difficult to argue that it exceeds the market economy in production, distribution, and consumption. It does exceed the market economy in the speed and consequences of inflation.

Discuss

20. If a Polish state store could sell at a reasonable price every bar of soap on its shelves, why wouldn't the state stock enough soap so that customers could buy a bar a week, instead of one bar every two months (the amount allowed by rationing in 1980–81)? Relate your answer to the laws of supply and demand.

21. Are there any black markets in the United States? If so, in what goods? How can black markets exist in a competitive economy?

22. If the masters of a command economy have absolute power, why can't they command producers to turn out whatever amount of goods the government wants—and get results? Why don't they order the farmers to grow enough food for everybody, and the makers of bicycles to supply enough bikes to every bicycle shop? Explain your answer, with reference especially to the four factors of production.

23. The Polish zloty, in 1981, would bring next to nothing in exchange for Western currencies (or for Japanese yen) at banks in New York, London, Paris, Brussels, Milan, Zurich, or Tokyo. Yet when the Polish government permitted Polish citizens to buy small

quantities of dollars (not more than four hundred dollars for travel overseas), it pretended that the zloty was worth nearly two cents. How is the actual value-in-exchange of any country's money determined? In 1988, the British pound was worth a dollar and eighty-five cents. If the British government said the pound was worth ten dollars, would American banks have to accept that figure?

What the Ludwikowskis experienced in Poland has been found by intelligent and honest observers in every command economy of the 1980s. In 1983, the Yugoslav scholar Mihaljo Mihajlov pointed out with sorrow and anger that inflation in Yugoslavia had reached 50 percent in the course of one year. Fourteen percent of Yugoslavia's population was unemployed. "Corruption has grown to unimaginable proportions," Mihajlov wrote. He remarked that in 1981 alone, the Yugoslav state had taken action against nineteen thousand cases of alleged "crimes against socialist property"—that is, theft and sabotage in state factories, bribery of managers and supervisors, and similar offenses.[5]

The faults of a command economy, apparently, are not Russian faults merely. They are failings natural to any economic system directed by central political authority.

The ogre Inflation is unimpressed by the theories of Karl Marx and other socialist ideologists. Inflation drubs the command economy even more mercilessly than it beats the market economy.

Secondary Causes of Inflation

Mistaken political policies are the most common and severe cause of massive inflation of prices. But other causes of inflation need to be mentioned.

Inflation of prices can result when a great many newcomers arrive in a region with no large supply of goods readily available. This

---

5. See Mihaljo Mihajlov, "The 'Third' Yugoslavia," *St. Croix Review*, August-September, 1983 (vol. XVI, No. 4), pp. 23–30; also Eric Bourne, "Yugoslavs face a tight squeeze under IMF austerity program," *Christian Science Monitor*, August 29, 1984, p. 11.

occurred in the California Gold Rush of 1849, described in chapter 10. Such phenomena have occurred repeatedly during recent decades in Asia, Africa, and much of Europe, when hundreds of thousands of people have fled from war, revolution, or persecution to neighboring countries—or even to other continents. In such circumstances, the demand for food, shelter, and clothing by the crowds of refugees often vastly exceeds the available supply of such goods; and prices inevitably soar upward.

Or powerful business groups, commonly called *cartels* or *trusts*, may join together to charge high prices to their customers throughout the world. When this happens, inflation of the price of some major commodity results. From time to time, this strategy has succeeded with petroleum, coffee, and even chocolate. Usually the cooperation or leadership of certain governments is necessary for such international combinations. Countries that cannot produce oil or coffee or chocolate of their own are compelled to pay inflated prices for these imported goods. Usually these international combinations last no longer than a few months or possibly a few years. Although such sudden price increases may contribute to a general inflation—particularly in the case of oil—international cartels were not a major cause of the worldwide inflation of the 1970s.

Or a very powerful labor union, or combination of unions, may send prices upward for a time by demanding and obtaining sudden wage increases that make production more costly. Such high costs of production may tend to deprive business and industry of the capital required for making production more efficient. At the same time, the higher wages paid to labor (or to members of the labor unions involved) will put more money abruptly into the pockets of one group of consumers, so creating demand for more consumer goods, and possibly adding to a general inflation.

Some economists state that something of this sort, over a period of years, happened to the American automobile and steel industries. Wages paid in those industries rose so high that very large price increases were charged to customers. Automobiles or steel manufactured in Japan or Europe became cheaper than American manufacturers. Therefore, the American automobile and steel industries, with their inflated prices, sank into a recession during the 1970s.

In France, during the years immediately following the Second World War, one important element in the general inflation appears to have been the demands of labor unions, repeatedly successful, for higher and higher wages. Wages went up; but prices promptly went up also; then more wage demands occurred. This unhappy cycle ended only when general inflation subsided considerably and the unions were persuaded to exercise restraint in what they asked. In general, nevertheless, strikes for higher wages appear to result from the higher prices of a general inflation in a country, rather than to be a principal cause of that inflation.

Natural disasters, such as crop failures in the arid regions of Africa during the 1970s and 1980s, also result in sharp inflation of prices for food, normal supply having been reduced suddenly and tremendously. And yet other causes of inflation, particularly of a local character, might be mentioned. But it remains true that *the worldwide phenomenon of inflation in the developed countries is the result of political causes primarily*.

Discuss

24. In England during the nineteenth century, when the price of bread rose sharply, sometimes crowds of poor people would gather to protest by throwing stones to break the windows of the houses of "corn factors"—that is, wholesalers and speculators who bought and sold grain on a large scale. Do you think that this was an effective way to reduce the price of bread? Can you compare this with occasional demonstrations by American housewives in the 1970s, in front of supermarkets, to protest sharp inflation of grocery prices?

25. During the Second World War, and on various other occasions, the United States government has endeavored to prevent inflation of wages and prices by governmentally set "ceilings" (maximum levels) or wage-and-price controls. If such measures were made permanent (rather than being used only in some emergency), would inflation be prevented?

Remedies for Inflation

Is the ogre named Inflation invincible? Will inflation of the price of goods continue, worldwide, until the world's economy stagnates or virtually collapses, and the relative prosperity of the twentieth century gives way to absolute poverty in the twenty-first century?

The answer to that inquiry depends upon how much economic intelligence and political imagination are applied in the near future to diminishing the causes of inflation. Remedies can be found; whether such remedies will be adopted throughout the world may be up to the young people now in high school and college.

Remember that inflation amounts to too much money chasing too few goods. To express this idea more formally, today economists tend to agree that inflation is a sustained increase in the price level or, put another way, a sustained decrease in the purchasing power of money. Those are the two sides of the coin of inflation: prices of goods keep going up, so any unit of money will buy fewer goods.

There exist three major ways to check inflation—even to get rid of it. (Inflation, after all, is not a normal condition: the inflation that the world experiences nowadays did not begin until after the Second World War. In the past, in most societies, most of the time, prices were fairly stable.) Below, we analyze briefly these three ways of dealing with inflation.

1. ***Increasing the supply of goods.*** If enough additional goods become available, demand is satisfied; then prices fall. This approach is popularly called **supply-side economics.** How does an economy go about increasing the supply of goods, and thereby lowering the prices of goods, and, therefore, ending inflation?

Supply may be increased by various means. Greater efficiency of production is one way; invention of new productive technologies is another; discovery of new sources of natural resources is a third; others may be suggested. During the past two centuries and longer, supply has been greatly increased by such nonpolitical means. The greater the supply, the lower the price.

But we have emphasized in this chapter that political measures have been the primary cause of recent inflation of prices. So if inflation is to be reduced or abolished during the remaining years of the twentieth century, presumably there will be needed political reforms that affect the economy.

What can governments do to increase the supply of goods, and so stop inflation? In the United States, the Reagan administration adopted supply-side economics for this purpose. The rate of inflation was reduced, although economists still argue as to whether this remedy will last. To encourage the increase of supply, the American government lowered income taxes in the expectation that private saving will lead to greater investment in the factors of production. If more capital is available to permit national increase of economic productivity, then supply will increase. Also, the Reagan administration endeavored to encourage more economic development through other measures, such as reducing certain forms of governmental regulation of business and industry that seem to hamper productivity. (Deregulation of the airlines and of natural-gas extraction are examples of such measures.) Similar encouragement of industry and business was undertaken in Britain during the 1980s.

Supply-side economists say that the general increase of productivity expected to result from such measures will help greatly to reduce governmental deficits and national debts. For if the gross national product increases, the government's revenues from taxation will increase without any need to increase the *rates* of taxation. With larger revenues from taxation, the government will not need to borrow so much money to finance its budget outlays; deficits then will decrease or vanish. (There might even occur, in one year or another, a surplus of receipts from taxation; that used to happen, as recently as one year of President Eisenhower's administration, in the United States and other countries.) When a surplus of revenue occurs, it can be used to reduce the national debt. When the debt is reduced, interest on the national debt also falls—so leaving more money that can be applied to the increase of productivity in the country or to public purposes.

Such is the plan of the supply-side economists. Whether this method will suffice to stop inflation of prices—why, we may learn that within the next few years. Probably it will be necessary to combine the supply-side solution with one or both of the other ways, described below, for dealing with inflation.

2. ***Reducing public expenditures.*** Earlier in this chapter, it was pointed out that the major cause of inflation in our time has been excessive governmental costs, paid for by deficit financing (borrowing); and that governmental borrowing often has resulted in "printing-press money," putting too much money into circulation through central banks or national treasuries. Also, those countries that borrow immense sums of money from foreign bankers have tended to inflate their currencies and now, with weakened economies, are unable to borrow more.

The spending of governments can be divided into defense (military) expenditures and domestic (nonmilitary) expenditures. In the fiscal year 1987, the United States government spent a total of nearly one trillion, four billion, six hundred million dollars. Of this, more than $282 billion went for national defense and more than $722.6 billion for the federal government's domestic costs and programs. There has been much talk in Congress of reducing both major items—but relatively little economizing has been accomplished. Interest groups of various sorts always are pushing for more spending, not less.

To suggest how rapidly government spending tends to increase, below we have a chart showing how the costs of Medicare (the federal program of hospitalization and other medical costs of the elderly) have grown since the program was initiated in 1967. These costs now come to eighty billion dollars annually. Attempts to reduce Medicare benefits and payments are opposed by many hospitals, physicians, and organizations representing the elderly. Few people favor excessive public spending in general; but any particular proposal for reduction of costs promptly rouses the opposition of the group of citizens affected by the intended economizing.

Federal Outlays for Medicare Benefits

Fiscal year	Outlay (billons)
1968	$ 5.332
1969	6.222
1970	7.149
1971	7.875
1972	8.819
1973	9.479
1974	11.348
1975	16.316
1976	17.779
1977	21.549
1978	24.934
1979	29.147
1980	35.034
1981	39.149
1982	46.568
1983	57.443
1984	63.220
1985	70.527
1986	70.164
1987	75.120
1988	78.857*

*estimated

Source: *Budget for the Fiscal Year* published each year by the Office of Management and Budget

Because Congress seems unable to restrain the increase of federal spending, a constitutional amendment has been proposed in the United States to require Congress to balance the federal budget annually—that is, to forbid deficit financing. A similar constitutional amendment has been proposed in Italy, worse afflicted by inflation than the United States. *Were there no annual public deficits, a major cause of inflation would disappear.*

3. ***Increasing taxation.*** This third means for checking inflation would decrease public deficits by raising more revenue for governments: a "pay as you go" policy. With increased receipts by the government, less borrowing would be required; deficits would go down; and the inflationary effect of deficit spending would be lessened.

A sharp increase of taxation, however, always is unpopular with the general public; it may result in the defeat of members of Congress or a national administration at the next election. Moreover, heavy taxation tends to deprive the private sector of capital for the increase of productivity—and therefore to diminish supply, or at least to reduce the increase of the gross national product. If supply diminishes, inflation increases. So great care must be exercised by any government concerning the rate of any tax increase and what form of new tax or added tax is levied.

Unless one or two or perhaps all three of the above measures are adopted in the major developed countries, worldwide inflation will continue until the world's economy is terribly shaken. It requires courage among political leaders, and intelligence on the part of the general public, to confront the ogre Inflation. The general public still does not understand either the causes or the cures of inflation: that is why we have given so much space to discussing this difficult subject.

Pollution, waste, and ugliness; galloping inflation of prices— these are two of the grave threats to continued economic prosperity throughout the world. Yet we need not despair. This book's concluding chapter will suggest the possibilities for economic progress.

CHAPTER 14

A Cheerful View of Our
Economic Future

Chapter 14

A Cheerful View of Our Economic Future

- •The Prophets of Doom
- •The World Is Not Growing Poorer
- •Killing the Goose That Lays the Golden Eggs
- •The Moral Foundation of Economics

The Prophets of Doom

E conomists endlessly discuss scarcity. Is scarcity growing worse in our time? Are the world's natural resources being exhausted? Is the world's population growing so rapidly that there will not be enough consumer goods to satisfy basic needs?

Certainly, as we have seen in the preceding three chapters, both market economies and command economies have experienced troubles in the latter half of the twentieth century. Even the countries with the more prosperous market economies have suffered depressions and considerable unemployment from time to time. Countries with command economies have endured severe scarcity of many goods. The problem of inflation has plagued every industrial nation and nearly all simpler economies.

Do these recent circumstances suggest that much of the world must sink into grim poverty before long? Should we believe the economic prophets of doom when they say that today's economy is going to decay and perhaps collapse?

No.

There is good reason not to agree with the prophets of doom.

Economic difficulties occur in our time, but it does not follow that these troubles must grow worse. It remains quite possible—very probable, indeed—that intelligent and diligent work will continue to relieve scarcity, to discover or create new resources, and to provide adequately for increasing populations.

The modern economy greatly needs two things. One of those two things is vigorous imagination. The other is adequate motives (or incentives) for economic production.

Depletion of natural resources and growth of populations are not the primary troubles of today's economy. Rather, the production of goods is impeded during these closing years of the twentieth century by political and moral confusion. If nations can be persuaded to concentrate upon political improvements and the recovery of good moral habits, the twenty-first century may know a general prosperity unequaled in any previous age.

Let us look first at some of the gloomy predictions made by certain writers, economists, and public leaders.

1. These pessimists argue that the world, or a great part of it, is running out of raw materials.

2. They say that food production will become insufficient and that much of the world may suffer famine within a few years.

3. They declare that the sources of energy supplying the modern economy soon may be exhausted.

4. They maintain that industrial pollution may ruin even the air we breathe and the water we drink.

5. They tell us the human race will increase so rapidly that the world's populations soon will be crowded uncomfortably together, with little to eat.

6. They insist that in an age of increasing poverty throughout most of the world, immigrants will pour into the United States and other developed countries, bringing with them scarcity and unemployment.

7. They hint that the accumulation of all these economic disasters will make necessary the establishment of totalist governments throughout the world.

Such are some of the more alarming predictions about the economy of the not-very-distant future. Let us ask whether these visions can be justified by proofs.

Discuss

1. At the end of World War I, totalist governments with command economies came to power in Russia and temporarily in several other countries. Just before, during, and after World War II, many other countries submitted to totalist governments and command economies. From your knowledge of history and politics, can you suggest why great wars cause harm to constitutional governments and market economies?

2. Throughout the nineteenth century, and until the First World War, most people in Europe and America seemed optimistic about the future: they believed that the world would make strong social and economic progress. A different mood affects many people in Europe and America today: they tend to think that social and economic conditions may grow worse. Can you suggest some political, economic, military, and religious reasons for this widespread change in attitude?

3. Does it seem to you that we live in an age of scarcity? Can you think of five goods that seem scarcer today than they were fifty years ago? Can you think of five goods that seem more abundant today than they were half a century ago?

4. From your knowledge of history, can you suggest a time when most people were better off economically than most people are today? Can you name a time when the rich had more advantages than the rich of today enjoy? Can you suggest times and places when and where the poorer classes may have been better off than the poor are in today's cities, even though their cash income may have been lower?

5. Will most young people growing up today be better off economically than their parents were, or worse off? Why? Explain your answer.

The World Is Not Growing Poorer

Let us consider the optimistic replies of some economists to statements made by the prophets of gloom and doom. Economics has been called the dismal science because it emphasizes scarcity. Yet not all economists take a dismal view of our prospects. Here are some cheerful responses to gloomy challenges.

> 1. Is the world running out of raw materials? Not so: the supply of raw materials has been increasing ever since human beings began to live in communities—because people continue to discover or invent new sources for producing goods. *Since the dawn of history, the cost of raw materials has been going down, not up.*

A few years ago, some geologists and economists predicted that copper ore would become so scarce that copper would be unavailable for most purposes. That has not happened. Mining technology, instead, has made it possible to mine veins of copper more efficiently, and scientific prospecting has discovered new deposits of copper ore. By comparison with the rate of wages since the year 1800, copper has gone down in price remarkably for more than a hundred eighty years: in short, copper is more abundant than it was two centuries ago. This is true of nearly all other raw materials. Human intelligence, century after century, has succeeded in increasing the supply of raw materials, and there is no reason to suppose that the human beings of our time are less intelligent than the men and women of previous centuries.

> 2. Is the production of food decreasing, so that ghastly famines (experienced during recent years in the Sahara and in eastern Ethiopia) will spread through much or most of the world before many years pass?

No, there seems to be no real sign of a coming general scarcity of food. Just the opposite: agriculture, grazing, and fishing are far more efficiently productive in our time than ever before in human existence. The supply of food has not merely kept up with the growth of population: in the technologically advanced countries, at least, far more food is available than ever before.

Those countries where massive famines still occur ordinarily are lands with primitive subsistence economies—that is, no reserves of food, no money to import food from abroad, and no tolerable means for transporting large quantities of food even if they could be purchased. When such regions are struck by a natural disaster—a prolonged drought, or a great flood—they suffer immediately. Many people endure malnutrition, and some starve. But that tragic event is not caused by any world scarcity of food or by modern agriculture: it results from a people's failure to advance in agricultural methods and in means of transportation.

Famines occurred far more frequently, and were far more terrible and widespread, a century ago. Since the Second World War, despite a rapid increase of population in most lands, per capita production of food has increased steadily because of improved agricultural methods and better transportation. There is reason to expect the world's population to be better fed (if present trends continue) in the twenty-first century than in the twentieth—even in those countries with subsistence economies. Obvious exceptions exist, especially in those countries dominated by Marxist regimes. Ethiopia and Cambodia are just two of many countries in which the Communist government has caused the starvation of millions of people.

3. Are the world's sources of energy being exhausted? Will future generations shiver in the dark because coal, petroleum, natural gas, and the other fossil fuels have been used up almost totally? Will forests be cut down so that no firewood remains available? Will all forms of energy except water power and wind power vanish in the twenty-first century?

That is not going to happen. Prospectors and scientists continue to seek out and develop previously unknown fuel deposits and to create new sources of energy. Since the temporary gasoline shortages of the 1970s, for instance, tremendous deposits of petroleum and gas have been tapped in regions—especially in Britain—where such resources were not even suspected to exist a few decades ago. Because of new mining techniques, a seemingly limitless supply of coal is available in countries that have been mining coal for centuries. Scientific forestry has been increasing the extent of woodland in much of the world; and technology has developed more efficient uses of wood or substitutes for wood products.

The industrially advanced countries are just beginning to develop nuclear-fission plants for peaceable uses and are arranging safe methods for disposing of radioactive wastes from such industrial plants. Presumably all societies of the twenty-first century will have available much more energy (usually in the immediate form of electricity) than had the advanced societies of the twentieth century. (Similarly, the twentieth century had more energy at its disposal than did the nineteenth century; and the nineteenth had more than the eighteenth. The world, it needs to be repeated, has been growing richer, not poorer, for some centuries.)

4. Is our industrial civilization going to pollute the air, the water, the land, and even human bodies to such an extent that the human race will be in danger of dying out? Certainly pollution has to be taken seriously.

Obviously, there is more industrial pollution today than there was in Adam Smith's time, before the development of much heavy industry. On the other hand, some forms of pollution were more common and more death-dealing then: for one thing, no town had a good system of sewers, let alone scientific disposal of sewage.

Yet today technology is available to reduce every sort of pollution, and the public is far more aware of the perils of pollution than were most people thirty or forty years ago. The five Great Lakes of the United States, which together form the largest body of fresh water in the world, are being redeemed from industrial pollution after one lake had been pronounced (erroneously) "dead" and another "dying." Many other examples of recent successful resistance to industrial pollution might be cited.

Various forms of pollution will trouble industrial countries a hundred years from now, but, in general, industrial pollution is less dangerous and oppressive today than it was in the nineteenth century or in the first half of the twentieth century.

Preventing pollution adds to the cost of production, and yet most forms of prevention do not so greatly increase costs as to damage seriously the efficiency of industrial and agricultural production.

> 5. Well, what about population? Won't the world of tomorrow be so crowded with people, like ants in a hill or bees in a hive, that life may not be worth living?

Probably there will be little such crowding. In much of today's world, the birth rate is static or even falling—or increasing more slowly than it once did. Although most countries are likely to have larger populations a half-century or a century from now, this growth means also that more people will be available for work, so increasing production of goods. Just now it appears that the United States of the near future may have too *few* young people—not enough to fill the jobs at present required for American prosperity. There may not be enough young men and women to support the costly Social Security system intended to assist the elderly.

Certainly, to make density of population tolerable, it is desirable to improve living conditions in cities and to improve the circumstances of rural life. The mere fact that a region's population has increased, nevertheless, is not necessarily an economic problem. It may be an economic benefit—an increase of human resources in many ways.

Nor are regions and countries with a high population density necessarily unpleasant places to dwell. The most densely populated country in the world, ever, is the island of Taiwan, off the coast of China. Yet Taiwan, economically prosperous, also is a beautiful land for the most part, attracting many tourists who come to see the island's charms. Belgium, the second most densely populated country, generally regarded as an attractive, civilized land, learned long ago how to get along peacefully and prosperously with a very numerous population. England, the first of all countries to develop large factories and new industrial methods, has densely populated areas—but also still the loveliest countryside in the world.

6. Will millions—or hundreds of millions—of people from the less prosperous countries shift into the industrialized advanced countries, taking away jobs from citizens and lowering everybody's standard of living—besides undermining a nation's old culture and unity?

Surely large shifts of population are in progress already. But the peaceful coming of people from abroad is not usually a cause of economic decay. Rather, such migrations mean that the host country is acquiring more human resources. Most such immigrants, especially in the history of the United States, have been hard-working, ambitious people who hoped to improve their economic condition. Often immigrants are willing to accept, at least in the beginning, hard, dangerous, or unpleasant work for which it is difficult to find sufficient labor within a country's established work force.

In the long run, most immigrants become strong upholders of the culture, the political system, and the economy to which they come. (Also, aspects of their cultures enrich our own.) America's present economic success is built, in no small degree, upon the hard, intelligent work of millions of immigrants, coming in wave upon wave, decade after decade. New waves of immigrants during recent years already are being absorbed into American social and economic patterns. Some are people who migrate from their native lands in search of employment, notably nowadays Mexicans and Central Americans. Others are political refugees—Cubans, Vietnamese, Cambodians, Ethiopians, Poles, Hungarians—many of them highly educated and able. It would not be unreasonable to cry, "The more, the merrier!"

> 7. Finally, as the world of the future sinks into desperate poverty, will not democracies and other forms of free or constitutional government be overthrown by Communist or fascist dictators, who will seize control of the means of production and determine who gets what goods? Will not all the countries of the world adopt harsh command economies?

Of course, they could, but this does not have to happen. We have just argued that the world probably will grow richer, not poorer. Yet even if there should be no gain in productivity—even if there should occur some shrinking in productivity—it does not follow that people who have to tighten their belts must choose a totalist command economy in preference to a market economy linked with a constitutional government.

For politics is more than merely economics. Even could it be shown that a totalist state with a command economy might achieve a greater gross national product than could a free country with a market economy, it still would be highly improbable that the free peoples of the United States, or Britain, or France, or Switzerland, or New Zealand, or any other long-established nation accustomed to freedom, might choose to enslave themselves in return for slightly higher annual incomes.

And in actuality, since command economies are almost always less productive than market economies, even in the depths of a major depression there would be small temptation for people living under free constitutional governments to prefer some new totalist government with a command economy. During the Great Depression, which began in 1929, dictators' promises of restoring prosperity indeed resulted in the overthrow of democratic governments in several important countries, but the consequences of such political and economic revolutions, in the long run, became desperately unpopular. Although most people today do not know as much history as they ought to, still the history of the rise of the twentieth-century dictators is widely known, and its lessons are fairly well understood. In short, economic dissatisfactions do not necessarily bring about ruinous political revolutions.

To put this subject in a nutshell, during the next hundred years the world (and not merely the major developed countries) probably will reduce scarcity and relieve poverty. Much of the world will become conspicuously more prosperous than it is now. (Here we are assuming that the world will not be widely devastated by wars or revolutions.)

The coming age will experience many social difficulties. Yet those troubles will not be economic troubles primarily.

Discuss

6. Is there less gold in the world than there was in 1776? What two countries are the largest producers of gold? Can you name any metal of which the source is exhausted or nearly exhausted?

7. When did the last famine occur in the United States? If a famine comes in Bangladesh or Ethiopia, what do Americans usually do about it? Where would the poor nations obtain famine relief if there were no rich nations?

8. Name two sources of energy used by human societies before the Middle Ages. Have those sources been exhausted? What sources of energy are used in the twentieth century that were not employed by the ancient Greeks, the Romans, or medieval people? (Be careful here.) What was the chief source of industrial energy during the nineteenth century? Has that source of energy been used up or abandoned?

9. Is your city, town, or neighborhood more polluted now than it was fifty years ago? If so, how? If pollution has diminished, how did that come about?

10. Try to compare the economies of the two countries described below, and attempt to give reasons why the country with the dense population is far more prosperous than the thinly populated country.

The country of Bolivia has about 5,600,000 inhabitants, approximately thirteen persons per square mile of Bolivian territory. Bolivian soil is rich in deposits of minerals: antimony, tin, silver, copper, lead, zinc, petroleum, natural gas, bismuth, wolfram, gold, iron, cadmium, borate of lime. Bolivia has 1.5 arable (cultivated) acres of land for every inhabitant. Of working Bolivians, some 67 percent are agriculturalists.

The country of The Netherlands has about 14,150,000 people, approximately one hundred persons per square mile. The Kingdom of the Netherlands has no mineral resources except a modest amount of natural gas. The Netherlands has about a tenth of an acre of arable land for every inhabitant. Of working citizens of The Netherlands, about 6 percent are agriculturalists.

The average family income in The Netherlands is several times greater than the average family income in Bolivia.

Can you guess what Bolivian political leaders desire: a larger population or a smaller population? Why, economically speaking?

11. Suppose that in the 1850s a farmer named Samuel Porter, from the Finger Lake country of upper New York state, homesteads a tract of 640 acres of virgin prairie in western Iowa. He and his wife bring with them their five sons and three daughters; Mrs. Porter gives birth to a sixth son during their first months of residence in Iowa.

After the Porters have begun to plow a part of their 640 acres, neighbors appear: a family named Shaughnessy, from County Galway in Ireland. Thomas Shaughnessy, when young, had served several years in the British army in India. The Shaughnessys, who take up a section of prairie, bring with them a dozen children of various ages.

The Porters have had two unpleasant brushes with Kiowa Indian raiders. Mrs. Porter does not care for Irish people: their speech and manners vex her.

Do you suppose that Mr. Porter would welcome the Shaughnessys in such circumstances, or that he would try to buy them out and persuade them to move on westward? Why, economically speaking? Relate your answer to human resources.

12. Suppose that the United States, in the year 2029, should fall into an economic depression worse than that which began in 1929. Suppose that a big and eloquent political leader should demand the abolition of Congress, the nationalizing of the stock market and of major industries, and "fair shares for all"—equal distribution to everybody of the national income.

Would you support him and his proposed reforms or oppose him? Why? Give your reasons systematically.

Killing the Goose That Lays the Golden Eggs

Perhaps we are growing too cheerful. It will not do to look forward complacently to an era of general wealth and security. "There's many a slip 'twixt the cup and the lip," a proverb instructs us: that is, to employ another proverbial phrase, "Don't count your chickens before they're hatched."

For political and moral errors can suffice to ruin even an economy that, taken by itself and its fruits, seems remarkably healthy. Political policies, or lack of sound political policies, ruined the economies of ancient Rome, of Spain in the sixteenth century, and of various Latin American states in the twentieth century.

And blundering policies may be undertaken in democratic nations that retain market economies. Burdens may be placed on industry, agriculture, and commerce that are too heavy to be borne. The majority of a democratic people may come to believe that the economy functions automatically: that no matter how much the means of production are taxed and interfered with by governments, still general prosperity will continue. The same people may think that it does not really matter how much a government spends or how a government gets its funds. "Well, after all," people may say, "if the government hasn't got credit, who has? If you can't trust the government, who can you trust?"

Yet the people who control governments, like the people who control banks or factories or farms or publishing companies, can make serious mistakes in policy. Governments are run by human beings, and a good many human beings, otherwise able and popular, understand very little about economics.

It is quite possible for governments or labor unions or certain pressure groups or indeed the general public to demand so much from industry, commerce, and agriculture that the whole economy may slip into a long-run depression—perhaps into a permanent decline. That can happen in the United States; indeed, that process may have commenced in America already.

For during the 1970s, the American economy became virtually static. That is, productivity increased somewhat, but slowly, while population also increased more slowly than it had increased during the 1950s and 1960s. Making allowance for the inflation of prices that occurred during the 1970s, there was little or no gain in productivity; neither was there any very appreciable loss of productivity. To put the matter another way, the American economy kept running as hard as it could, just to remain where it was. The average citizen was no better off than he had been a few years earlier—but not really worse off, either. (Though he might think he was worse off, because of the higher prices he had to pay for goods and because of higher taxes.)

What had happened was this: the gross national product had ceased to increase. For many years Americans had expected a substantial increase annually in the gross national product of the United States—which would mean that their own private incomes, too, probably would go up. But in terms of *constant dollars* (that is, allowing for inflation), the typical American citizen ceased, sometime in the 1970s, to be better off than he had been before.[1]

In short, that marvelous American system of economic productivity was not behaving so marvelously as it once had. Conceivably, the gross national product might diminish if this trend were to continue: then all Americans would be tightening their belts. Industry, commerce, and agriculture were no longer expanding noticeably. Prices continued to rise, interest rates continued to rise, unemployment payments continued to rise, governmental expenditures continued to rise.

But productivity was *static:* that is, it did not increase or decrease. Why had the vigor begun to go out of American productivity?

---

1. **Constant dollar:** a fixed value of the dollar, determined by what a dollar would buy during a certain "base year," in the way of certain commodities. Because of inflation, the dollar of 1988, say, was worth less than the dollar of 1958: that is, the dollar of 1988 bought fewer goods and services than did a dollar of thirty years earlier. To understand what value a dollar has in any particular year, that year's dollar must be compared with the constant dollar. The device called the *constant dollar* is a way of measuring the dollar's real purchasing power.

For a part of the answer to that question, we can look at an imaginary, yet typical, American industrial firm: Gray Iron Fabricating Company of Mortmain, Michigan. The president of this foundry is Herbert McCullough. He and members of his family own most of the stock in this moderate-sized industrial corporation.

During World War II and for some years thereafter, Gray Iron Fabricating (founded 1921) balanced its books rather handsomely at the end of each fiscal year: that is, the business paid very satisfactory dividends to its stockholders and good salaries to its executives, Mr. McCullough chief among them; also, the firm held an excellent credit rating with three Michigan banks.[2]

But in about 1967, the foundry began to experience difficulties. There were troubles with two strong unions that had been certified by the National Labor Relations Board (NLRB) for collective bargaining with Gray Iron's management. Mr. McCullough found himself compelled to pay very high hourly wages—higher than in any other country in the world. Also, competition from abroad was becoming formidable. Some of Gray Iron's old customers began to mutter that they could buy cheaper from Japan or Germany, thousands of miles distant. Gray Iron's equipment, acquired mostly during the Second World War, needed replacement if production was to be efficient.

As the next few years passed, Gray Iron ceased to pay substantial dividends to its stockholders; Mr. McCullough reduced his own salary and the salaries of junior executives but could not reduce his bill for daily wages: that kept going up. Everything that Gray Iron had to buy was vastly more expensive than Mr. McCullough had expected it could become. The foundry, as business diminished, laid off nearly forty employees: the firm's payments to the Michigan Employment Security Commission had to be increased proportionately.

McCullough, who was not growing younger, found himself in trouble with a federal agency, the Occupational Safety and Health

---

2. **Fiscal year:** any annual period at the end of which a firm, a government, or some other agency measures its financial condition. Usually a fiscal year is not identical to the calendar year. For instance, a fiscal year may run from July 1 to the following June 30.

Administration (OSHA), because his equipment allegedly was not so safe as newer equipment would be. He was compelled to pay a substantial fine to the federal government. He was also forced into negotiation with another agency of the federal government, and into litigation with a woman junior executive, because he had promoted a young man over the woman's head. A third misfortune fell upon Gray Iron: a workman who had ignored safety instructions was electrocuted, and his widow sued for three million dollars' damages. The lawyers' fees were heavy, and the suit prolonged; then came appeals to higher courts; the whole thing became a heavy worry.

Meanwhile, Gray Iron Fabricating did not find it easy to meet its obligations to the banks; interest payments were kept up by strenuous efforts, but only minor sums of principal could be repaid. Orders from customers slowly diminished. Outwardly, Gray Iron Fabricating looked healthy enough, with handsome offices, a tidy oldfangled foundry surrounded by lawns and trees, and a big, amicable president who dressed well. But Herbert McCullough was now sixty-eight years old and tired, and his wife would have liked to move to St. Augustine, Florida.

By 1980, the books of Gray Iron Fabricating Company showed a loss. The foundry still was turning out plenty of production (though not so much as once) and retained many old customers; it was a going concern, in no immediate peril of bankruptcy. But its situation was uneasy. Having gone over his account books, Herbert McCullough made a list of what he called "fringe" costs. (By "fringe" he meant something not essential to production and sales.) In the box on page 360 are some of his fringe items.

"Fringe" Obligations of Gray Iron Fabricating

- federal and state unemployment insurance (required by federal and Michigan statutes)
- workmen's compensation insurance (required by state statute)
- medical and dental insurance for all employees except executive staff (required by contract with unions)
- payments to union pension fund (required by contract with unions)
- vacation pay for all employees except executives (required by contract with unions)
- Social Security payments for every employee (required by federal statute: this was the heaviest "fringe" burden)
- "affirmative action" measures to hire more "minority" employees (required by federal regulations)
- improvements to foundry thought unnecessary by McCullough, but demanded by OSHA (federal agency)
- wages for more security guards to protect plant and employees against increasing vandalism and violent crime (suggested by city police force, busy with other responsibilities)
- sudden increase of foundry's real-property tax assessment by 30 percent, to pay for rising costs of county and city government

---

At this point, Mr. McCullough ceased to compile his list of fringe obligations, the process being too dismal. He called a conference of his chief stockholders to put before them the following list of possible courses of action.

The McCullough Choices

1. Borrow five million dollars from banks at high interest rates, enlarge and modernize the foundry, and hire a larger and better sales force; so increase the gross income of the firm.

2. At the earliest possible opportunity allowed by NLRB, terminate the firm's contracts with the unions; insist upon diminishing union fringe benefits before signing a new contract; face a strike, if necessary.
3. Sell Gray Iron Fabricating to some large corporation—if any might be interested. Accept payment in stock of the bigger corporation that would absorb the family firm; no payment in money.
4. Go out of business; sell site and buildings of firm for whatever sum might be got; retire to St. Augustine and live on savings.
5. Offer Gray Iron Fabricating as a gift to the two unions or to the federal government. They act as if they already owned the business, anyway.

The firm of Gray Iron Fabricating Company is imaginary. But the troubles of many American industrial firms are far from imaginary. In recent decades, major American industries have been heavily taxed, have conceded high wages to labor unions, have been perplexed by numerous governmental regulations, and sometimes have found themselves short of capital for improvements. Small businesses have complained even more loudly of their difficulties.

When costs of production and distribution are forced upward by various demands and pressures, producers and sellers try to shift their increased costs to consumers through charging higher prices. But in a truly competitive economy, no one producer can charge higher prices than his competitors and hope to attract customers—except by superior quality or sometimes by superior advertising.

If all producers and distributors in a country find it necessary to raise their prices, then foreign competitors enter the market, offering lower prices if their costs of production and distribution are lower. The president of Gray Iron Fabricating found himself losing business to Japanese and German firms. A whole industry within a country thus may find itself backed against the wall by imported goods; foreign firms may become the principal suppliers of important products.

Discuss

> 13. What choice or choices should the McCullough family make? What would you do, in their shoes? How does this example illustrate the difficulties of a relatively small firm in recent years? In this imaginary example, do you think that Gray Iron's difficulties are typical of American business, or exaggerated?
>
> 14. Herbert McCullough was required to pay out large sums of money to a variety of individuals and organizations. Who was required to pay money to Mr. McCullough?

The resources of even the biggest industrial and commercial firms are limited. Demands upon them by public authority and claims by other groups may remind you of the fable of the goose that laid the golden eggs.

Aesop, an obscure Greek slave, is supposed to be the author of this lesson. In some versions of the story, the bird is a hen, not a goose, and its owner is a woman or a man rather than a couple. But in all versions, the moral is the same. Below you will find the fable in the recent rendering by an English poet, Paul Roche. As Roche expresses the moral, "Greed destroys the source of good."

The Goose That Laid the Golden Eggs

> The phenomenon
>   had been going on
>   for several weeks.
> Yes, the Goose actually laid golden eggs:
>   huge nuggets smooth as wax
>   and heavy as lead.
> The Man and his Wife went down on their knees
>   and thanked Hermes[3]
>   for having so rewarded their years
>   of poverty and piety . . .
> "But we could do with a bigger house,"
>   said the wife. "Of course,"
>   the Man replied.

---

3. **Hermes:** in Greek mythology, the messenger of the gods; also himself the god of luck and of wealth.

And after a few days
    and a few more golden eggs,
    they both said:
"Why not servants and a carriage? . . .
Then there's that dowry for our beloved daughter's
   marriage."
Soon the golden eggs could hardly keep pace
    with the couple's galloping desires.
They became rapacious
    and they gave themselves airs.
"We must have money," was the Wife's cry.
"Put pepper in the Goose's mash:
    perhaps
    it will then lay two eggs at a time . . .
    I need a new costume."
Then one day the Wife
    nudged her man with a terrible gleam in her eye.
"Cut it open," she said, cold:
    "it's an enormous bird
    and full of gold."
"I can't," he said.
So she put in his hands a knife.
"Go on," she said:
    "I owe the dressmaker, the hairdresser, the grocer,
    the chemist, the wine shop, the jeweller . . .
    we simply must have more money—
    or do you want me to borrow?"
"All right," he said, "but it's damnable."
So he laid the Goose on the kitchen table,
    stunned it and opened it up.
Then he gave a great booming laugh, dismally unfunny.
"My dear, you'll never guess,"
    he said; and his tears of rage, frustration and
      sorrow
    broke in a flood.
"There's nothing inside the Goose
    but ordinary flesh and blood."

The greed of the foolish couple in this fable is paralleled sometimes—and especially in the twentieth century—by the rash eagerness with which governments try to extract more and more money from the producers of goods. In some socialist countries, this foolish covetousness sometimes has taken the form of "capital levies"—that is, compelling all owners of property to pay to the state, annually, some percentage of the market value of their holdings.

After a few years, the practical result of such a public policy is the confiscating of the capital a nation must have for its production. Private ownership is destroyed or, at best, reduced to small proportions. Then the state has lost its sources of revenue. To keep the economy operating at all, the state (or some syndicate or corporation authorized by the state) must become itself the producer and distributor of most goods—or else undo in some way the mischief accomplished by the capital levy.

Few people in the United States desire to confiscate private property or to damage the market economy that has helped to make them prosperous. Yet public expenditures and regulatory policies that go so far as to place heavy burdens upon corporations, partnerships, individual enterprises, and professions can crush an economy into poverty—without anyone having intended that result.

Discuss   15. Medieval moralists listed Seven Deadly Sins, one of which was *avarice*, the greedy desire for wealth. Can you think of recent or historical examples of people who lost nearly everything by demanding too much, too soon? Can governments, as well as individuals, fall into the vice of avarice?

16. Can you complete the analogy between the goose and the market economy by showing what would happen to public and private incomes if suddenly a government should seize the means of production? (Karl Marx predicted that Communists would so seize both industrial and agricultural properties once they had taken power by revolution.)

The Moral Foundation of Economics

Some people would like to separate economics from politics, but they are unable to do so. Another name for economics is *political economy*. As we mentioned in earlier chapters, a sound economy cannot exist without a political state to protect it. Foolish political interference with the economy can result in general poverty, but wise political encouragement of the economy helps a society toward prosperity.

Similarly, some people would like to separate economics from morals, but they are unable to do so. For unless most men and women recognize some sort of moral principles, an economy cannot function except in a small and precarious way. Moral beliefs, sometimes called moral values, make possible production, trading, saving, and the whole economic apparatus.

All human creations and institutions have some connection with moral ideas and moral habits, for human beings are moral creatures. Concepts of right and wrong haunt us in everything we do—whether or not we wish to be concerned with moral questions.

So it is that the final section of this final chapter of this book on the first principles of economics suggests that *material prosperity depends upon moral convictions and moral dealings*.

Adam Smith, the principal founder of economic science, was a professor of moral philosophy. He took it for granted that moral beliefs should affect economic doings.

The success of economic measures, like the success of most other things in human existence, depends upon certain moral habits. If those habits are lacking, the only other way to produce goods is by compulsion—by what is called slave labor. Let us examine briefly some of the moral qualities that make possible a prosperous economy.

Any economy that functions well relies upon a high degree of *honesty*. In the market, buyers and sellers must be able to trust one another. Of course, some cheats and charlatans are found in any society, yet, on the whole, in a prospering economy most people behave honestly. "Honesty is the best policy," Benjamin Franklin wrote in the eighteenth century, echoing an old English proverb. He meant that honesty pays, in an economic sense.

For any advanced economy is based upon *contracts:* agreements to sell or to buy, promises to pay, deeds of sale, all sorts of "commercial instruments." Many commercial contracts are oral, rather than written. Today's markets especially depend upon *implied* contracts (as distinguished from detailed written contracts). You may have seen a public auction, at which a bidder may pledge a large sum merely by raising one hand or nodding his head. The auctioneer trusts the bidder to keep his promise to buy at a certain price. On a much vaster scale, the complex apparatus of stock markets depends on such implicit contracts—and on ordinary honesty.

On the other hand, those societies in which theft, cheating, and lying are common do not ordinarily develop successful economies. If production and distribution can be carried on only under armed protectors and without any certainty of being paid, then little will be produced and distributed above the level of subsistence. When bargains are not kept and loans are not repaid, prices are high and interest rates are higher—which discourages production and distribution.

Another moral quality or habit important for the success of an economy is the custom of doing good work—of producing goods of high quality. The Romans had a word for this: *industria,* a moral virtue, from which our English word *industry* is derived. Goods should be produced, and services rendered, for the sake of turning out something satisfactory or even admirable—not for the sake merely of cash payment. This affection for quality is bound up with the hope of pleasing or helping the purchaser or customer: doing something kindly for other people, even though producer and distributor may never see most of the customers. This belief in working faithfully and well is connected with the virtue called *charity.* For charity is not a handout, primarily; the word means "tenderness or love, affection for other people." The producer who creates first-rate goods is serving other people and can take satisfaction in that service.

One more virtue of the marketplace is a kind of courage: what the old Romans used to call *fortitude*. This economic courage includes the willingness to take risks, the ability to endure hard times, the talent to hold out against all the disappointment, harassment, ingratitude, and folly that fall upon people in the world of getting and spending.

It would be easy enough to list other moral beliefs and customs that are part of the foundation of a prosperous economy, but we draw near to the end of this book. So instead we turn back, for a moment, to one vice we discussed earlier—and to the virtue which is the opposite of that vice.

The vice is called *envy*; the virtue is called *generosity*.

Envy is a sour emotion that condemns a person to loneliness. Generosity is an emotion that attracts friends.

The generous man or woman is very ready to praise others sincerely and to help them instead of hindering them. Generosity brings admiration of the achievements and qualities of other people.

Now, generosity, too, is a moral quality on which a sound economy depends. Producer and distributor, when they are moved by generosity, do not envy one another: they may be competitors, but they are friendly competitors, like contestants in some sport. And in a society with a strong element of generosity, most citizens do not support public measures that would pull down or repress the more productive and energetic and ingenious individuals.

A spirit of generosity toward others is still at work in America. But in much of the world, a very different spirit has come to prevail. In Marxist lands, envy is approved by the men in power. Private wealth and personal success are denounced on principle. The Marxist indoctrinator deliberately preaches envy. By appealing to that strong vice, he may be able to pull down constitutions, classes, and religions.

Because the market brings substantial success to a good many individuals, the Marxist hates the market. A consistent Marxist declares that when two people exchange goods in any market, both are cheated. Yes, *both*—that is what the Marxist says. Exchange itself is "capitalist oppression," the Marxist propagandist proclaims. Certainly there is little profitable exchange in Communist countries. Envying the market's popularity and success, the Marxist denounces the market furiously.

In the long run, the envious society brings on proletarian tyranny and general poverty. In both the short run and the long run, the generous society encourages political freedom and economic prosperity.

Also, a successful free economy makes possible material generosity: it creates a material abundance that gives wealth to private charities and enables the state to carry out measures of public welfare.

From the generous society comes plenty. The old Greeks often represented in their sculptures and paintings the symbol of the *cornucopia*, the horn of plenty, a large goat's horn overflowing with flowers, fruit, and grain. To this day, the cornucopia is the symbol of a prospering economy.

The American market economy, whatever its shortcomings, has put a cornucopia into most households in the United States. The rewards of the market economy have been generous.

If the horn of plenty is to continue to overflow with good things, it must be cherished with courage and intelligence. Crushing taxation, imprudent meddling, malicious envy, or revolutionary violence might destroy the horn. To protect the cornucopia, it is necessary to understand economics tolerably well. Otherwise, a society of generosity may give way to a society of envy.

In our time of troubles, many strange economic doctrines are preached. Yet there is reason to believe that the productive market economy will be functioning well a century from now. The errors of command economies and the blunders of utopian welfare states have become obvious to a great many people, while Adam Smith continues to make economic sense.

So long as many people work intelligently, with good moral

habits, for their own advantage and for the prosperity of a nation, an economy will remain healthy. But hard work and sound habits may be undone by foolish public policies or by the violent envy of totalist states. There is a strong need for watchfulness on behalf of the economy.

This book has not been able to tell you everything about the Goose with the Golden Eggs. But we have been able to offer some information about the care and feeding of this creature; and we have cautioned you not to slaughter her.

Nowadays this Goose goes by the name of Market Economy. It seems probable that she still will be preening her feathers when you are ready to take your part in the world of work. If you treat her kindly and intelligently, she will continue to lay for you.

GLOSSARY

Some words have many meanings. This list gives mainly the meanings of words as they are used in this book. To find other meanings of these words, look them up in a dictionary.

A

absolute advantage: superiority in the ability to perform in one or more areas.

abundance: plenty; more than is sufficient. Although in the long run all goods are scarce, temporarily or under certain circumstances there may exist a large stock of some particular good, exceeding local demand for that good. This we call abundance. Under circumstances of abundance, prices tend to fall.

accounting profit: the surplus of income over outgo, as shown on a firm's account books.

allocate: to set apart for a particular purpose; assign or allot.

allocating the factors of production: allotting amounts or quantities of natural resources (land and raw materials), labor, capital, and management needed to produce a good. Properly allocating these factors helps to increase economic efficiency by reducing real cost. (See *real cost.*)

alternative foregone: the good or service that a producer or a buyer gives up when he decides to obtain instead some good or service that he wants more.

American market: the exchange of goods within the economic structure of the United States; all the buyers and sellers in the country.

antitrust laws: statutes to prevent combinations of individuals or firms that would reduce economic competition.

assembly line: a method of production in which the product being made moves along from worker to worker, each worker doing one special job.

assets: total resources of a person or business, such as cash, inventories, good will, machinery, real estate, etc.

authoritarian government: a government possessing great power, which citizens are compelled to obey.

B

balance of trade: the difference between the value of exports and imports of a country. A country having a *favorable* balance of trade exports more goods than it imports.

Bank of the United States: a bank chartered by Congress primarily to handle money matters for the national government. The first bank operated 1791–1811; the second bank, 1816–36.

barter: the direct exchange of one good for another good, without money passing from hand to hand.

basic needs: things necessary to stay alive and well: food, clothing, shelter.

birth rate: proportion of the number of babies born per year to the total population; usually expressed as a quantity per 1,000 of population.

black market: a market in which goods are exchanged illegally. Often, scarce goods appear in the black market and are sold for very high prices.

board of governors: group of persons who direct and supervise the Federal Reserve System. Board members are appointed by the President and confirmed by the United States Senate.

bond: a certificate issued for sale by a government or by a private company that promises to repay the bondholder after giving him or her an agreed rate of interest for a certain period.

bondholder: one who invests money in the government or in a business by buying certificates (bonds) issued by the government or business.

boom: in economics, a time when goods are in great demand, the demand is greater than the supply, businesses expand, and prices probably increase.

bureaucracies: systems of public employees.

Bureau of Engraving and Printing: the part of the United States Department of the Treasury that makes paper money.

Bureau of the Mint: the part of the United States Treasury that makes coins.

business cycle: a series of changes in business activity: prosperity, or boom, is followed by slump (recession or depression), which is then followed by recovery.

business fluctuations: marked changes in the volume of production, distribution, employment, and other aspects of commerce and industry.

C

capital: in economics, savings (in money or goods) that can be used to make more goods and more money; capital goods.

capital goods: anything used in the production and distribution of goods, including services, e.g., machines, buildings, tools, transportation; producer goods; capital.

capitalism: an economic system in which there is private or corporate ownership of the means of production; investments determined by private decision rather than by state control; and prices, production, and the distribution of goods determined mainly in a free market.

capitalist: anyone who owns producer goods or a share in some business that produces goods.

captains of industry: heads of large business firms.

cartels: powerful international business groups that join together with the intention of raising prices.

chartered: given written permission by a government to conduct business.

checking account: money that a person deposits in a bank and which the person withdraws from the bank by writing checks; demand deposits.

civilization: a stage of human society marked by the following: efficient food production, much division of labor, learned persons, many capital goods, and towns or cities.

civil liberties: freedoms that protect citizens against arbitrary power.

civil service: government employees appointed to jobs on the basis of competitive examinations rather than by political patronage; most government employees outside the armed forces.

classical economics: economic theories, developed by Adam Smith and other British economists late in the eighteenth century and early in the nineteenth century.

closed shop: an arrangement by which union membership is a condition of hiring as well as of continued employment, or one in which the employer must call on the union to furnish employees.

collective bargaining: the process by which wages, hours, rules, and working conditions are discussed and agreed upon by a union (which represents the employees) and an employer.

collective farms: large agricultural areas organized as units and worked by laborers under the supervision of the government.

collectivist state: a country in which the factors of production are controlled by the government.

collectivization: the act of organizing the means of production under the control of the state (nation). The term refers to forcing farmers to give up land and to join collective farms.

combination in restraint of trade: an alliance, or joining, of businesses for the purpose of reducing competition; any attempt by producers to reduce competition.

command economy: a system in which prices, production and distribution of goods, and savings and investment are determined by the government; planned economy; directed economy.

commerce: trade; an exchange of goods and money.

commercial banks: banks specializing in checking accounts and private loans.

Commercial Revolution: the great expansion of trade that began in the sixteenth century between Western Europe and other parts of the world, including the Far East and North and South America.

commodity: anything that is bought or sold; or, as generally used in the United States, standard raw materials, such as grains, animal products, and other unprocessed goods.

common stocks: certificates held by owners of a corporation which entitle them to share in whatever profit remains after all other costs have been paid.

Communism: (1) a system under which most or all property is owned by the state or community; (2) the name given to totalitarian systems based on the Marxist-Leninist ideology, as in the Soviet Union and People's Republic of China.

Communist: a person who belongs to the political party that believes in Communism; anything pertaining to Communism or to the Communist party.

Communist bloc: all the nations that are governed under Communism.

comparative advantage: the idea that one (person, business, region, country) is most successful when specializing in the job that one does best.

comparative efficiency: similarities and differences in productivity between methods of production.

competition: a contest for some prize, honor, or advantage; in economics, a contest among sellers and among buyers. (See *economic competition, imperfect competition,* and *open competition.*)

competitive economy: (See *market economy.*)

compound interest: money earned on an investment and on the interest added to the investment.

compulsory saving: saving that is directed and enforced by the government, e.g., Social Security taxes.

concentration camp: a guarded camp where prisoners or aliens are held.

conservative: one who prefers old and tested institutions to new and untried ways; one who believes that there are basic values that need to be conserved.

constant dollar: dollar of which the value does not change; a fixed value of the dollar that makes possible comparison of wages, production, gross national product, etc., from year to year. Constant dollars eliminate distortion of values caused by inflation or deflation in current (present-day) dollars. (See *current dollars.*)

constitutional government: a system in which political power is limited by law.

consumer goods: things produced for direct use by consumers.

consumers: people who use goods, including services.

consumption: the act of using or using up. Consumer goods are for consumption.

contract: an agreement between two or more parties to do, or not to do, a specified thing or things. Contracts may be written or oral, and they are enforceable by law.

corporation: a business organization owned by many people. Each owner investing in the corporation can vote at corporation meetings and is entitled to a share of the corporation's profits. Possible losses of each owner are limited to the extent of his or her actual investment.

cost of production: the amount a producer must pay for all the things (factors of production) needed to make or provide a good.

credit: trustworthiness; confidence in a purchaser's ability and intention to pay, shown by letting a person buy goods without paying for them immediately.

credit card: an identification card issued to an individual by a bank or other business, which allows the individual to buy goods now and pay for them later.

creditor: lender; one to whom money is owed.

culture: a people's way of life, including their work and other activities, language, ideas, religions, government, education, arts.

current dollar: the actual value of a dollar in a particular year, as contrasted with constant dollar.

D

debased: reduced in value.

debtor: borrower; one who owes something, such as money.

deferred payments: payments that are postponed until some future date.

deficit budget: the planned spending by a government of more than it receives from taxes or other sources of revenue.

deflation: a condition of falling prices and a rise in the value of money; the opposite of inflation.

demand: the amount of a good that people will buy at a certain price.

demand deposits: money deposited in banks in checking accounts; deposit money. Demand deposits are re-

moved from banks when depositors write checks.

deposit money: (See *demand deposits.*)

depreciate: diminish (lessen) in market value.

depression: in economics, a time during which supply is greater than demand. Prices fall, production slows down, many workers are laid off, and business is poor. (See *recession.*)

devaluation: reduction in the exchange value of a country's monetary unit in terms of gold, silver, or foreign monetary units.

developed countries: countries having many large industries and scientific, mechanized agriculture. In developed countries, most people work in industry; only a small percentage work in agriculture.

dialectical materialism: the Marxist theory that looks upon history as a process of conflict between classes. It maintains that this struggle is about ownership of the means of economic production.

dictator: a person who exercises absolute authority over a country—usually by suspending the country's constitution.

diminishing marginal valuation: the decreased worth of a good as the quantity of the good is increased; diminishing marginal utility.

diminishing scarcity: increasing prosperity, by increasing the supply of goods.

directed economy: (See *command economy.*)

disinflation: a condition of falling prices

and a rise in the value of money; the opposite of inflation; deflation.

distribution: the activities involved in the exchange of goods among producers and consumers, including shipping, storing, advertising, and selling.

dividends: money or shares of stock paid to people who own stock (shares) in a business. Dividends are paid from a company's earnings; the amounts paid vary with changes in earnings.

division of labor: the separation of workers into different jobs so that more and better goods can be produced; specialization.

double-digit inflation: a swift increase of general prices at a rate between 10 percent and 99 percent.

durable goods: things not soon consumed or destroyed in use, which can be used over a number of years; for example, printing presses or railroad cars.

duties: taxes levied by governments on imports or exports.

E

easy-money policy: action taken by the Federal Reserve to increase the amount of money in circulation, usually involving decreased interest rates on bank loans to encourage people to borrow money from the banks. (Compare *tight-money policy*.)

ecology: a branch of biology that deals with the relation of living things to their environment and to each other.

economic competition: a contest among producers and among consumers to succeed in industry and commerce.

economic growth: the expanding of production at a faster rate than the growth of population.

economic motive: the desire for goods and services as an incentive; the goal of acquiring goods as a motive for human action.

economic policies: plans for achieving objectives concerning the economy.

economics: the study of how goods are produced, distributed, and consumed; the science that studies how people satisfy their wants from the limited resources available.

economic theory: ideas about the laws or principles or political economy.

economists: scholars concerned with the study of producing, distributing, and consuming goods; experts on economic matters.

economy: (1) skill in the production, distribution, and consumption of goods; from Greek words meaning "management of the household." (2) a whole system of production, distribution, and consumption, extending to great numbers of people. Every nation has its own economy, or economic system.

efficiency: productiveness, or the power of producing intended results. People who are efficient get good results from what they do. (See *comparative efficiency*.)

elastic demand: demand that increases or decreases as prices change. If the price of a good goes down, people will buy more of that good, which increases demand. If the price of a good goes up, people buy less of it, which decreases demand.

emergent nations: countries that have recently become politically independent.

enterprise: a bold undertaking or attempt; in economics, a company organized for commercial or industrial purposes.

entrepreneur: a person who organizes and manages any enterprise, especially a business, usually with considerable initiative and risk; enterpriser.

ethnic origin: the cultural source or group from which a person comes.

exclusive franchise: permission from a manufacturer to be the only one to sell his products.

export: (noun) a good sent out of a country for sale or trade; (verb) to send goods to other countries for sale or trade.

extended family: in addition to parents and children, such a larger family includes grandparents, aunts, uncles, cousins, and other connections by birth, adoption, or close association.

F

face value: the amount printed on the front of stocks, bonds, money, other; the asserted value.

factors of production: the four things needed to produce goods: natural resources, labor, capital, and management.

famine: a disastrous shortage of food, causing the malnutrition or starvation of many people.

fascist: in economics, a term describing a system of government in which property is privately owned, but industry and business are regulated by a strong national regime. The chief example is that of Italy under the dictatorship of Benito Mussolini.

favorable balance of trade: a condition that exists when a country sells abroad (exports) goods of greater value than the value of goods it buys (imports) from other countries.

federal government: (1) a form of government in which the political authority is distributed between the central government and smaller state or provincial governments; (2) name often given to the national government (as opposed to state governments) in the United States.

federalism: a system of government in which power is divided between national and state authorities, as in the United States or Switzerland.

Federal Reserve Board: (See *board of governors*.)

Federal Reserve notes: paper money issued by the Federal Reserve System.

Federal Reserve System: the central banking system of the United States.

fiat money: currency backed only by government command.

fiscal year: any yearly period at the end of which a business, government, etc., determines its financial condition without regard to the calendar year.

Five-Year Plan: a plan specifying goals to be reached within a period of five years, designed to bring about a rapid increase in industrial capacity, the development of natural resources, etc., by central planning and intensive utilization of capital goods and labor.

fixed expenses: payments, such as rent, which stay the same over a fairly long time.

fortitude: patient courage no matter what happens; moral strength or endurance.

Forty-Niners: people who went to California in 1849 to find gold.

fossil fuels: petroleum, natural gas, coal, lignite, and peat, which were once masses of plants, now used to produce energy.

franchise: permission from a manufacturer to sell his products.

free enterprise economy: economic system based on private property and profit in a free market; how the private sector works. (See *market economy.*)

free market: a market in which price and quality are determined by the laws of demand and supply, not by government intervention.

free trade: commerce unhampered by high taxes or by other governmental limitations, particularly international trade.

G

galloping inflation: an economic condition in which the rate of inflation goes up with great speed.

geographic specialization: division of labor among regions and countries.

goods: material things or services that people find valuable; things or services that people want and are willing to pay for.

governmental grant: a gift of money from a government for particular purposes.

Great Depression: the period of low business activity and widespread unemployment that began with the stock market crash of October 1929 and lasted until World War II (1939–45).

Gresham's Law: an economic principle that is summed up in the words "Bad money drives out good"; that is, depreciated money will drive sound money off the market—people will hoard the good money.

gross national product (GNP): the total money value of all goods, including services, produced and paid for in a nation in one year.

H

hard money: medium of exchange consisting of metallic coins (precious metals) or of notes exchangeable for coins of precious metal.

hoard: to accumulate money, food, or other things in a hidden or carefully guarded place for preservation or for future use.

I

immigrant: a person who comes to a country to settle.

imperfect competition: a market condition marked by a limited number of sellers or buyers. When there are few buyers in the market, for instance, they may try to settle upon the price they are willing to pay to sellers. (Compare *open competition.*)

import: (noun) a good brought from another country for sale or trade;

(verb) to buy goods from other countries.

income tax: the part of one's income given to the government.

industrialization: the act of converting a region's economy (usually from agriculture) to one based primarily on manufacturing.

Industrial Revolution: a period of great changes in industry, as people began to use power-driven machines in factories to make goods; began in England about 1750.

industry: systematic work; the use of power-driven machines to make goods in factories; factories that produce a certain good, such as the automobile industry.

inelastic demand: when prices change, such demand changes little or may not change at all. For example, despite sharp increases in the price of gasoline, most drivers may continue to buy as much gasoline as before.

inflation: an economic condition in which too much money is in circulation, causing prices to rise rapidly.

input: the total cost (in time or money) needed to produce a good. (Compare *output.*)

insurance policy: a guarantee of payment for loss or harm from certain occurrences (fire, accident, death, disablement, etc.) in return for the payment of sums of money called premiums; a form of savings investment.

intelligence: mental ability; the ability to reason, to understand, or to perform similar forms of mental activity.

interest: payment on loans; money paid for the use of money belonging to

others. (Compare *principal.*)

Internal Revenue Service (IRS): the division of the United States Department of the Treasury that collects taxes for the national government and enforces tax laws.

international relations: various connections between countries, including political and economic agreements.

intrinsic value: natural worth.

invest: to put capital to use in a way offering profitable returns in the form of profits, dividends, or interest.

investments: the using of money or capital in order to make a profit, especially interest or income.

investors: people who put savings to work in something offering profitable returns; for example, savings accounts, shares in corporations, government bonds.

L

labor: handwork, brainwork, or a combination of both kinds of work; workers.

labor union: an organization formed by workers to deal with managers or owners of businesses.

laws of economics: general rules or principles concerning the production, distribution, and consumption of goods.

laws of supply and demand: the economic laws according to which prices will rise if the demand is greater than the supply, and prices will fall if the supply is greater than the demand.

legal tender: notes or bills issued by

governments or by approved banks for use as a medium of exchange.

legislation: (1) the act of making or enacting laws; (2) a law or a body of laws enacted.

legislators: lawmakers.

legislature: the organ of government that has the power to make laws.

liberal: in politics, a person who favors change and experiment, as opposed to a conservative.

limited liability: the legal rule that if a corporation goes bankrupt the owners of shares cannot lose more than the value of their shares.

liquid investments: savings that can be converted into cash without much difficulty or delay.

loss: that which is lost; in economics, often used as the opposite of *profit.*

M

macroeconomics: "big" economics; studies the total wealth of a society— its income, its savings, and the state of its total economy; also deals with national economic policy and the role of government.

managed currency: monetary system in which the supply of money is determined by governmental officials.

management: one of the four factors of production; the work of persons who plan and direct production.

marginal: situated on the border or edge.

market: a process by which people exchange goods (including money) so that buyers and sellers can get what they are seeking for themselves; a place where buyers and sellers meet to exchange goods.

market clearing price (equilibrium price): in any particular market, at any particular time, the price at which the whole available supply of a good can be sold; the point at which demand and supply meet, resulting in a price that "clears the market."

market economy: an economy or part of an economy based on producing and selling what people will buy; also called competitive economy; the opposite of command economy. (See *free enterprise economy.*)

market mechanism: an automatic system for communicating information about the exchange of goods; test of the market. Consumers' buying decisions tell producers what goods are in demand.

market price: the general price of a good as determined by open competition among many sellers and buyers.

market research: the gathering and studying of data relating to consumer preferences, purchasing power, etc., especially preliminary to introducing a product on the market.

mass market: a very large number of people to whom large quantities of products are sold.

mass production: the system of making many products quickly in volume by using machines and a detailed division of labor. Mass production depends upon a mass market. (See *mass market.*)

means of production: (See *factors of production.*)

measure of value: a kind of ruler to determine the worth of something. Using a standard unit of money, such as the American dollar, we can tell how much one good is worth compared with some other good.

medieval times: the period of European history from c. A.D. 500 to 1500; the Middle Ages.

Medicare: a program of the federal government that provides hospitalization and some other medical benefits for American citizens sixty-five years of age or older, regardless of the individual's financial means.

medium of exchange: means or way for exchanging goods. Money is a medium of exchange and includes bills, coins, checking accounts, savings accounts, and credit cards.

mercantile system: an economic system under which a country tries to accumulate much gold and silver by exporting the largest possible quantity of its products and importing as little as possible, thus establishing a favorable balance of trade; economic policy followed by the principal states of Europe from the early sixteenth century to about the end of the eighteenth century.

mercantilism: mercantile system.

Mercantilist: a person who believed in elaborate regulation of the country's economy. (See *mercantile system.*)

microeconomics: "little" economics; the scientific study of the activity of many small parts of economic activity and their relation in the market; deals with the behavior of smaller economic units—individuals, households, and firms. It is the study of the market. (Compare *macroeconomics.*)

middlemen: traders or merchants who buy goods from producers and then sell them, usually at a profit, to retail traders. Commercial wholesalers and jobbers are middlemen.

migration: the act of going from one country or region to another.

mineral raw materials: metals or other things found in the ground that can be used in manufacturing or as sources of energy.

mixed economy: an economy that is a mixture of a market economy and a state-regulated economy.

moderate: "middle of the road" politicians who are opposed to extreme changes.

monetary system: the plan by which money is managed in the national economy.

money supply: all the money in the United States that is in circulation or deposited in banks; includes coins and paper.

monopoly: a condition in which some industry or business is dominated by just one firm. Under monopoly, there is no competition. (Compare *oligopoly.*)

monopoly of force: governmental control of police and troops which allows a government to keep the peace and enforce the laws.

moral: concerned with right conduct or the distinction between right and wrong.

morals: principles or habits with respect to right and wrong conduct.

N

national income: the sum of wages, salaries, profits, and other incomes received by the population of a country during a certain period of time (usually one year).

nationalism: the feeling of strong loyalty to one's country.

nationalist government: a government that takes command of the economy in order to strengthen the nation, especially in military power.

nationalized: private property taken over by the government.

natural disaster: occurrences in the natural environment over which humans have no control; for example, cyclones, earthquakes, floods.

natural laws: rights and duties that all human beings share. These laws are presumed to be derived from human nature and divine will, rather than from man-made statutory law.

natural monopoly: a business in which it would be technologically difficult to have competition, usually a public utility (electricity, water, gas).

natural resources: things found in the natural environment that people have learned to use; one of the four factors of production.

near-money: an economic term applied to time deposits (savings accounts) and credit cards.

needs: necessities. (Compare *wants.*)

O

obsolescence of inventory: out-of-date goods on hand.

oligopoly: a condition in which some industry or business is dominated by a very few firms. Under oligopoly, there is imperfect competition. (Compare *monopoly.*)

open competition: a condition of the market in which there are many sellers and many buyers, and no one seller or buyer, or group of sellers or buyers, can exert enough influence to affect the price or the quality of a good.

opportunity cost: an element in the real or true cost of a good or service. (Real cost includes both money price and opportunity cost.) Opportunity cost signifies the cost of foregoing the next-best good available to a producer or a buyer—that is, what good the producer or buyer must give up in order to obtain the good he chooses to acquire.

outgo: expenses.

output: how much is produced.

overproduction: an economic condition in which more goods are produced than the market can dispose of, supply being greater than demand.

P

partnership: an association of two or more people who own a business and share the profits or losses according to the amount of money each has invested in the business.

payment for abstinence: the reward that one acquires for having postponed consumption of money or other goods.

pension plan: a financial system to

provide for the support of people when they retire after having worked for a certain length of time.

per capita income: total national income for a particular time divided by the total number of people in a country.

Physiocrats: the first group to try to create a science of economics; French economists in the eighteenth century who were opposed to mercantilism, believing that government interference in the economy should be strictly limited.

planned economy: (See *command economy.*)

platform: in political science, the official position taken by a political party on the issues.

policy: a plan of action for achieving an objective.

political liberties: in the United States, guarantees of freedom from the possessors of power, as in the Bill of Rights of the federal Constitution.

political party: a group of citizens united to promote, through representative government, their own ideas of what is best for the nation.

pound, British: the British unit of money, originally worth a pound's weight of silver. Until the Second World War, the British pound was worth nearly five dollars in American money.

postponing consumption: delaying purchases of goods in order to save for the future.

preferred stocks: shares in a company that generally give holders the right to payment of dividends before such payments to holders of common stocks.

premiums: money paid to an insurance company by the buyer of an insurance policy.

price: the value that the seller and the buyer agree upon when a good changes hands.

price-fixing: setting the prices of goods at certain levels, regardless of supply and demand.

price signals: changing prices, which tell of changes in supply or in demand or in both.

priming the pump: increasing public spending to build up the demand for goods.

principal: in economics, an amount of capital as distinguished from interest or profit.

principle: an accepted or professed rule of action or conduct.

priorities: in economics, the order in which wants are purchased. For example, food is the highest priority of most people.

private capitalism: an economic system in which the owners of capital are many private individuals.

private enterprise: business owned and run by private individuals, not by the government.

private enterprise economy: (See *free enterprise economy.*)

private sector: the part of the economy that is made up of private businesses, such as partnerships, corporations, and individual enterprises; makes decisions about its own private production; the opposite of public sector.

producer goods: goods used to make other goods; capital goods.

producers: people who work to provide goods.

production: the making of goods.

productivity: efficiency; getting the largest possible output of goods from a given input of the factors of production.

profit: any sort of gain; any reward for labor or cleverness; in economics, the excess of the price paid by the buyer over the total costs of the good to the seller; the excess of income over outgo (expenses).

profit motive: the hope of gain by an exchange of goods.

proletarian tyranny: oppressive rule by the proletariat, or revolutionary working class.

proletariat: the industrial working class, lacking property, in Marxist terminology.

prosperity: economic success; the condition of enjoying many goods, including services.

public sector: the part of the economy connected with governmental expenditure and under governmental direction.

public utility: an organization providing essential public services and to some extent regulated by government; for example, companies providing electricity, water, gas.

R

radical: fundamental or extreme, as a radical change; one who believes that society should be changed completely and quickly, using violence if necessary. (Compare *conservative, liberal.*)

ration: to reduce consumption by permitting consumers to obtain only a limited amount of goods.

raw materials: goods from which other goods are made, for example, iron ore, steel, milk, cotton.

real cost: the total true cost of a good, including both its price in money and the opportunity cost involved (accounting cost plus opportunity cost). (See *opportunity cost.*)

real property: property consisting of land and the things on or in it, such as buildings, crops, minerals.

recession: in economics, a moderate business reversal; less severe than a depression. (Compare *depression.*)

refugee, political: one who flees from danger or trouble, especially from a foreign country, as in time of a great change in government.

relative scarcity: a condition that exists when particular wants are greater than a particular supply of goods that could satisfy them.

resources: sources of supply, support, or aid; the collective wealth of a country or its means of producing wealth.

retail centers: a store or group of stores selling goods to consumers, usually in small quantities.

retail sellers: people who sell goods to consumers in small quantities. (Compare *wholesaler.*)

revenues: the income of a government from taxes and other sources.

revolution: in politics, history, and economics, a big, sudden change or upheaval in society.

revolutionaries: persons who work or fight to overthrow the government of a country.

reward of abstinence: the satisfying of a want after one has postponed that satisfaction; for instance, interest paid upon a savings account at a bank.

right-to-work law: a statute providing that a worker does not have to belong to a union to be employed.

S

saboteur: one who commits underhanded acts to interfere with production or with a cause.

saving: postponing the spending of money; postponing the use of a good.

savings account: money saved in a bank and which earns interest at specified times so long as it stays on deposit at the bank.

scale of production: the size of a business or operation.

scarcity: smallness of supply. All goods that have value are scarce, in the sense that they must be paid for: more demand exists for them than can be supplied readily. Some goods are almost always scarce, everywhere: the more popular cuts of meat, for example. Other goods may be relatively scarce, such as water in New York City or Los Angeles; or the same goods may be painfully and permanently scarce, such as water in desert countries.

serfdom: the condition of a peasant who is tied to the land and who passes from one owner to another with the land.

serfs: persons who were bound to stay and work on the land where they were born. Serfs could not be sold off the land, unlike slaves.

service industries: organizations that offer personal services to consumers, rather than offering material things; for example, work done by doctors, lawyers, repair firms, schools, theaters, hotels.

services: actions that people perform for others; dry cleaning, for example, or hairdressing.

servile labor: unfree workers; people who must do whatever work they are assigned, at what wages people in authority set for them, and under such conditions as their employers provide.

shares: (See *stocks.*)

shortage: a condition in which there is temporary lack of a good that ordinarily can be supplied in response to demand. This occurs when demand considerably exceeds supply because of unusual conditions.

signals of the market: consumers' buying decisions, which constitute demand and which tell producers the kinds and quantities of goods they should produce.

socialism: government ownership and control of the means of production.

socialist: a person who believes that the community as a whole should own all means of production.

social organization: the way a society or community is fitted together, so that people know what part they have in the society.

Social Security system: a program of social insurance by the federal government to protect wage earners and their dependents against major economic hazards; for example, poverty in old age, crippling injuries, loss of parents in childhood. The United States Social Security system was begun with the Social Security Act of 1935.

Social Security taxes: money paid by wage earners and self-employed persons to the federal treasury; a form of compulsory saving.

society: the group of people who live in a community.

soviets: committees of workers in the Soviet Union.

specialization: the concentrating of one's efforts in a particular activity or field. (See *division of labor.*)

specie: money made of metal.

speculation: trading in goods, land, stocks, etc., in the hope of making a quick profit from changes in the market price; engagement in business transactions involving considerable risk but offering the chance of large gains.

speculator: one who deals in stocks or other goods in the hope of making a quick profit.

stagflation: a journalistic term to describe a state of the economy in which demand is stagnant or sluggish, but prices continue to rise.

standardized goods: commodities that are identical in size, shape, color, quality, weight, and the like.

standard of living: a pattern of consumption to which classes or individuals become accustomed.

state: an organized political community, usually with a definite territory, and independent of the rule of any higher authority. States have governments; but the state is permanent, while governments change from time to time. Germany, Britain, France, Brazil, and Egypt, to name a few, are examples of states. In the United States of America, the word state usually means one of the fifty states that make up the federal Union.

state capitalism: economic system in which the government owns most of the capital (producer goods).

statutes: written laws of a state.

stockholder: a person who owns shares in a business, but does not own all the business. Most big corporations are owned by thousands of stockholders.

stock market: a place for buying and selling shares (stocks) in businesses.

stocks: investments in some industrial or commercial company or corporation; shares in a company.

strike: in labor, a work stoppage. Workers refuse to work until management agrees to make certain changes in working conditions, wages, or benefits.

subsidies: grants of money in aid of some project, whether furnished by government or by private organizations.

subsistence economy: a system of production that provides only the necessities of life.

supply: the quantity of a good for sale at

a certain price; also the amount of materials being produced.

supply-side economics: a term to describe economic policies that emphasize a swift and steady increase in the supply of goods—often as a means to reduce inflation of the currency and public deficits.

T

tariffs: taxes on goods bought from outside a country's boundaries.

technological unemployment: lack of jobs caused by changes in methods of production.

technology: a way of getting things done or of producing goods in a society; in modern times, the application of science in industry and commerce.

test of the market: (See *market mechanism.*)

Third World: a term to describe those countries today that say they are not under the influence of either the Soviet Union or the "Western bloc" (the United States and Western European states). Many of the Third World countries have command economies with relatively little industrial development.

tight-money policy: action taken by the Federal Reserve to decrease the amount of money in circulation, usually by increasing interest rates on bank loans to discourage borrowing. (Compare *easy-money policy.*)

time deposits: bank savings accounts.

totalist government: a government possessing total power over the citizens, who have no real rights in such a society; totalitarian government.

traditional society: economically, a society in which production is determined by old custom.

trend: general direction or development.

triple-digit inflation: a swift increase of general prices at a rate between 100 percent and 999 percent.

true cost: (See *real cost.*)

true profit: the gain of a firm or other enterprise after all expenses of production and distribution have been deducted from gross income. Such expenses include, among other items, interest on capital invested, the factor of risk, and the wage of management.

trust: a type of business organization that controls many companies or corporations.

U

underdeveloped country: a country that does not have a high degree of industrialization.

underproduction: not producing enough goods to meet demand.

utopia: Greek word meaning "nowhere"; the ideal state described by Sir Thomas More.

V

value: in economics, what people are willing to pay for a good; worth; in philosophy, those things (including ideas and qualities) that we believe are good and important.

value-in-exchange: price; the trading worth of a good; trading value.

value-in-use: the worth of a good to its owner, determined by what use the owner can make of the good.

vegetal raw materials: substances derived from plants, such as cotton, flax, and cereal grains, which can be used to produce goods.

voluntary saving: free choice of whether to save and by what means to save.

W

wage of management: money paid to the hired manager of a business.

want: a human desire to have a certain good or kind of good.

wealth: all the things that have value: all goods—money, property, capital goods, consumer goods.

welfare state: a society in which many of the people's material wants and services are supplied by the state itself.

Western democracies: representative governments in Western Europe and in North and South America.

Western Europe: those countries west of (and including) Italy, Austria, West Germany, and Denmark; sometimes used to include only those European countries north of the Pyrenees Mountains and bordering on the Atlantic Ocean or the North Sea.

wholesaler: one who sells goods in large amounts, as to retailers or jobbers rather than directly to consumers.

Index

A

Abraham 39
absolute advantage
    155–158
abstinence 176–177
accounting cost 255
accounting profit 105
accumulated capital 34
advantage
    absolute 155–158
    comparative 154–158
    economic 154
Aesop 169, 362
Afghanistan 267
agricultural economics
    331–332
agriculture 30, 174, 260,
    283
    as an industry 45, 50, 60,
    234, 264, 331–332
    efficiency in 153, 171–172
    inefficiency in 290, 292,
    305, 331–332
Albania 267
allocating factors of
    production 147–148

alternative foregone 106,
    255
American Fur Company
    62
American market 96
Amish 124
anarchy 231, 284
Andropov, Yuri V. 289
Angola 267, 299
antitrust law 136
Arab Oil Embargo 137, 303
Argentina 277, 324
Aristotle 180, 202
authoritarian government
    101, 241, 277, 287, 334
    (*see also* central
    government, command
    economy)

B

Babbitt, Irving 47, 124
balance of trade 28
Bangladesh 56
bank 177, 182, 206–207,

    212, 304, 324
    central banking system
    62, 214, 215–218, 261,
    263, 278, 317, 339
bankruptcy 108, 237, 243,
    264, 267
bargaining 48, 50 (*see also*
    collective bargaining)
barter 69, 198–199
base metals 204
Belgium 49, 252, 352
Benton, Thomas Hart 210
Bevan, Aneurin 296
Bible
    Genesis
        41 172; **47** 172–173
    Proverbs
        6:6–8 171; **6:6–11** 47
        10:4 47; **10:5** 171
        13:11 47; **12:24, 27** 47
        13:4 47; **14:23** 47
        15 223; **15:16** 223
        15:19 47; **16** 223
        16:8 223; **16:16** 223
        19:24 47; **20:4, 13** 47
        21:5, 25–26 47

P

partnership 185
patent 115, 117
Paul 222
payment for risk 178
pension fund 193
pension plan 193
per capita 35
per capita income 269
Peron, Juan Domingo 277
personal property 174
Peru 324
physiocracy 28, 30–31, 205
Physiocracy 29
Pilgrims 5
pine-tree shillings 199–200
Pitt, William 34
Plain People 124
planned economy 100, 293
Plato 228
plenty 36, 280 (*see also* prosperity)
Poland 87, 267, 291–292, 324, 326–334
political economy 22, 229, 238, 365
political freedom 257, 265–268
political protection 227–231, 240–241, 245
Polk, James Knox 230
pollution 304–308
Polmos 291–292
pound 6
poverty 18, 245, 264, 271–272
    causes of 192, 291, 323, 331, 337, 349, 365, 368
    examples of 250, 281–282, 283, 291
preferred stock 185–186
premium 183
premium for risk 186
President of the United States 215, 217–218,

230, 231, 235, 237, 318
price 47–48, 72–92, 96–97, 105, 121–122, 132–136, 252–265, 286, 309–341
    competitive 125–126, 132
    control 309
    defined 72
    equilibrium 91
    fixed 86–87, 241, 293–297, 329, 336
    governmental regulation of 86–92, 132, 135, 296, 309
    increase 96–97, 230–232, 243, 309–341
    inflation of 230–232, 258–259, 309–341, 357
    market 72, 82–83, 125, 290, 293
    market-clearing 91
    work 252–257
private enterprise economy 95 (*see also* market economy)
private sector 102, 175, 228, 235, 237, 278, 306, 311–312, 322, 341
prodigality 14
producer 9, 99, 143
production 249, 260–268, 271–273, 303, 305, 309, 322
    absolute advantage 156–158
    assembly-line 160
    comparative advantage 154–158
    controlled by government 277, 278, 290, 292
    cost of 75–77, 131, 335, 351, 361
    decrease in 132
    efficiency 18, 33, 49, 132, 143–166, 191, 249, 337, 349
    factors of 43–64, 146–147, 172, 322, 338
    for profit 266–268, 291
    for use 266–268, 291

increase in 27
input 143–144
marginal 153
mass 52, 148, 159, 288
output 143–144
scale of 158–161, 191
underproduction 285, 312, 322, 328–332
productivity 49, 143, 240, 244, 252–254, 260–273, 284, 285, 292, 321–322, 357
    decreased 290, 331–333, 341
    increased 288, 338, 349, 351, 357
profit 104–118, 265–268, 288, 291
profit motive 104, 117, 235, 288
proletariat (*see* dictatorship of the proletariat, Karl Marx, Marxism)
promissory notes 206
property 174, 235, 251, 277–279, 284, 288, 290, 293–294, 364
    personal 174
    private 37, 235, 251, 277, 278, 279, 284, 288, 290, 364
    real 57, 174, 284
    rental 88–92, 293–294
prosperity 125, 249–250, 258, 271, 291, 293, 298, 322, 346, 365
    examples of 262–264, 269, 337
    sources of 35–38, 44, 50, 122, 192, 242, 273, 304
Proverbs (*see* Bible)
public sector 228, 235, 237
public utility 135, 183

R

radical 61
Randolph, John 210–211
rationing 278, 282, 286, 288, 329–331